Survi

GLOBAL POLITICS AN

Volume 64 Number 2 | April

'The war in Ukraine may thus be the first crisis in decades in which all sides see core interests at stake which they cannot abandon. This was never quite true of Cold War crises. In Europe, the West accepted Soviet imposition of brutal but (in the short term) stable outcomes on Eastern bloc uprisings. The various Berlin crises were resolved through mutually acceptable and stabilising compromises.'

Nigel Gould-Davies, Putin's Strategic Failure, p. 13.

'To a degree unusual for a US president, moreover, Nixon had developed a realist world view that minimised the importance of ideology and of a state's domestic political system. He knew perfectly well that Mao had been a bloody and capricious mass killer, but what was there to gain by criticising the Chinese system?'

John L. Harper, Nixon in China, February 1972: Revisiting the 'Week that Changed the World', p. 46.

'To what extent nuclear weapons could dampen pressure towards conflict depended on the numbers deployed and the ease with which they could be used. The major powers learned to act cautiously in their presence.'

Lawrence Freedman, SALT 50 Years On: Strategic Theory and Arms Control, p. 76.

Survival
GLOBAL POLITICS AND STRATEGY
Volume 64 Number 2 | April–May 2022

Contents

Cover: Sergey Bobok/AFP via Getty Images

On the cover
A Russian armoured personnel carrier burns next to the body of an unidentified soldier in Kharkiv, Ukraine, on 27 February 2022.

On the web
Visit www.iiss.org/publications/survival for brief notices on new books on Culture and Society, the Middle East and the United States.

***Survival* editors' blog**
For ideas and commentary from *Survival* editors and contributors, visit www.iiss.org/blogs/survival-blog.

Survival

GLOBAL POLITICS AND STRATEGY

The International Institute for Strategic Studies

2121 K Street, NW | Suite 600 | Washington DC 20037 | USA
Tel +1 202 659 1490   Fax +1 202 659 1499   E-mail survival@iiss.org   Web www.iiss.org

Arundel House | 6 Temple Place | London | WC2R 2PG | UK
Tel +44 (0)20 7379 7676   Fax +44 (0)20 7836 3108   E-mail iiss@iiss.org

14th Floor, GBCorp Tower | Bahrain Financial Harbour | Manama | Kingdom of Bahrain
Tel +973 1718 1155   Fax +973 1710 0155   E-mail iiss-middleeast@iiss.org

9 Raffles Place | #49-01 Republic Plaza | Singapore 048619
Tel +65 6499 0055   Fax +65 6499 0059   E-mail iiss-asia@iiss.org

Pariser Platz 6A | 10117 Berlin | Germany
Tel +49 30 311 99 300   E-mail iiss-europe@iiss.org

Survival Online www.tandfonline.com/survival and www.iiss.org/publications/survival

Aims and Scope *Survival* is one of the world's leading forums for analysis and debate of international and strategic affairs. Shaped by its editors to be both timely and forward thinking, the journal encourages writers to challenge conventional wisdom and bring fresh, often controversial, perspectives to bear on the strategic issues of the moment. With a diverse range of authors, *Survival* aims to be scholarly in depth while vivid, well written and policy-relevant in approach. Through commentary, analytical articles, case studies, forums, review essays, reviews and letters to the editor, the journal promotes lively, critical debate on issues of international politics and strategy.

Editor **Dana Allin**
Managing Editor **Jonathan Stevenson**
Associate Editor **Carolyn West**
Assistant Editor **Jessica Watson**
Editorial Assistant **Charlie Zawadzki**
Production and Cartography **Kelly Verity**

Contributing Editors

Målfrid Braut-Hegghammer	**Russell Crandall**	**John A. Gans, Jr**	**Hanns W. Maull**	**Angela Stent**
Ian Bremmer	**Chester A. Crocker**	**Melissa K. Griffith**	**Jeffrey Mazo**	**Ray Takeyh**
Rosa Brooks	**Toby Dodge**	**John L. Harper**	**Teresita C. Schaffer**	**David C. Unger**
David P. Calleo	**Bill Emmott**	**Matthew Harries**	**Steven Simon**	**Lanxin Xiang**
	Mark Fitzpatrick	**Erik Jones**	**Karen Smith**	

Published for the IISS by
Routledge Journals, an imprint of Taylor & Francis, an Informa business.

Copyright © 2022 The International Institute for Strategic Studies. All rights reserved. No part of this publication may be reproduced, stored, transmitted or disseminated, in any form, or by any means, without prior written permission from Taylor & Francis, to whom all requests to reproduce copyright material should be directed, in writing.

About the IISS The IISS, a registered charity with offices in Washington, London, Manama, Singapore and Berlin, is the world's leading authority on political–military conflict. It is the primary independent source of accurate, objective information on international strategic issues. Publications include *The Military Balance*, an annual reference work on each nation's defence capabilities; *Strategic Survey*, an annual review of world affairs; *Survival*, a bimonthly journal on international affairs; *Strategic Comments*, an online analysis of topical issues in international affairs; and the *Adelphi* series of books on issues of international security.

Director-General and Chief Executive
John Chipman

Chair of the Trustees
Bill Emmott

Chair of the Council
Chung Min Lee

Trustees
Caroline Atkinson
Neha Aviral
John O. Brennan
Chris Jones
Kurt Lauk
Catherine Roe
Grace R. Skaugen
Matt Symonds
Matthew Symonds
Jens Tholstrup

IISS Advisory Council
Joanne de Asis
Caroline Atkinson
Shobhana Bhartia
Linden P. Blue
Garvin Brown
Alejandro Santo Domingo
Thomas Enders
Michael Fullilove
Yoichi Funabashi
Alia Hatoug-Bouran
Badr Jafar
Bilahari Kausikan
Thomas Lembong
Eric Li
Peter Maurer
Charles Powell
George Robertson
Andrés Rozental
Mark Sedwill
Grace R. Skaugen
Debra Soon
Heizo Takenaka
Marcus Wallenberg

SUBMISSIONS

To submit an article, authors are advised to follow these guidelines:

- *Survival* articles are around 4,000–10,000 words long including endnotes. A word count should be included with a draft.
- All text, including endnotes, should be double-spaced with wide margins.
- Any tables or artwork should be supplied in separate files, ideally not embedded in the document or linked to text around it.
- All *Survival* articles are expected to include endnote references. These should be complete and include first and last names of authors, titles of articles (even from newspapers), place of publication, publisher, exact publication dates, volume and issue number (if from a journal) and page numbers. Web sources should include complete URLs and DOIs if available.
- A summary of up to 150 words should be included with the article. The summary should state the main argument clearly and concisely, not simply say what the article is about.

- A short author's biography of one or two lines should also be included. This information will appear at the foot of the first page of the article.

Please note that *Survival* has a strict policy of listing multiple authors in alphabetical order.

Submissions should be made by email, in Microsoft Word format, to survival@iiss.org. Alternatively, hard copies may be sent to *Survival*, IISS–US, 2121 K Street NW, Suite 801, Washington, DC 20037, USA.

The editorial review process can take up to three months. *Survival*'s acceptance rate for unsolicited manuscripts is less than 20%. *Survival* does not normally provide referees' comments in the event of rejection. Authors are permitted to submit simultaneously elsewhere so long as this is consistent with the policy of the other publication and the Editors of *Survival* are informed of the dual submission.

Readers are encouraged to comment on articles from the previous issue. Letters should be concise, no longer than 750 words and relate directly to the argument or points made in the original article.

ADVERTISING AND PERMISSIONS
For advertising rates and schedules

USA/Canada: The Advertising Manager, Taylor & Francis Inc., 530 Walnut Street, Suite 850, Philadelphia, PA 19106, USA Tel +1 (800) 354 1420 Fax +1 (215) 207 0050.

UK/Europe/Rest of World: The Advertising Manager, Routledge Journals, Taylor & Francis, 4 Park Square, Milton Park, Abingdon, Oxfordshire OX14 4RN, UK Tel +44 (0) 207 017 6000 Fax +44 (0) 207 017 6336.

SUBSCRIPTIONS

Survival is published bimonthly in February, April, June, August, October and December by Routledge Journals, an imprint of Taylor & Francis, an Informa Business.

Annual Subscription 2022

	UK, RoI	US, Canada Mexico	Europe	Rest of world
Individual	£180	$303	€ 243	$303
Institution (print and online)	£648	$1,113	€ 951	$1,194
Institution (online only)	£551	$963	€ 808	$1,015

Taylor & Francis has a flexible approach to subscriptions, enabling us to match individual libraries' requirements. This journal is available via a traditional institutional subscription (either print with online access, or online only at a discount) or as part of our libraries, subject collections or archives. For more information on our sales packages please visit http://www.tandfonline.com/page/librarians.

All current institutional subscriptions include online access for any number of concurrent users across a local area network to the currently available backfile and articles posted online ahead of publication.

Subscriptions purchased at the personal rate are strictly for personal, non-commercial use only. The reselling of personal subscriptions is prohibited. Personal subscriptions must be purchased with a personal cheque or credit card. Proof of personal status may be requested.

Dollar rates apply to all subscribers outside Europe. Euro rates apply to all subscribers in Europe, except the UK and the Republic of Ireland where the pound sterling rate applies. If you are unsure which rate applies to you please contact Customer Services in the UK. All subscriptions are payable in advance and all rates include postage. Journals are sent by air to the USA, Canada, Mexico, India, Japan and Australasia. Subscriptions are entered on an annual basis, i.e. January to December. Payment may be made by sterling cheque, dollar cheque, euro cheque, international money order, National Giro or credit cards (Amex, Visa and Mastercard).

Survival (USPS 013095) is published bimonthly (in Feb, Apr, Jun, Aug, Oct and Dec) by Routledge Journals, Taylor & Francis, 4 Park Square, Milton Park, Abingdon, OX14 4RN, United Kingdom.

The US annual subscription price is $1,085. Airfreight and mailing in the USA by agent named WN Shipping USA, 156-15, 146th Avenue, 2nd Floor, Jamaica, NY 11434, USA. Periodicals postage paid at Jamaica NY 11431.

US Postmaster: Send address changes to Survival, C/O Air Business Ltd / 156-15 146th Avenue, Jamaica, New York, NY11434.

Subscription records are maintained at Taylor & Francis Group, 4 Park Square, Milton Park, Abingdon, OX14 4RN, United Kingdom.

ORDERING INFORMATION

Please contact your local Customer Service Department to take out a subscription to the Journal: **USA, Canada:** Taylor & Francis, Inc., 530 Walnut Street, Suite 850, Philadelphia, PA 19106, USA. Tel: +1 800 354 1420; Fax: +1 215 207 0050. **UK/Europe/Rest of World:** T&F Customer Services, Informa UK Ltd, Sheepen Place, Colchester, Essex, CO3 3LP, United Kingdom. Tel: +44 (0) 20 7017 5544; Fax: +44 (0) 20 7017 5198; Email: subscriptions@tandf.co.uk.

Back issues: Taylor & Francis retains a two-year back issue stock of journals. Older volumes are held by our official stockists: Periodicals Service Company, 351 Fairview Ave., Suite 300, Hudson, New York 12534, USA to whom all orders and enquiries should be addressed. *Tel* +1 518 537 4700 *Fax* +1 518 537 5899 *e-mail* psc@periodicals.com *web* http://www.periodicals.com/tandf.html.

The International Institute for Strategic Studies (IISS) and our publisher Taylor & Francis make every effort to ensure the accuracy of all the information (the "Content") contained in our publications. However, the IISS and our publisher Taylor & Francis, our agents, and our licensors make no representations or warranties whatsoever as to the accuracy, completeness, or suitability for any purpose of the Content. Any opinions and views expressed in this publication are the opinions and views of the authors, and are not the views of or endorsed by the IISS and our publisher Taylor & Francis. The accuracy of the Content should not be relied upon and should be independently verified with primary sources of information. The IISS and our publisher Taylor & Francis shall not be liable for any losses, actions, claims, proceedings, demands, costs, expenses, damages, and other liabilities whatsoever or howsoever caused arising directly or indirectly in connection with, in relation to or arising out of the use of the Content. Terms & Conditions of access and use can be found at http://www.tandfonline.com/page/terms-and-conditions.

The issue date is April–May 2022.

The print edition of this journal is printed on ANSI-conforming acid-free paper.

THE ADELPHI SERIES

JAPAN'S EFFECTIVENESS AS A GEO-ECONOMIC ACTOR

Navigating Great-power Competition

Yuka Koshino and Robert Ward

available at
amazon

OR

R Routledge
Taylor & Francis Group

Adelphi 481–483; published March 2022; 234x156; 168pp; Paperback: 978-1-032-32139-4

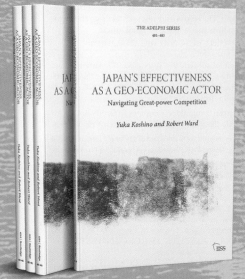

In this *Adelphi* book, Yuka Koshino and Robert Ward draw on multiple disciplines – including economics, political economy, foreign policy and security policy – and interviews with key policymakers to examine Japan's geo-economic power in the context of great-power competition between the US and China. They examine Japan's previous geo-economic underperformance, how Tokyo's understanding of geo-economics has evolved, and what actions Japan might feasibly take to become a more effective geo-economic actor. Their conclusions will be of direct interest not only for all those concerned with Japanese grand strategy and the Asia-Pacific, but also for those middle powers seeking to navigate great-power competition in the coming decades.

'In foreign affairs, Japan is often thought of as a big country acting like a small one. Yet that is to miss the significance, range and effectiveness of Japan's economic statecraft, in which the country not only acts its true size but also does so with much more autonomy and agency than it does in classic diplomacy. Yuka Koshino and Robert Ward shine a truly illuminating light on how Japan thinks and behaves as a geo-economic actor, whether through trade, investment, aid, rule-setting or, crucially, technology. This *Adelphi* book deserves to be widely read, for it adds greatly to our understanding of a much neglected and under-appreciated aspect of Japanese strategy.'

Bill Emmott, Chairman of the IISS Trustees; Chairman of the Japan Society of the UK; and author of *Japan's Far More Female Future* (Oxford University Press, 2020)

Putin's Strategic Failure

Nigel Gould-Davies

> As exposure to the atmosphere reduces all mummies to instant dissolution, so war passes supreme judgment upon social organizations that have outlived their vitality.
>
> Karl Marx on the Crimean War, 1855[1]

War is the ultimate test of a society's resources, leadership and will. It reveals what forms of power matter and which countries possess them. War's consequences are legion and unforeseen and, in modern times, have above all surprised those who start it.

Russian President Vladimir Putin's war in Ukraine is teaching Russia these lessons anew. At the time of writing, barely three weeks in, it was already clear that his 24 February invasion of Ukraine was a grand strategic error. This war has unleashed forces that are weakening his country's, and his own, position, on every political front.

Comprehensive opposition

Firstly, Putin underestimated Ukraine's cohesion and will to resist. When he declared war, he called on Ukrainian forces to lay down their arms. Many

Nigel Gould-Davies is IISS Senior Fellow for Russia and Eurasia and Editor of *Strategic Survey*. From 2000–10, he served in the UK Foreign and Commonwealth Office, including as ambassador to Belarus. He later held senior government-relations roles in the energy industry. He is author of *Tectonic Politics: Global Political Risk in an Age of Transformation* (Brookings, 2019).

Survival | vol. 64 no. 2 | April–May 2022 | pp. 7–16   https://doi.org/10.1080/00396338.2022.2055818

have died rather than surrendering, while many Russian soldiers have done the opposite – indeed, some have deserted. Doubling down on his delusion, Putin then called on the Ukrainian military to overthrow President Volodymyr Zelensky. Instead, Ukrainians who have never used a gun are now learning to do so, and to make Molotov cocktails, in defence of their country. The invasion remade Zelensky, whose popularity had fallen to 25% before the invasion, as an inspirational war leader who has united his country and rallied Western support.[2] Putin is inadvertently completing the work he began in 2014 of uniting Ukrainian society and reinforcing its national identity.

Secondly, Putin underestimated Western cohesion and resolve. It is the third time in living memory that Russia's growing threat to Europe has unleashed the West's latent strength. In the late 1940s, Soviet ambition and overreach triggered the founding of NATO, a trebling of the US defence budget and United Nations intervention in the Korean War. Growing Soviet power in the late 1970s prompted NATO to deploy intermediate-range nuclear weapons in Europe, and the Carter and Reagan administrations to begin a new military build-up. Russian aggression has now provoked an even stronger and more united transatlantic response. The earlier mobilisations of Western power had been controversial, opposed in the late 1940s by large European communist parties, and in the late 1970s by the peace movement. But this time, support for Ukraine and opposition to Russia are virtually unanimous. Corporate, sporting and cultural boycotts amplify Russia's unprecedented diplomatic isolation.

Beyond the West, Russia enjoys almost no support. Major Asian states have signed up to new export controls on semiconductors, and Singapore has imposed wider sanctions. China's abstention on the United Nations Security Council resolution condemning the Russian invasion made a mockery of the Putin–Xi declaration of friendship with 'no limits' three weeks earlier. Except for Belarus, a co-belligerent, Russia enjoys no visible support even among post-Soviet autocracies. Only four countries joined Russia in voting against the UN General Assembly (UNGA) resolution condemning the war. This is just 2% of the UNGA vote, compared to the 12% that supported the Soviet Union after its 1979 invasion of Afghanistan.[3]

This isolation is not only more comprehensive but will be far more costly, more quickly. Russia now faces a range of coercive economic measures never inflicted on a major economy. They include the freezing of central-bank assets; full blocking sanctions on several major banks and their exclusion from the SWIFT international network; a US ban on domestic purchases of Russian oil and new energy investments; a ban on semiconductor and other high-technology sales; and international cooperation to seize oligarchic assets. The United States had prepared these sanctions during the four months of Russian military build-up, and warned Russia of unprecedented measures in the event of invasion. But the European response is path-breaking. The European Union committed itself to funding arms supplies, and German policy underwent a revolution in a weekend by suspending the Nord Stream 2 gas pipeline, agreeing to send weapons and increasing the defence budget to a twenty-first-century high of 2% of GDP. Ukraine is midwife to the birth of a geopolitical EU.

The European response is path-breaking

Thirdly, Putin underestimated domestic opposition. His war against fellow Slavs is the most unpopular decision he has ever made. The stated aims – to 'denazify' a country with a democratically elected Jewish president, and to stop a 'genocide' that does not exist – lack credibility.[4] Despite a severely repressed civil society, demonstrations began on the first day of the invasion, with more than 10,000 arrests made already. Restrictions on speech have become even more draconian. The authorities have closed more media outlets and are slowly suffocating social channels. Mention of 'war' rather than a 'military operation' risks 15 years in prison. These are not the actions of a regime in confident control of the information space. It is too soon to know how far the war will turn public opinion against the authorities. But it is already clear that the costs in blood (casualties) and treasure (sanctions) of the war pose an unprecedented challenge to the regime, and that the regime knows it.

Perhaps more significantly, Russian elites are disquieted. Anxiety radiated from senior government figures whom Putin browbeat and humiliated at an extraordinary televised meeting of the Security Council on 21

February. Technocrats like Central Bank governor Elvira Nabiullina have since appeared to be in something like shock. Several celebrities and influencers have expressed their opposition to the war. The tsunami of sanctions will hurt the entire business class, not only the oligarchs, whose signalling of unease has not protected them from asset freezes, property seizures and the work of a new US 'klepto-capture' unit to pursue their overseas wealth. Even among the *siloviki* (security officials) there are growing tensions. The head and deputy head of the foreign-intelligence branch of the Federal Security Service (FSB) have reportedly been put under house arrest. Putin has ordered military prosecutors to punish officials responsible for sending conscripts to fight in Ukraine.

Deeper dynamics

All this matters because war is a contest of wills as well as arms. On the battlefield and the home front, the contrast of Russian misgivings and Ukrainian morale will shape the course of the conflict. But opposition to the war matters for domestic reasons, too. The invasion, its human costs and the pain of sanctions will weaken Putin's regime from below and within.

Russia's political misjudgements are interlocking and reinforce one another. Ukraine's success in preventing a rapid Russian victory bought time for the West to concert its response – in particular, for Europe to harden its sanctions far beyond Russia's, and perhaps its own, expectations. Zelensky's video call with EU leaders on 25 February, in which he told them that it 'may be the last time you see me alive', reportedly hastened their historic policy shift.[5] Without Ukraine's resistance and Western sanctions, the Kremlin would in turn face few strains from the war at home.

But Russia's war has not only unleashed countervailing strength on Russia's domestic, regional and international fronts. With astonishing speed, it has also shattered myths about Russia's own strength. Over the previous decade, Russia had burnished its reputation as an increasingly formidable and effective power. It appeared to have identified disintegrative forces within the West before anyone else, and learned to exploit them with disinformation and cyber power. The divisions and demoralisation of the Western alliance during the Trump years, the 6 January insurrection at the

Capitol in Washington and strategic defeat in Afghanistan all appeared to confirm the West's disarray and loss of confidence.

Meanwhile, Russia exploited its own growing strength by invading and occupying parts of Georgia in 2008 and Ukraine in 2014, and intervening in the Syrian civil war in 2015. These operations were audacious, risky and successful. By acting swiftly and decisively, Russia threw the West off balance and forced it to react to faits accomplis. Military reform and operational experience in Syria appeared to have built highly capable armed forces. Russia also challenged the West more provocatively and directly – most flagrantly by using radioactive polonium in 2006, and the military nerve agent Novichok in 2018, against its enemies on British soil. Western responses rarely disconcerted Russia and never caused it to reappraise its strategy.

As Russia increasingly confronted the West, Moscow established close ties with Beijing, cordial relations across the Middle East and a growing military presence in Africa. Putin gained admirers as an effective strongman and strategist, including among some right-wing democratic parties. Russia's one obvious weakness was its economic stagnation, and it seemed not to matter. Russia was viewed 'not as a declining power but as a persistent one' that would sustain a potent challenge across regions and domains. Decline was a 'myth'.[6]

Against this background of advances in every direction, Russia faced only one adverse trend, but one that mattered disproportionately to Putin. Ukraine, a country and people he did not consider legitimately distinct from Russia, was moving steadily out of its orbit. Ukraine's economic and security cooperation with the West deepened; national identity strengthened; the 2014–15 Minsk agreements failed to give Russia's proxies in the Donbas a veto over Ukrainian national politics; and in early 2021 Kyiv began to clamp down on the Kremlin's cat's paw (and Putin's friend), member of parliament Viktor Medvedchuk.[7] Russia found itself in the unfamiliar position of reacting to, rather than dictating, the rhythm of events. It responded by escalating its threats and demands in response to successive setbacks. In early 2021, Russia sought to coerce Ukraine into complying with its interpretation of the Minsk agreements by breaking the ceasefire in Donbas. In March and April, following Kyiv's moves against

Medvedchuk, Russia conducted a major force build-up on Ukraine's border. In October it began an even larger and more systematic mobilisation, and presented sweeping and unsatisfiable security demands to the US and NATO. When this year-long campaign of escalating compellence – the threat of force to induce policy change – failed, Putin went to war.

Putin had not used compellence before – it is the opposite of his favoured modus operandi of initiating force to achieve rapid faits accomplis – and there is almost no Soviet precedent for it.[8] Few observers realised that the novelty of its use reflected Russia's limited options for trying to halt Ukraine's drift away from its remaining pull. Even in early February 2022, many believed that Putin was merely bluffing and had achieved his goals simply by reasserting Russia's significance. This drew a false distinction – rather than equivalence – between the threat of force and its credible use. It also underplayed the political and psychological importance – obsession is not too strong a word – of Ukraine for Putin, and thus the unprecedented risks he was prepared to take.

The consequence is a war that has exposed fundamental Russian weaknesses: serious failures of military planning and execution on the battlefield; economic vulnerability and dependence that sanctions have targeted; early and emphatic defeat in the information war; and the failure to use cyber power. Russia's decline now seems more truth than myth after all.

Since Russia is already far worse off than it was before the invasion, the consolation of victory is more important than ever to Putin. As he did repeatedly in the pre-war crisis, he will therefore meet setbacks with escalation. This is already taking many forms: full deployment of forces mobilised for the war, indiscriminate attacks on civilian areas, recruitment of Syrian mercenaries, reported requests to China for help and the threat to cut gas supplies to Europe. Together, these convey determination that verges on desperation.

Conversely, any outcome short of subordinating Ukraine would mark a severe political and psychological defeat. Since the one priority higher for Putin than controlling Ukraine is the survival of his own regime, he might accept this only if he concludes that continuing the war would imperil his rule. Even in this case, it is not clear how Russia could credibly commit to a negotiated settlement, even if it wished to, given its past violations of assurances to Ukraine and systematic dissembling in the run-up to the war.

But the West, too, has much at stake. A Russian victory would put four EU and NATO members in the sights of an aggressive pariah, deeply hostile to both organisations, that has clearly signalled its intent to roll back the European security order. It would also be a recipe for regional instability. Since a pro-Russian puppet government would lack legitimacy, its rule would merely turn an inter-state war into a national liberation struggle – an eventuality now foreshadowed by the mass peaceful demonstrations in towns that Russia has occupied.

*   *   *

The war in Ukraine may thus be the first crisis in decades in which all sides see core interests at stake which they cannot abandon. This was never quite true of Cold War crises. In Europe, the West accepted Soviet imposition of brutal but (in the short term) stable outcomes on Eastern bloc uprisings. The various Berlin crises were resolved through mutually acceptable and stabilising compromises. In more peripheral Third World conflicts, one superpower or the other could ultimately accept defeat and withdrawal that, however traumatic, was not existential.

For these reasons, and because Ukraine's 43 million citizens will continue to demand a say over their future, mooted compromises of Ukraine's partition or neutralisation do not yet feel like stable solutions whose terms all sides will accept. Instead, the dynamic is one of parallel escalation: by Russia to defeat Ukraine's forces and inflict civilian costs that coerce the Zelensky government to end the war; and by the West to provide weapons to Ukraine that prevent its defeat, and impose severe costs on Russia with sanctions. This dynamic raises two risks. Firstly, parallel escalation could lead to a direct clash. Russia's threat to target arms supplies bound for Ukraine makes this more likely. Secondly, Russia, fearing defeat, could radically escalate and cross the nuclear threshold. Putin is already exploiting this fear. He issued a barely veiled threat to go nuclear if impeded by outside powers when he announced the invasion, and has since put nuclear forces on a 'special combat duty regime'.[9] The more frustrated he is on the battlefield, the more severe his tests not only of Ukrainian but of Western resolve will be. The limits of the latter have served him well many times before.

But even if Russia out-escalates the West, defeats Ukraine or bludgeons it into submission, and then somehow limits the ensuing resistance with the mass arrests and executions that Western intelligence has reported it is planning, sanctions will drastically and rapidly weaken Russia's economy, and more can be imposed. Putin has compared them to 'war', the term he forbids in describing his own aggression.

The costs of any victory will therefore be very large. But whether Russia wins, loses or finds a compromise in the field, the most fateful uncertainty of the war is its effect on the home front. Like Marx's mummies exposed to air, Putin's war has laid bare many weaknesses of Russia's power. Will it also pass its 'supreme judgement' on his regime?

Notes

1   Karl Marx, 'Another British Revelation', *New York Herald Tribune*, 24 September 1855.

2   On Zelensky's domestic problems before the war, see Olga Rudenko, 'The Comedian-turned-president Is Seriously In Over His Head', *New York Times*, 21 February 2022, https://www.nytimes.com/2022/02/21/opinion/ukraine-russia-zelensky-putin.html.

3   The UN General Assembly vote on 2 March 2022 condemning the invasion of Ukraine was 141 for, five against and 35 abstentions. The UNGA vote in January 1980 condemning the invasion of Afghanistan was 104 for, 18 against and 18 abstentions.

4   For Putin's televised speech containing these terms and accusations, see Max Fisher, 'Putin's Case for War, Annotated', *New York Times*, 24 February 2022, https://www.nytimes.com/2022/02/24/world/europe/putin-ukraine-speech.html.

5   See, for instance, Steven Erlanger, 'How Volodymyr Zelensky Rallied Ukrainians, and the World, Against Putin', *New York Times*, 27 February 2022, https://www.nytimes.com/2022/02/27/world/europe/volodymyr-zelensky-ukraine-russia.html.

6   Michael Kofman and Andrea Kendall-Taylor, 'The Myth of Russian Decline: Why Moscow Will Be a Persistent Power', *Foreign Affairs*, vol. 100, no. 6, November/December 2021, pp. 142–52.

7   In May 2021, Putin held a Security Council session devoted to this issue, at which he said that 'Ukraine is slowly but surely being turned into

some kind of antipode of Russia, into some kind of anti-Russia'. President of Russia, 'Soveshchaniye s postoyannymi chlenami Soveta Bezopasnosti' [Meeting with permanent members of the Security Council], 14 May 2021, http://www.kremlin.ru/events/security-council/65572.

8   A rare exception was the threat to crush the Solidarity trade union in Ukraine's western neighbour, Poland, in 1981. This led the Polish government to, in effect, invade its own country by declaring martial law.

9   'Putin Orders "Special Service Regime" in Russia's Deterrence Force', TASS, 27 February 2022, https://tass.com/defense/1412575?utm_source=google.com&utm_medium=organic&utm_campaign=google.com&utm_referrer=google.com.

Copyright © 2022 The International Institute for Strategic Studies

A Useful Failure: Macron's Overture to Russia

Eglantine Staunton

Throughout his presidency, French President Emmanuel Macron has promoted a rapprochement between the European Union and Russia. While he was not the first French president to attempt an overture, the proposal was considered controversial by many within and beyond France. For Macron, the rapprochement was not intended to be an end in itself, but rather a means to two ends: the strengthening of the EU and the protection of what he referred to as 'European civilisation'. As Macron argued, 'I am not pro-Russian, I am also not anti-Russian, I am pro-European'.[1] Russia's invasion of Ukraine indicates that his overture has failed. As a result, Macron has readjusted his objectives with respect to Russia. Broader aspects of his European policy, however, remain as relevant as ever.

Macron's gamble

Only two weeks after his election in May 2017, Macron invited Russian President Vladimir Putin to Versailles to celebrate the Franco-Russian friendship. Two years later, in August 2019, on the eve of the G7 Summit in Biarritz, he again hosted Putin, this time at the Fort de Brégançon, a French presidential retreat to which very few foreign visitors are invited, to discuss the future of EU–Russia relations. These high-profile exchanges were not isolated events but rather illustrated Macron's determination to promote

Eglantine Staunton is a Senior Lecturer (Fellow) in the Department of International Relations at the Coral Bell School of Asia Pacific Affairs at the Australian National University.

Survival | vol. 64 no. 2 | April–May 2022 | pp. 17–24   https://doi.org/10.1080/00396338.2022.2055819

a redefinition of the relationship between the two states and, more importantly, between the EU and Russia. He articulated this goal unambiguously at the 2019 Conference of the Ambassadors, the annual meeting in which the French president reflects on France's foreign policy and outlines its future objectives. Macron confirmed that a shift towards Russia was one of the main priorities of his foreign policy, warning the ambassadors not to push back and reminding them that foreign policy remained his *domaine réservé*.[2]

In justifying the overture, Macron argued that the EU and Russia needed each other more than ever. One of his core priorities was to strengthen the EU. In his opinion, this could not be done without Russia, since it was key to the stability of the European continent, and the EU needed it to make progress on key issues in which Russia was implicated such as Syria, counter-terrorism and cyber security. Conversely, he argued, Russia needed the EU in order to remain a great power rather than becoming the 'junior ally of China'.[3]

More grandly, Macron framed the need to strengthen the EU–Russia relationship on civilisational grounds. He claimed that 'European civilisation' was under threat, and that this was problematic because Europe was 'the only geographical area that has put humanity with a capital H at the heart of its project'.[4] He said that the EU and Russia needed to work hand in hand to protect this civilisation because they were both a part of it. Like Charles de Gaulle, Macron explained that 'Russia is European, very deeply so' because 'it is Europe in the historical sense of the term, from the Atlantic to the Urals' and 'from Lisbon to Vladivostok'.[5] Putin himself had used the latter expression.[6] While Macron promised French diplomats he would not be naive and acknowledged that a redefined relationship would take time, he contended that over the next decade the EU–Russia partnership could and should be reinvented, and promoted a deeper Franco-Russian relationship as a first step to get there.[7]

The proposed rapprochement took many French diplomats and commentators by surprise. Although Macron had acknowledged the need for some dialogue with Russia during his 2017 election campaign, he had mainly deplored his opponents' 'fascination' with Putin, declaring that the Russian leader 'does not share our values and has not fulfilled his responsibilities when it comes to international conflicts'.[8] Macron and Putin indeed sharply clashed on several issues, including Iran, Syria, Ukraine and Russia's alleged interference in various elections, including France's.

The Franco-Russian relationship had deteriorated during the presidency of his predecessor, François Hollande, due to core differences over Syria and Ukraine, and even before that period the two countries clashed over many issues, including Georgia, Iran, Kosovo and Libya. But the roots of the relationship go back to the seventeenth century, and several earlier attempts to establish warmer ties had been made during the post-Cold War era. In the early 1990s, president François Mitterrand promoted the creation of a 'European confederation'. Similarly, Jacques Chirac tried to forge a strong partnership between the EU and Russia, and the Founding Act on Mutual Relations, Cooperation and Security between NATO and the Russian Federation was signed in Paris in 1997. He also developed a strong personal relationship with both Boris Yelstin and Putin, facilitated by France and Russia's common positions on major strategic issues such as the Iraq War. Despite his Atlanticist sensibility, Nicolas Sarkozy was also determined not to isolate Russia, and, as a result, strengthened Paris's economic partnership with Moscow and even supported then Russian president Dmitry Medvedev's call for a pan-European security pact.

A frustrated overture

Despite the recent record of French government outreach to Russia, many argued that Macron's eager approach would simply repeat the mistakes of his predecessors and other Western leaders.[9] His strategy of audacity and risk-taking, as he characterised it, failed to inspire his European partners and merely upset them. Eastern European states such as Poland and Romania objected to the proposed rapprochement.[10] In June 2021, Macron and Angela Merkel, then the German chancellor, had to abandon the idea of holding an EU–Russia summit owing to the strong backlash from other EU members. By the end of 2021, Macron's strategy vis-à-vis Russia appeared to be impeding his larger objective of strengthening European sovereignty and endangering France's self-proclaimed status as European leader. The French president, however, kept emphasising that he was not naive, that the shift he was urging would take time and that the potential gains were worth the risk.

Macron's overture has not panned out. Despite his facilitation (with Merkel) of the return of Russia to the Parliamentary Assembly of the Council of Europe in June 2019 and dangling EU sanctions relief if progress were achieved on key issues, the relationship between the EU and Russia is now at its lowest point since the end of the Cold War.

What brought the relationship to its nadir, of course, was Putin's decision to invade Ukraine. In December 2021, he demanded that Ukraine and other states never be able to join NATO and that NATO remove its troops from Eastern Europe, essentially going back to the 1997 status quo. By sending more than 100,000 troops to the Ukrainian border, he warned the West that he was willing to use force to back up his demands. Macron was seen as the EU's main interlocutor with Putin during the crisis. Some hoped that his strategy was finally starting to pay off when the Russian president appeared willing to talk. On 7 February 2022, after several phone exchanges, Macron and Putin met in person in Moscow for over six hours. As Macron hinted in the press conference that followed, this meeting was possible because of the personal relationship the two leaders had built.[11] While no solution to the Ukraine crisis was formally agreed, they insisted that diplomacy was still a viable option and that some of Macron's proposals – he did not specify which ones – appeared plausible. Similarly, on 20 February 2022, Macron seemed to have convinced Putin to meet with US President Joe Biden during a summit on the security of Europe and argued that de-escalation was still possible.

Macron was relying on a strategy he has also used in the Indo-Pacific: offer a third way between escalation and capitulation, which he labelled 'demanding dialogue'.[12] With respect to Ukraine, he aimed to find a compromise that would address Putin's concerns by offering 'tangible security guarantees' while rejecting 'the use of force' and 'spheres of influence', and guaranteeing 'the territorial integrity of states' and their 'freedom of choice' to join alliances.[13] Putin crushed Macron's hopes when he recognised the independence of two separatist regions in eastern Ukraine on 21 February 2022, hours after Macron announced that Putin and Biden had agreed to a summit. Russian forces began the invasion of Ukraine three days later.

If a war on the European continent were not enough, Russia has challenged France and the EU in Syria and Mali. Russia's numerous vetoes at the United Nations Security Council and its support for Syrian President Bashar al-Assad's brutal regime have helped perpetuate the lengthy and bloody conflict, and impeded humanitarian aid and counter-terrorism operations. In Mali, Russian mercenaries from the Wagner Group have interfered with French counter-insurgency operations initially undertaken in 2013, and indirectly contributed to the expulsion of the French ambassador to Mali in January 2022.[14]

Moving forward

In light of these frustrations, Macron has begun to make necessary adjustments to his foreign policy towards Russia. France's presidency of the Council of the EU for the first half of 2022 has afforded him an opportunity to anchor Europe's response to Putin's aggression in Ukraine. Macron has coordinated EU sanctions against Russia, committed more French troops to NATO and agreed that France will lead a new NATO forward-presence deployment in Romania.

To an extent, Macron's determination to play a central role in addressing the Ukraine war is a function of his desire to distance perceptions that he fell for Putin's duplicity, especially considering that the French presidential election is imminent. More importantly, though, Macron wants to sustain the ambitious vision of the EU and France's role within it that he has held throughout his presidency, and to justify France's self-proclaimed status as an indispensable leader of the EU. At the very least, he has been able to establish France's leadership on Europe–Russia relations. This has been possible not only because of the diplomatic rapport he has built with Putin over the years, but also because Macron has avoided any appearance of unilateralism, for which he was earlier criticised, by extensively consulting with other European partners, the United States and NATO since the beginning of the Ukraine crisis.

Even though Macron's rapprochement with Russia has failed, other aspects of his foreign policy remain eminently relevant. In particular, Macron has advocated greater European strategic autonomy throughout his presidency, and Ukraine's situation confirms that the EU needs to be stronger diplomatically and militarily. The fact that Putin tried to deal exclusively with the United States at the beginning of the crisis and the EU's dependency on NATO for security matters tended to validate Macron's claim that the EU needed to step up if it wanted to 'decide its own future' and 'be a power of equilibrium'.[15] Some observers have construed Macron's behaviour as divisive.[16] In fact, his objective has not been to exclude NATO or the US from the negotiations, but merely to make sure that the EU itself has a roughly equal voice and can address major tensions taking place on the continent. The United States shares this objective as it seeks to focus on China and the Indo-Pacific.

The crisis in Ukraine has also shown the need to negotiate what Macron has called a new 'collective security order' by way of a much broader discussion on the stability and security of the continent. As Macron hinted in his speech to the European Parliament on 19 January 2022, the extent and nature of the discussions cannot be as ambitious as he had originally hoped, but basic issues of stability and security must be on the table.

*   *   *

Putin has been caught off guard both by Ukraine's capacity to slow down the invasion and by the EU's response to it. The speed, scale and scope of the EU's sanctions are noteworthy and can be seen as participating in economic warfare. Additionally, for the first time in history, the EU has taken the decision to deliver weapons to a non-member state. The war in Ukraine has dislodged the complacency of EU members about European defence. Even reluctant states such as Germany appear to be on board, and Chancellor Olaf Scholz announced that the country would overturn its post-Second World War defence policy by spending more than 2% of its GDP on its military. In the meantime, the EU is working to strengthen the European pillar of NATO. When the time comes, it will also be in a stronger position to define a new collective security order with Russia because it is looking at ways to reduce its dependence on Russian gas: the Nord Stream 2 pipeline is dead, alternative sources have already been sought out and there is a push under way towards nuclear alternatives and renewable energy. It is uncertain when and how the conflict will end. But it does seem clear that despite his failed attempt at rapprochement – and to some extent because of it – Macron will continue to lead the EU's effort to deal with Russia.

Notes

1   Emmanuel Macron, 'Discours à la conférence de Munich', Élysée, 15 February 2020, https://www.elysee.fr/emmanuel-macron/2020/02/15/conference-sur-la-securite-de-munich-faire-revivre-leurope-comme-une-puissance-politique-strategique.

2   See Emmanuel Macron, 'Conférence des ambassadeurs', Élysée, 27 August 2019, https://www.elysee.fr/emmanuel-macron/2019/08/27/discours-du-president-de-la-republique-a-la-conference-des-ambassadeurs-1.

3   Ibid.

4   Macron, 'Conférence des ambassadeurs'. See also Eglantine Staunton, '"France Is Back": Macron's European Policy to Rescue "European Civilisation" and the Liberal International Order', Third World Quarterly, vol. 43, no. 1, November 2021, pp. 18–34.

5   Emmanuel Macron, 'Déclaration conjointe avec Vladimir Poutine', Élysée, 20 August 2019, https://www.elysee.fr/emmanuel-macron/2019/08/20/declaration-de-presse-demmanuel-macron-president-de-la-republique-avec-vladimir-poutine-president-de-la-federation-de-russie; and Emmanuel Macron, 'Discours devant le Conseil de l'Europe', Élysée, 31 October 2017, https://www.elysee.fr/emmanuel-macron/2017/10/31/discours-du-president-de-la-republique-emmanuel-macron-devant-le-conseil-de-leurope-a-strasbourg.

6   See, for instance, 'President Vladimir Putin's Speech at the Meeting of the Customs Union Heads of State with President of Ukraine and European Union Representatives', Permanent Mission of the Russian Federation to the European Union, 26 August 2014, https://russiaeu.ru/en/president-vladimir-putins-speech-meeting-customs-union-heads-state-president-ukraine-and-european-un.

7   See Macron, 'Conférence des ambassadeurs'.

8   Emmanuel Macron, 'Discours de la politique de lutte contre le terrorisme', En Marche, 10 April 2017, https://en-marche.fr/articles/discours/meeting-macron-politique-lutte-contre-le-terrorisme.

9   See, for example, James Nixey and Mathieu Boulègue, 'On Russia, Macron Is Mistaken', Chatham House, 5 September 2019, https://www.chathamhouse.org/expert/comment/russia-macron-mistaken.

10   See, for instance, Robin Emmott, John Irish and Andreas Rink, 'EU Divisions over Russia Mount as France, Germany Seek Peace in Ukraine', Reuters, 6 October 2019, https://www.reuters.com/article/us-ukraine-russia-eu-idUSKCN1WL04D.

11   See Emmanuel Macron, 'Déplacement du Président de la République en Russie', Élysée, 8 February

2022, https://www.elysee.fr/emmanuel-macron/2022/02/08/deplacement-du-president-de-la-republique-en-russie/.

12 See, for instance, Colin Dwyer, 'Macron Opens a "Demanding" Dialogue with Putin in France', NPR, 29 May 2017, https://www.npr.org/sections/thetwo-way/2017/05/29/530575368/macron-opens-a-demanding-dialogue-with-putin-in-france.

13 Emmanuel Macron, 'Discours devant le Parlement Européen', Élysée, 19 January 2022, https://www.elysee.fr/emmanuel-macron/2022/01/19/discours-du-president-emmanuel-macron-devant-le-parlement-europeen.

14 See 'Mali: Wagner pille "déjà" le pays mais ne cherche pas à remplacer les Européens, affirme Jean-Yves Le Drian', Le Figaro, 30 January 2022, https://www.lefigaro.fr/flash-actu/wagner-pille-deja-le-mali-mais-ne-cherche-pas-a-remplacer-les-europeens-affirme-paris-20220130.

15 Macron, 'Discours devant le Parlement Européen'.

16 See, for instance, Mehreen Khan et al., 'Macron Floats EU Security Pact with Russia, Risking Western Split over Ukraine', Financial Times, 19 January 2022, https://www.ft.com/content/0db12864-a154-4607-a0e8-c9722e956424.

Copyright © 2022 The International Institute for Strategic Studies

Protecting US Interests in Afghanistan

Laurel Miller

The time has passed when Washington could hope to exert much sway over how Afghanistan is governed. With the Taliban in charge since their mid-August 2021 takeover, the United States has little leverage to shape how the former insurgents, who withstood US military, diplomatic and sanctions pressure for two decades, will run the country.

The Taliban regime now ruling from Kabul is not entirely immune to outside influences. In its public statements, it appears intent on portraying itself as a responsible power both at home and in its foreign relations.[1] The regime desires legitimacy and needs financial help to restore a semblance of functionality to the country's devastated economy.[2] But it remains disinclined to give much ground on American and other Western demands – for instance, that it rule in a more inclusive fashion and restore to women all of the freedoms to study and work that they enjoyed for 20 years.

For the foreseeable future, Afghanistan will not have anything like the kind of state that the US planned for, invested in and wanted to see take hold during two decades of counter-insurgency and nation-building. There will be no fledgling democracy under a constitution promising equal rights and protections for women and minorities, and no security partner for the US. Even the more limited current aims that Biden administration officials have articulated – a 'more representative government'

Laurel Miller is Director of the Asia Program at the International Crisis Group. From 2013 to 2017, she was deputy and then acting Special Representative for Afghanistan and Pakistan at the US State Department.

Survival | vol. 64 no. 2 | April–May 2022 | pp. 25–34   https://doi.org/10.1080/00396338.2022.2055820

that respects 'the rights of all Afghans'[3] – are likely out of reach, at least as Washington would define them.

But the US does still have some choices about the relationship it can have with Afghanistan. Failure to define a 'good enough' relationship in terms of US interests and a path for establishing it risks policy drift.

Isolation vs engagement

The collapse of the US-supported government and the Taliban's ascent to power triggered an immediate US policy of isolation. This included cutting off all non-humanitarian foreign aid, closing the US Embassy, freezing over $7 billion of Afghan foreign-exchange assets held in the US and broadly applying long-standing sanctions on the Taliban to the entire country. These and similar steps by other Western states produced an enormous economic shock that, combined with drought and persistent fragility, pushed more than half the population into acute food insecurity and plunged the already poor country deeper into poverty.[4] (Collectively, Western aid to the prior government had paid for about three-fourths of public spending, including most civil-servant salaries.) At the same time, to salve these effects, the US has been the top contributor to a large humanitarian-aid response, running to a total of nearly $2bn in 2021, with $4.4bn requested for a United Nations-coordinated response plan for 2022.[5]

In the months since the political upheaval and the end of the war, driven largely by the urgency of the humanitarian and economic crises, the US has relaxed its policy of isolation in several ways. In particular, it has made exceptions to the sanctions regime through US Treasury Department 'general licenses', undertaken intermittent diplomatic engagement with regime officials outside of Afghanistan and loosened restrictions on access to World Bank trust-fund money for healthcare, education and agriculture.[6] Washington also may release some of the frozen central-bank reserves, but has not yet determined how they might be used.[7]

The current policy approach is thus a hybrid of isolation and engagement, whereby Washington is seeking to ease the effects of economic disruption while avoiding any financial transfers to or through public institutions. Although carve-outs from sanctions and recent clarifications of the sanctions' scope have been important for enabling the flow of humanitarian aid and removing some impediments to ordinary economic activity, a broader lifting of sanctions does not appear to be on the horizon. A partial return of the Afghan central bank's reserves and a plan for restoration of normal central-banking functions probably is not imminent. And there are no signs that diplomatic interaction will become more regular.

After losing a 20-year war with the Taliban, the United States' rapid shift from isolation – the default response – to normalised engagement would have been unusual and unexpected. If not for Afghanistan's rapid descent into what – at least until the Russian invasion of Ukraine – had been shaping up as the world's most dire humanitarian crisis, a posture even more severe than the current one would have been probable. The Taliban's conduct as a government so far, although not as harsh as its moral policing of the 1990s, neither accords with US values nor seems susceptible to real change. The group has not yet expressed a political vision, much less one involving pluralism or representative government, and how it will perform in suppressing terrorist groups present in Afghanistan remains uncertain. Similar realities are not a bar to bilateral relations with governments elsewhere in the world, but obviously do not make the Taliban regime an attractive partner or beneficiary.

Nevertheless, the logic of keeping isolating measures in place, even if some degree of engagement moderates them, is elusive. Given how resilient the group proved against much more powerful US pressure during the war, sanctions, asset freezes and limitations on diplomatic interaction are unlikely to shape the Taliban's behaviour to any significant degree. If the purpose of those policies is to starve the regime of resources, the effects are more likely to be visited on the population, which didn't choose to live under Taliban rule, than on the regime itself. If limiting the regime's ability to raise funds is intended to curtail its spending power, that raises questions about the degree to which the US wishes to hobble the new regime and for what purpose. While isolation does express moral opprobrium, it seems largely decorative, since the US decision to withdraw from Afghanistan was projected to lead to a Taliban victory anyway. Some may believe that the Taliban still deserve punishment for hosting al-Qaeda leaders while they plotted the 9/11 attacks, but there have been no indications that the Biden administration has deliberately chosen a policy of retribution.

Lifting the sanctions and asset freezes would make the US less complicit in Afghanistan's economic hardship and mitigate the risk of growing anti-Western sentiment. But it would not solve the problem of the country's lack of economic self-sufficiency. The government and economy have historically been dependent on externally provided resources. Although preventing the state's degeneration into utter dysfunctionality is crucial for Afghans, who need an effective public sector, and would increase regional stability, it is politically implausible for the US to allocate large-scale foreign assistance directly to the Taliban-led government. The crisis in Europe may have imperilled even funding for the UN's humanitarian appeal for 2022, which should not be subject to political considerations.

There is also the problem of aid conditionality. Policymakers in Washington and other capitals who are focused on Afghanistan appreciate that humanitarian aid alone provides a bandage but cannot staunch an increasingly impoverished population's bleeding.[8] Donor governments have considered the idea of formulating a conditionality framework in restoring some aid beyond basic needs to shore up the public sector and boost economic activity. Donors have not yet determined what they would expect from the Taliban in exchange for broader aid programmes, however, and they are unlikely to be able to establish a mutually satisfactory formula. The Taliban are highly reluctant to be seen as wanting or needing foreign support and simply assume Western governments will help the Afghan people to the extent they care about the population's welfare, so any conditions they might agree to would likely be unacceptably minimal to those governments.

So far, the US has articulated general goals – more representative government and respect for human rights, including free movement of Afghans who wish to leave the country, a clampdown on reported reprisal killings and universal girls' education (currently available on a limited basis at the secondary-school level) – but without any clarity, at least publicly, on what the Taliban might get in return. Any counter-terrorism demands Washington may be making have not been openly disclosed, but probably resemble the

February 2020 US–Taliban deal's provisions calling on the Taliban to keep a lid on terrorist groups, including al-Qaeda, present in the country.

The US goals are all worthy of continued pursuit. They do not, however, add up to a clear vision of a US–Afghanistan relationship, especially given that the Taliban are not likely to loosen their unilateral grip on power or diverge from their brand of religiously and culturally based social conservatism.

US interests

The United States has several reasons to want a more serviceable relationship with Afghanistan, even under Taliban rule. Firstly, the US has an ongoing security interest in preventing Afghanistan from becoming a base for transnational terrorist groups operating there that could harm the US or its allies.[9] Secondly, the US has a moral and reputational interest in securing the departure of Afghans endangered because of their past involvement in American efforts in the country, as well as in helping the population at large preserve some of the social and economic advances of the last two decades. Thirdly, the US has a political and security interest in tamping down anti-Western sentiment in and around Afghanistan by ameliorating the country's humanitarian and economic degradation.

A more representative form of government is desirable from a democratic perspective, but it is not necessarily a core US interest. If the Taliban took Western advice and did broaden the composition of their government, that might help bolster the regime's durability by defusing the grievances of ethnic and regional groups who feel unable to influence the new political arrangements. But it is not certain that inclusivity would lead to a durably more peaceful Afghanistan because the potential would remain for violent competition over political power and economic resources.

At least for the time being, however, Taliban regime collapse would not be advantageous for the US. It would surely produce more chaos in the security environment, more bloodshed and greater humanitarian disaster. Although the US may not wish to shore up the Taliban regime, it would be prudent for it to avoid actively delegitimising it or undermining its stability. Simply neglecting Afghanistan might be the path of least resistance, but that course would not enable the US to satisfy any of its interests. Washington needs to affirmatively define the relationship it wishes to have and actively work to establish it.

Defining a steady-state relationship

Perhaps the most obvious lesson from US involvement in Afghanistan is that ambitions should be kept well in check. Any relationship that Washington could realistically establish in the near to medium term would be limited, and should have four main features. Firstly, the relationship should involve persistent and routinised diplomatic engagement by US government personnel, based in Kabul, through an interests section housed within another country's embassy. Secondly, beyond providing humanitarian aid, it should incorporate a modest development-assistance programme focused on supporting livelihoods and well-being in areas such as healthcare, education, agriculture and rural development. Thirdly, the US should amend the sanctions architecture, tailoring it to specific activities of concern, such as arms transfers to Afghanistan or terrorist-group financing. Finally, direct engagement of US personnel with specific high-level Taliban figures whom Washington regards as politically or morally inappropriate interlocutors based on past or ongoing actions should be limited.

A relationship with these characteristics could enable the US to protect its interests by maintaining open lines of communication on US counter-terrorism concerns and offering the Taliban sufficient diplomatic normalisation and foreign aid to incentivise the regime to reduce the risks of terrorist activity in Afghanistan. It would also give the US a diplomatic platform for persistent engagement to, among other things, facilitate the exit of Afghans who had been promised a path towards immigration to the US. In addition, it would enable the United States to help prevent worst-case humanitarian outcomes, and afford it influence in international efforts to reduce Afghanistan's aid dependency over time.

Such a relationship also would provide the US with diplomatic means – limited, but more robust than they currently are – to press its concerns about governance and human-rights issues. Though results in these areas would probably be marginal, the Taliban's desire for international legitimacy might at least give the US and other outside actors enough collective leverage to rein in the most egregious conduct. The persistent engagement envisioned here would also enable the US to gain, develop and maintain a better understanding of facts on the ground than it currently has.

The policy basis for sustaining such a relationship would not be that the Taliban are satisfying US desires for how the group governs, but rather that the group is willing to engage with Washington on matters relevant to US interests. To be viable, Washington would probably need to dangle the possibility of full recognition and reciprocal re-establishment of embassies, even though that is not likely to be politically feasible for some years.

One tempting question is whether the United States' relationship with Afghanistan could evolve roughly along the lines of its bilateral relationship with Vietnam after the war, to the point where the US State Department referred to Afghanistan, as it now refers to Vietnam, as one of America's 'trusted partners with a friendship grounded in mutual respect'.[10] It's not impossible, but full normalisation of that relationship and lifting of a trade embargo did not happen until 20 years after the war. It is premature to plot out the longer-term evolution of the US–Afghanistan relationship, not least because it is not yet clear how and for how long the Taliban regime will govern. But the Vietnam example does counsel that the US should remain alert to any opportunities for expanded normalisation.

Potential disrupters

There are several important potential disrupters of the United States' ability to sustain a satisfactory steady-state relationship with a Taliban-run Afghanistan. The most damaging would be a terrorist attack tied to the country. In that event, there would be no way to seriously punish the Taliban without resorting to the use of force. Ratcheting up sanctions or other economic pressure would harm the population but have little impact on a regime that is already well practised in surviving such pressure. Even without once again dislodging the regime, the US could launch punitive attacks, but obviously any semi-normalised relationship would be broken.

A rise in domestic armed opposition to the Taliban could also disrupt the relationship. It would be naive to assume that the violent contest for power in Afghanistan has permanently ended. If an armed opposition group gained traction, political momentum might build within the US to support it, particularly if the Taliban were not conducting themselves in ways that accommodated US interests and values.

If Taliban governance becomes egregiously bad for Afghans, say with a return to the harshest forms of moral policing and violence against sectors of the population, opposition to engagement in Washington could become overwhelming. Finally, the Taliban – through incompetence, malign intent or both – could come to pose a threat to Afghanistan's neighbours and more broadly to regional security serious enough to preclude a normal US diplomatic relationship with the regime.

* * *

So far, the Taliban claim to want a relationship of mutual respect with the US and formal recognition of their regime's legitimacy. But they are reluctant to convey what, if anything, they are willing to do to attain those goals. For the time being, their priority remains consolidation of power and suppression of potential challengers. Having just won the war and given the strong current of nationalist pride in their rhetoric, they are loath to accommodate US interests – or at least to appear to do so. Nevertheless, the US should pursue a relationship with the group without expecting too much in return. Such an initiative would not merely be a favour to Afghans, though no doubt they would benefit. Rather, it would be mainly a way for the United States to secure a reliable means of protecting US interests that the alternative – no relationship beyond occasional ad hoc problem-solving – would not allow.

Notes

1   After the Russian invasion of Ukraine, for instance, the Ministry of Foreign Affairs issued a statement calling for restraint, expressing concern about civilian casualties and noting its 'foreign policy of neutrality'. Islamic Emirate of Afghanistan, Ministry of Foreign Affairs, 'Statement Concerning Crisis in Ukraine', 25 February 2022, https://twitter.

com/QaharBalkhi/status/1497104 807932272647?s=20&t=8e_2j6am SdA-8CYBMg0a9w.

2   See Christina Goldbaum, 'Facing Economic Collapse, Afghanistan Is Gripped by Starvation', *New York Times*, 4 December 2021, https://www. nytimes.com/2021/12/04/world/asia/ afghanistan-starvation-crisis.html.

3   'U.S. Aims to Restore Modes of Transportation Out of Afghanistan, Tom West Says', Rachel Martin Interview with US Special Representative for Afghanistan Tom West, NPR, 2 March 2022, https://www.npr. org/2022/03/02/1083881226/u-s-aims-to-restore-modes-of-transportation-out-of-afghanistan-tom-west-says.

4   See International Crisis Group, 'Beyond Emergency Relief: Averting Afghanistan's Humanitarian Catastrophe', 6 December 2021, https://www. crisisgroup.org/asia/south-asia/ afghanistan/317-beyond-emergency-relief-averting-afghanistans-humanitarian-catastrophe; and World Food Programme, 'Afghanistan', https://www.wfp.org/ countries/afghanistan.

5   See UN Office of the Coordinator for Humanitarian Affairs, 'Afghanistan Flash Appeal 2021' and 'Afghanistan Humanitarian Response Plan 2022',

available at https://fts.unocha.org.

6   See World Bank, 'World Bank Announces Expanded Approach to Supporting the People of Afghanistan', 1 March 2022, https://www.worldbank.org/en/ news/press-release/2022/03/01/ world-bank-announces-expanded-approach-to-supporting-the-people-of-afghanistan.

7   See Christina Goldbaum, Safiullah Padshah and Taimoor Shah, 'Biden's Decision on Frozen Funds Stokes Anger Among Afghans', *New York Times,* 13 February 2022, https://www. nytimes.com/2022/02/13/world/asia/ afghanistan-funds-biden.html.

8   See 'David Miliband's Testimony to the Senate Foreign Relations Committee Subcommittee on Afghanistan', Rescue.org, 9 February 2022, https://www.rescue.org/ press-release/david-milibands-testimony-senate-foreign-relations-committee-subcommittee-afghanistan.

9   See Joshua T. White, 'Nonstate Threats in the Taliban's Afghanistan', Brookings Institution, 1 February 2022, https://www.brookings.edu/blog/ order-from-chaos/2022/02/01/nonstate-threats-in-the-talibans-afghanistan/.

10 US Department of State, 'US Relations with Vietnam, Bilateral Relations Fact Sheet', 9 April 2021, https://www. state.gov/u-s-relations-with-vietnam/.

Copyright © 2022 The International Institute for Strategic Studies

South Korea's Aircraft-carrier Debate

Jeongseok Lee

Amid an accelerating naval arms race in the Asia-Pacific, South Korea is preparing to build its first aircraft carrier. After years of rumours, in August 2020 Seoul officially announced its plan to commission a 'light' carrier with a displacement of 30,000 tonnes around 2033.[1] According to the South Korean navy, the vessel will have a flight deck 254 metres long and 43 metres wide capable of handling ten to 12 vertical take-off and landing (VTOL) fighters.[2]

In October 2021, South Korean President Moon Jae-in revealed his enthusiasm for the new carrier by confidently declaring that it would speed up the South Korean navy's transformation into a blue-water navy.[3] Since the early 2000s, South Korea has acquired three *Aegis* destroyers and two amphibious assault ships. Along with six more 'mini-*Aegis*' destroyers and eight more KSS-III-class advanced submarines to be commissioned over the next two decades, the new carrier would significantly increase the South Korean navy's capability to carry out operations in distant waters.[4]

Not everyone in South Korea is enthusiastic about this ambitious plan. Since the announcement of the carrier programme, the country's politicians, defence analysts and news media have engaged in a heated debate over the programme's practicality and desirability. This ongoing conversation extends beyond the issue of military procurement to South Korea's grand strategy.

Jeongseok Lee is a visiting scholar in the Department of Political Science at James Madison University, focusing on Asia-Pacific security and US–Asia relations. His work on this article was supported by the Albritton Center for Grand Strategy at Texas A&M University.

Survival | vol. 64 no. 2 | April–May 2022 | pp. 35–44   https://doi.org/10.1080/00396338.2022.2055821

Affordability

As in many other carrier debates, the first point of contention is the programme's cost. According to a government estimate, the cost of building the vessel will be about two trillion won (approximately $1.7 billion).[5] Civilian defence experts who support the programme offer similar projections. Onboard aircraft will cost an additional 3trn won ($2.55bn), more than doubling the effective cost.[6]

Yet opponents of the carrier programme charge that the government is significantly underestimating the expense of the overall platform. For instance, Representative Shin Won-sik of the South Korean National Assembly contends that acquiring fixed-wing VTOL aircraft alone will cost up to 4trn won ($3.4bn), while procuring escort ships will require an additional 12trn won ($10.2bn). The programme's total cost will reach 30–40trn won ($26–34bn), he argues, if the operating cost of a carrier battle group is included.[7]

The large gap between these cost breakdowns arises from different approaches to budget assessment. Both the government and critics tend to agree that the initial acquisition of a carrier and onboard aircraft will require 5–6trn won ($4.25–5.1bn). The jaw-dropping figure of 30–40trn won suggested by critics includes the cost of acquiring escorts and the operating costs of the entire carrier battle group over its full lifespan. Factoring in the latter is somewhat inequitable since adding long-term operating costs would significantly bloat any defence programme's price tag. Furthermore, the estimate may exaggerate the marginal cost of establishing a carrier group insofar as the South Korean navy already operates, or will soon commission, several advanced destroyers and submarines that could be used to complete the group. And although the initial acquisition cost of 5–6trn won is itself substantial, it will be spread over the next 13 to 15 years. South Korea spends 16–17trn won on the acquisition and development of weapons systems every year, so the multi-year outlay for the carrier programme does not seem prohibitive.[8]

Strategic utility

Critics also view building an aircraft carrier as an unnecessary diversion of resources. This line of argument comes mostly from those who believe Seoul's strategy should be focused on North Korea, which still poses the greatest threat. They contend that an aircraft carrier will add little value in addressing that threat, since South Korea itself would serve as an 'unsinkable aircraft carrier' in a conflict with the North.[9]

The South Korean navy and supporters of the carrier programme claim that an aircraft carrier could serve as a useful deterrent and defence against the North by functioning as a 'mobile airfield at sea'.[10] The South Korean air force's bases are vulnerable to surprise attacks as fixed targets, they say, whereas the air assets on a carrier would be able to avoid such strikes.[11] In fact, when the South Korean government first announced the carrier programme in 2020, it presented it as part of the acquisition plan for enhancing the capacity to attack strategic targets in North Korea.[12]

This rationale, however, seems to have been developed mainly to defend the project from critics. Deterring North Korea can hardly be the main purpose of building the aircraft carrier. In a war with the North, the carrier could offer more strategic options by providing credible amphibious capacity and flexible air support for ground forces.[13] But the South Korean military already has capabilities that are sufficient to overwhelm North Korea's air defences. In addition, the entire territory of North Korea already lies within the mission radius of the South Korean military's *Hyunmu*-series missiles and F-15K fighters.

The central, and more convincing, basis for the carrier programme is that it would be a key strategic asset in addressing Seoul's growing concerns about regional maritime security. While South Korea is not one of the disputants, it has been warily watching the increasing tensions in the East and South China seas. As the country depends heavily on oil and gas imports transiting these waters, the perception that it cannot remain a passive spectator has gradually emerged in Seoul over the past decade.[14] Concerns about Beijing's maritime expansion have also grown with the increasing frequency of Chinese intrusion of South Korea's exclusive economic zone (EEZ) and air-defence identification zone. Former US president Donald Trump's public complaints about America's burden of protecting global shipping lanes and doubts about the value of its alliances have also bolstered the case for a South Korean blue-water navy.[15] Although Trump is gone now, worries about a potential US retreat remain very real in Seoul. Without a blue-water capability of its own, the diminution of America's maritime presence would require South Korea to depend on China and Japan, which have substantial naval capacities, to keep East Asian shipping lanes open and safe. Given China's increasing assertiveness and South Korea's long-standing friction with Japan over historical and maritime issues, however, relying on these neighbours would be an unattractive option for Seoul.

The Moon government's shift in defence policy indicates that the main reason for the carrier programme is to expand the South Korean navy's operational focus beyond the Korean Peninsula. Until Moon came to power in 2017, Seoul's defence policy had been practically confined to North Korea for decades, and the South Korean navy had remained a small, brown-water force for coastal defence. Moon has tried to change this traditional defence policy. While easing tensions with Pyongyang with a dovish approach to North Korea, his government has accelerated the modernisation of air and naval forces to address 'potential regional threats' beyond the North.[16] The carrier programme is part of this effort. With Moon's strong endorsement, the South Korean navy now envisions building a 'strategic mobile fleet' consisting of three maritime task forces that will carry out operations outside the littoral waters around the Korean Peninsula. Each task force will operate six destroyers and two submarines, and the new carrier will reportedly lead one of the task forces as the flagship.[17]

Considering its small size and design, South Korea's new carrier could provide only limited power-projection capacity in a distant theatre such as the South China Sea, and its survivability in a full-scale war remains questionable. Nevertheless, the carrier and its strategic mobile fleet would serve as effective deterrents or tools of coercion in medium- and low-intensity disputes near the border of South Korea's EEZ and beyond.[18] The carrier programme would also help Seoul catch up with its neighbours in an accelerating naval-aviation contest. China already operates two carriers, and a third is expected to enter service around 2025.[19] Japan recently launched its own aircraft-carrier programme, under which its two helicopter-carrying destroyers will be transformed into fixed-wing carriers.[20] The development of a carrier would thus allow South Korea to join a prestigious club of regional carrier operators and, in theory, give it a useful strategic card to play in potential maritime disputes with Beijing and Tokyo.

Risk of entanglement

Some opponents of the carrier programme worry that it may increase the risk of entanglement in a US–China confrontation. They warn that even if South Korea does not contemplate China as a target of the new carrier now, Beijing – already wary of emerging US-led naval coalitions such as the Quadrilateral Security Dialogue and AUKUS – may see a South Korean carrier as a strategic asset that the United States could potentially marshal against China.[21]

This seems a valid concern. Although the United States has not officially weighed in on Seoul's carrier programme so far, once the carrier is completed Washington is likely to press Seoul to participate in the American and allied effort to contain Beijing's maritime expansion. Despite its relatively small size and limited power-projection capabilities, South Korea's new carrier could pose a substantial challenge to China in certain multilateral settings. Shin Won-sik raised this possibility in a parliamentary debate in December 2020, arguing that the South Korean carrier would be used mostly to support US Indo-Pacific Command's naval missions directed at China rather than carrying out independent missions.[22] In a similar vein, former representative Kim Jong-dae, a prominent defence analyst, observed that it would be difficult for Seoul to refuse such a demand from Washington.[23] While China too has remained silent on South Korea's carrier programme, critics suspect that Beijing will raise questions about Seoul's real intentions as the programme progresses. In fact, a few Chinese journalists and civilian analysts have already begun to voice suspicions that South Korea's carrier group could be used against China.[24]

At the same time, some supporters of the programme suggest that the development of a carrier would strengthen South Korea's alliance with the United States by signalling Seoul's intention to participate in the US Indo-Pacific strategy.[25] However, this is not an easy decision for South Korea to make. In the recent feud between Seoul and Beijing over the deployment of the United States' Terminal High Altitude Area Defense (THAAD) system in South Korea, Seoul learned that antagonising Beijing could be very costly. In response to South Korea's decision to deploy the system, China imposed harsh economic sanctions that substantially damaged South Korean businesses. This punishment lasted more than a year, ending with Seoul's implicit pledge not to form a trilateral alliance with Washington and Tokyo against Beijing.[26] In light of the significant geopolitical implications of South Korea's aircraft-carrier programme, it could become another THAAD.

*   *   *

Whether South Korea will have its own aircraft carrier in the early 2030s, as planned, remains to be seen. Sceptical lawmakers remain an obstacle. Soon after the carrier programme was officially launched in 2020, South Korea's National Assembly almost killed it by cutting 99% of the 2021 budget requested by the navy for the programme.[27] Although the programme's 2022 budget survived the parliamentary deliberation, before the approval the National Assembly's National Defense Committee had attempted to cut 93% of the requested budget.[28] The opposition People Power Party, which has traditionally supported the North Korea-focused defence policy, has voiced the most vehement opposition to the programme. While the ruling Democratic Party of Korea has generally supported Moon's defence reform and expansive strategic vision, many of its members are worried that the carrier programme will burden a government budget already strained by the COVID-19 pandemic. In addition, Moon, who has championed the programme and sustained its momentum despite the National Assembly's doubts, is leaving office this spring.

Arguably superseding partisan domestic political factors, however, is the increasingly urgent question of South Korea's grand strategy. For decades, South Korea has stuck to the strategy of 'America for security, China for economy'. This has worked quite well thanks to relatively stable US–China relations. Washington has continued its extended deterrence against North Korea without demanding that Seoul carry a regional security burden beyond the Korean Peninsula, and Beijing has provided enormous economic benefits to South Korean businesses without asking Seoul to distance itself from Washington. However, as tension between the United States and China has grown, the Biden administration has pressured its Indo-Pacific allies to do more to counter Beijing's ambitions.[29] Moon has remained silent about Seoul's position, but his successor will have to formulate a clear response.

If South Korea opts to participate more actively in emerging US-led regional initiatives aimed at China, the carrier programme is likely to get a boost. If it opts to retain its North Korea-focused grand strategy and distances itself from anti-China coalitions, the programme will probably lose momentum. A South Korean aircraft-carrier programme would not fundamentally change the balance of naval power in the Asia-Pacific. But its fate does provide a window into South Korea's strategic soul-searching.

Notes

1   Ministry of National Defense of the Republic of Korea, '21–25 Gukbang Junggyi Gyehoek Bogo' [National defence mid-term plan 2021–25], 10 August 2020, https://www.mnd.go.kr/user/boardList.action?command=view&page=1&boardId=O_59748&boardSeq=O_256039&titleId=null&id=mnd_010403000000&siteId=mnd.

2   Rear Admiral Chung Seung-kyun, 'Gyeonghangongmohameui Jakjeon Jeonryakjeok Yuyongseong' [Operational and strategic utilities of a light aircraft carrier], Light Aircraft Carrier Seminar co-sponsored by the Republic of Korea Navy and Chungnam National University, 4 February 2021, https://www.youtube.com/watch?v=sSocWSbr_yU.

3   'Je 73 junyeon Gukguneui Nal Ginyeomsa' [President's address for the 73rd National Armed Forces Day], Republic of Korea Cheong Wa Dae, 1 October 2021, https://www1.president.go.kr/articles/11184.

4   On South Korea's mini-*Aegis*-class destroyer programme, see 'South Korea Starts Bidding Process for ROK Navy's KDDX Future Destroyer', *Naval News*, 4 June 2020, https://www.navalnews.com/naval-news/2020/06/south-korea-starts-bidding-process-for-rok-navys-kddx-future-destroyer/. The South Korean navy's KSS-III next-generation submarine project involves nine attack submarines, and the first vessel was commissioned last year. See 'KSS-III (*Jangbogo*-III) Class Attack Submarines, South Korea', *Naval Technology*, 21 January 2022, https://www.naval-technology.com/projects/kss-iii-jangbogo-iii-class/.

5   'Jeong Kyeong-doo: Gyeonghangmo Geonjo, 50 Nyeon Naedabon Gyehoek … Gukbang Yesan Chungdang Ganeung' [Jeong Kyeong-doo: construction of light aircraft carrier is for the next 50 years … defence budget can cover the programme], *Dong-A Ilbo*, 25 August 2020, https://www.donga.com/news/Politics/article/all/20200825/102634888/1.

6   See Gil Beyongok, 'Gyeonghangongmohameui Gukga Anbo Jeonryak Mit Gukga Gyeongje-e Michineun Pagub Hyogwa' [Light

aircraft carrier's national security strategy and its effects on national economy], Light Aircraft Carrier Seminar co-sponsored by the Republic of Korea Navy and Chungnam National University, 4 February 2021, https://www.youtube.com/watch?v=fYzrIpcZQOk.

7   'Gyeonghangmo Saeop, Anbo Wihyepgwa Mugwanhan Yesan Nangbi' [Light-carrier programme is waste of budget not related to security threats], *Hangyereh*, 25 August 2020, http://www.hani.co.kr/arti/politics/defense/959255.html.

8   For weapons development and procurement, South Korea spent about 16.6trn won and 17trn won in 2020 and 2021, respectively. The 2022 budget for that category is 16.6trn won. 'Gukbang Yesan Chuyi' [National defence budget trends], E-Narajipyo [E-National Indicators], http://index.go.kr/potal/stts/idxMain/selectPoSttsIdxMainPrint.do?idx_cd=1699&board_cd=INDX_001. For the overall trend in South Korea's defence spending, see International Institute for Strategic Studies (IISS), *The Military Balance 2022* (Abingdon: Routledge for the IISS, 2022), p. 283.

9   See Yang Sang-hoon, 'Gojong Heose Saenggak Naneun Mooneui Yukjo Gyeonghangmo Sho' [Moon's 6trn-won show reminds us of King Gojong's bluff], *Chosun Ilbo*, 7 January 2021, https://www.chosun.com/opinion/column/2021/01/07/GFHGEYQ WJBERLAABFDKT4UO2UY/.

10 Chung, 'Gyeonghangongmohameui Jakjeon Jeonryakjeok Yuyongseong' [Operational and strategic utilities

of a light aircraft carrier]; and Gang Jinbok, 'Haegun Gyeonghangmo Saeobeui Dangwiseong' [Necessity of the navy's light aircraft-carrier programme], *Sisa Mirae Shinmun*, 16 March 2021, http://www.sisamirae.com/news/article.html?no=42859.

11 See Republic of Korea Navy Planning and Management Department, 'Q&A Ro Araboneun Gyeonghanggongmoham' [Explaining the light aircraft carrier with Q&A], 10 May 2021, p. 53, http://www.navy.mil.kr/ebook/ebook05/assets/index.html; and Kim In-seung, 'Hangukhyeong Hanggongmoham Doipgyehoekgwa 6.25 Jeonjaenggyi Haesang Hanggong Jackjeoneui Hameui' [The naval air operations during the Korean War and their implications for the Korean aircraft-carrier programme], *Gukbang Jeongchaek Yeongu* [National defence policy studies], vol. 35, no. 4, 2020, pp. 131–2.

12 See Ministry of Defense of the Republic of Korea, '21–25 Gukbang Junggyi Gyehoek Bogo' [National defence mid-term plan 2021–25].

13 See Republic of Korea Navy Planning and Management Department, 'Q&A Ro Alaboneun Gyeonghanggongmoham' [Explaining the light aircraft carrier with Q&A], p. 48.

14 See Min Gyo Koo, 'The Hegemonic Competition in the Indo-Pacific Region and the Making of South Korea as a Middle Sea Power', *Korean Journal of Defense Analysis*, vol. 32, no. 1, March 2020, pp. 1–17.

15 See, for example, Brett Samuels, 'Trump Calls on Foreign Countries to Protect Their Own Oil Tankers',

Hill, 24 June 2019, https://thehill.com/homenews/administration/449978-trump-calls-on-foreign-countries-to-protect-own-oil-tankers.

16 See Jeff Jeong, '4 Questions About South Korea's Weapons Wish List', *Defense News*, 2 June 2019, https://www.defensenews.com/interviews/2019/06/03/4-questions-about-south-koreas-weapons-wish-list/.

17 See Gil Yoon-hyeong, 'Haegun, 3 Gae Gidongjeondaero Guseongdoen "Gidong Hamdae" Mandeunda' [The navy will establish 'Strategic Mobile Command' consisting of three task forces], *Hangyeore*, 2 September 2021, https://www.hani.co.kr/arti/politics/defense/1010157.html.

18 See Republic of Korea Navy Planning and Management Department, 'Q&A Ro Alaboneun Gyeonghanggongmoham' [Explaining the light aircraft carrier with Q&A], pp. 47–54, 58–9.

19 See Liu Xuanzun, 'China's Third Aircraft Carrier Expected to Launch in 2021', *Global Times*, 17 January 2021, https://www.globaltimes.cn/page/202101/1213074.shtml.

20 See Kosuke Takahashi, 'Japan Begins Refitting First of Two *Izumo*-class Carriers to Support F-35B Operations', *Janes Defence News*, 30 June 2020, https://www.janes.com/defence-news/news-detail/japan-begins-refitting-first-of-two-izumo-class-carriers-to-support-f-35b-operations.

21 See Gil Yunhyeong, 'Hangukyi Gongdeulyineun Gyeonghangmo, Mi Jeonryak-e Dongwondoel Ganeungseong' [South Korea's light aircraft carrier may be used for American strategy], *Hangyeore*, 10

September 2020, https://news.naver.com/main/read.nhn?mode=LSD&mid=sec&oid=028&aid=0002512307&sid1=001.

22 See Jeong Seung-im, 'Gyeonghangmo Doyiphamyeon Migun-e Kulyeodaninda' [With light aircraft carrier, South Korea will be dragged into US naval missions], *Hanguk Ilbo*, 6 December 2020, https://www.hankookilbo.com/News/Read/A2020120416430004604.

23 See Gil, 'Hangukyi Gongdeulyineun Gyeonghangmo, Mi Jeonryak-e Dongwondoel Ganeungseong' [South Korea's light aircraft carrier may be used for American strategy].

24 See Li Wen, 'Hanguo Guofang Guihua Yu Qianzhi Zoubian?' [Does South Korea's defence plan seek to contain its neighbours?], *Huanqiu Shibao*, 11 August 2020, https://world.huanqiu.com/article/3zQ3pWoWktv; and Sina Military, 'Hangguo Yaozao Hangmu Duikang Riben Haizi Tongshi Dui Zhongguo Ye Zaocheng Weixie' [South Korea seeks to build carrier to counter Japan's Maritime Self-Defense Forces; it also poses threat to China], *Xinlang Junshi*, 29 July 2019, https://mil.news.sina.com.cn/jssd/2019-07-29/doc-ihytcitm5392366.shtml.

25 See Hong Gyu-deok, 'Cheot Quad Jeongsanghoeeuiwa Hanguk Gyeonghangmoeui Jeonryakjeok Gachi' [The first Quad summit and the strategic value of South Korea's light aircraft carrier], *Joongang Ilbo*, 19 March 2021, https://news.joins.com/article/24015466.

26 See Jeongseok Lee, 'Back to Normal? The End of the THAAD Dispute Between China and South Korea',

China Brief, vol. 17, no. 15, November 2017, https://jamestown.org/program/back-normal-end-thaad-dispute-china-south-korea/.

27 See Yang Seung-sik, '101 Eok Yoguhaetda 100 Eok Sakgamdoen Gyeonghangmo Yesan' [10bn out of 10.1bn-won carrier budget was cut], *Chosun Ilbo*, 4 December 2020, https://www.chosun.com/politics/diplomacy-defense/2020/12/04/HZPAAI3QOJFNXL2HTS3FIZ42TA/.

28 See Gyeonghangmo, '72-eok Yesan Buhwallo Gisahoesaeng: 10-nyeon Dwi Mule Teunda' [7.2bn budget for light aircraft carrier revived from near death: it will be commissioned in 10 years], *NoCut News*, 4 December 12, https://www.nocutnews.co.kr/news/5668028.

29 See Jack Detsch, 'Biden Looks to Contain China – But Where's the Asian NATO?', *Foreign Policy*, 26 March 2021, https://foreignpolicy.com/2021/03/26/biden-china-asian-nato/.

Copyright © 2022 The International Institute for Strategic Studies

Nixon in China, February 1972: Revisiting the 'Week that Changed the World'

John L. Harper

It is well to remember the state of US–China relations when Richard M. Nixon came to power for a pair of reasons. Firstly, it does justice to the remarkable changes Nixon and his Chinese counterparts wrought in the space of a few months in 1971–72. Secondly, it serves as a warning: to paraphrase William Shakespeare, what is past may be prologue.

Relations between China and the United States had been frozen in bitter hostility since they had fought each other to a standstill in Korea. Unlike London and Paris, Washington had never normalised relations with Peking, as it was then known, instead recognising the Taiwan-based Nationalist Chinese regime as China's legitimate government. In 1954, Washington and Taipei signed a mutual-defence treaty, calling on the US to defend the island. Washington refused even to use the term 'People's Republic of China', referring disparagingly to the country as 'mainland China' or 'Red China'.

Nixon's informed gambit

Although national security advisor Henry Kissinger became Nixon's indispensable collaborator, the China move was the president's brainchild. On first hearing of it, Kissinger is said to have asked whether Nixon had taken leave of his senses. Why did Nixon decide to pursue the opening, and how did he manage to pull it off? There is no doubt something to the conventional wisdom: he was the right man at the right time. This doesn't mean

John L. Harper is Emeritus Professor of American Foreign Policy at the Johns Hopkins University SAIS Europe, and a contributing editor to *Survival*. He is the author of *The Cold War* (Oxford University Press, 2011).

Survival | vol. 64 no. 2 | April–May 2022 | pp. 45–51   https://doi.org/10.1080/00396338.2022.2055822

that only Nixon could, or would, have done it. But he was well positioned and determined to reap the projected domestic political benefits before somebody else had the chance.

Nixon had been a hard-fisted anti-communist from the start of his political career, a member of the pro-Chiang Kai-shek 'China lobby' and a supporter, even if not a close friend, of senator Joseph McCarthy, the notorious anti-communist witch-hunter. Nixon could afford to be flexible and pragmatic on China because he had the confidence of the right in the US, and nobody could reasonably accuse him of being soft on communism. Mao Zedong himself noted this when he told Nixon during their one meeting, 'I voted for you' and 'I like rightists'.[1] Mao meant that he liked Western politicians who were anti-Soviet and politically able to do deals that would stick.

To a degree unusual for a US president, moreover, Nixon had developed a realist world view that minimised the importance of ideology and of a state's domestic political system. He knew perfectly well that Mao had been a bloody and capricious mass killer, but what was there to gain by criticising the Chinese system? As he said to Mao: 'What is important is not a nation's internal political philosophy. What is important is its policy toward the rest of the world and toward us.'[2]

Unlike Donald Trump, who is occasionally compared to him, Nixon had acquired a wealth of experience in foreign affairs as vice president, and given considerable thought to the China question. In a 1967 article, written after a tour of Asia, he floated the idea of a new approach, observing: 'The world cannot be safe until China changes.'[3] He didn't mean by this that China must evolve in the direction of political pluralism and capitalism. His comparison was with the Soviet Union, which had adopted a policy of peaceful coexistence with the West, and whose international behaviour had mellowed in recent years.

Although the new approach proceeded in fits and starts, the time was right in the early 1970s for two reasons: even before their 1969 border clashes, China and the Soviet Union had come to see each other as deadly enemies. Several informed observers in the West favoured reviving a notion seriously discussed in the Truman administration State Department in the late 1940s, but abandoned in 1950: China as an 'Asian Yugoslavia', a communist counterweight to the Soviet Union.[4] The second reason was the dire condition of the United States itself. It was bogged down in a hopeless stalemate in Vietnam, torn apart domestically and urgently in need of a relaxation of pressure on its imperial periphery. Nixon's overriding priority as president was to get the country out of Vietnam while preserving a minimum of face.

Nixon's goals

What, more specifically, did Nixon hope to accomplish during his week-long state visit from 21 to 28 February 1972? His immediate aim was to launch a process of normalisation and foster a new climate in which to negotiate what had been the intractable conflicts between the two sides. Thanks partly to carefully orchestrated photo opportunities and displays of cordiality – a beaming Nixon shaking hands with Mao, toasting the suave Zhou Enlai and, with his entourage, touring the Forbidden City and the Great Wall – the trip's atmospheric dimension was far from unimportant and a brilliant success. White House chief of staff H.R. Haldeman, a former advertising executive, acted as stage manager. A fellow staffer called the China trip 'Haldeman's masterpiece, his Sistine Chapel'.[5]

Simultaneously, Nixon intended to send a sharp message to the Soviets, hoping Moscow's fear of a Sino-American combination would make it more malleable on issues like arms control. He remarked to White House aide John Ehrlichman just before the trip: 'We're playing the Chinese [the weaker of the two communist powers] because of the Russians ... This is the game.'[6] According to Kissinger, even before Nixon's departure, the prospect of a US–China partnership had shaken the Russians: 'Other [US–Soviet] nego-tiations deadlocked for months began magically to unfreeze.'[7] This is an obvious exaggeration. But the China opening undoubtedly made Soviet leader Leonid Brezhnev more eager to pursue detente with Washington, including by hosting Nixon in Moscow in May 1972 and concluding the SALT I interim accords.

A concomitant aim was to exploit Beijing's fear of Moscow in order to gain leverage over China – on Vietnam, for example – and coax it into a kind of quasi-alliance. Although military and intelligence cooperation would later develop, the Chinese were wary of becoming dependent on the United States, and probably feared the Russians less in 1972 than they had in 1969. It was clear from Kissinger's talks with Zhou before the trip that Beijing had little or no intention of helping Washington to extract itself from Vietnam, and would have been unable to twist Hanoi's arm hard enough even if it had tried. The Chinese delivered a blunt message on the subject: get out of Vietnam, and we'll move on from there. On Taiwan, the most pressing issue for Beijing, the Chinese were equally blunt, insisting the US break with Chiang and withdraw its forces (and tactical nuclear weapons) from the island. In the Shanghai Communiqué issued on the last evening of Nixon's visit, the US acknowledged that Chinese on both sides of the strait recognised that there was one China, including Taiwan. The US did not challenge that position, accepting, in effect, the principle of 'one China'.[8] Ultimately, and thanks to Ronald Reagan, Nixon's rival on the Republican right, the US would refuse to phase out arms sales to Taiwan, a bitter pill for Beijing to swallow.[9]

Overall, the outcome of the February 1972 visit was mixed, but clearly positive in terms of Nixon's aims. The domestic US reaction was enthusiastic, exactly as Nixon and his choreographers had planned. The trip began a process of normalisation, even if that process turned out to be slower and more tortuous than expected. Even if China was no help on Vietnam, having Beijing as a de facto partner rather than an enemy would lessen the impact of losing the war on the US. The opening began a shift in the international power balance decisively in favour of the West, more than offsetting whatever gains Moscow made on the Cold War chessboard in the later 1970s.

Should Nixon be seen as the originator of a later policy that assumed China would move towards political pluralism, and become a pillar of the international system created by the US and its friends? This may have been his hope at times, but not his expectation or his aim. Shortly before going to China, Nixon had invited André Malraux to the White House for a briefing. The French novelist and China expert told him: 'Think of the 16th century explorers who set out for a specific objective but often arrived at an entirely different discovery. What you are going to do, Mr. President, might well have a totally different outcome from whatever is anticipated.'[10]

The conversation seems to have left Nixon with a feeling of foreboding, a lingering fear of unforeseen consequences. Something he saw in China reinforced that sense: a spectacular display by Chinese athletes and gymnasts. He wrote afterwards in his diary: 'Not only we but all the people of the world will have to make our very best effort if we are to match the enormous ability, drive, and discipline of the Chinese people.'[11] Nixon agreed with Kissinger's contemporaneous assessment that although China was weaker than the Soviet Union, it was the greater threat over the long run, and the US would probably have to lean towards the Soviets to counter the Chinese.[12]

*   *   *

What would Nixon's China policy be in the age of Xi Jinping? Until recently, probably exactly that: lean towards Russia, even at the cost of tolerating a Russian sphere of influence. Denying the reality of spheres of influence in international politics, he might point out, is like denying the law of gravity in physics. He spelled out his views on the matter in April 1972, when giving marching orders to Kissinger, who was about to leave for Moscow to prepare the US–Soviet summit: 'Now what we're really saying to them [the Russians] is in effect, look, we'll divide up the world, but by God you're going to respect our side or we won't respect your side.'[13] Nixon would no doubt be outraged by Russia's invasion of Ukraine, but as a realist, he would believe that the war was avoidable, and partly the result of Western errors. Instead of declaring that Ukraine would become a member of NATO, the US and its allies might either have acknowledged Russian hegemony over Ukraine, or pursued its neutralisation along the lines of Austria in the Cold War.

In any case, Nixon would no doubt see a policy that has driven China and Russia into each other's arms as the height of geopolitical incompetence. On Taiwan, it's conceivable that he would have come full circle, insisting as he did as a China lobbyist that the US must defend the island, not for the sake of democracy, but as a strategic outpost against Chinese expansionism. But it's equally possible that, as a realist, he'd argue that under no circumstances should the United States involve itself in a war, or series of wars, to prevent China from retaking Taiwan. While expressing the hope that it would be accomplished peacefully, he conceded that China would sooner or later absorb Taiwan. A war, or series of wars, to prevent the inevitable from happening would probably destroy the US position in East Asia, not to mention Taiwan itself.

Notes

1. 'Mao Zedong Meets Richard Nixon, February 21, 1972', declassified transcript, USC US–China Institute, https://china.usc.edu/mao-zedong-meets-richard-nixon-february-21-1972.

2. Quoted in John L. Harper, *The Cold War* (Oxford: Oxford University Press, 2011), p. 166.

3. Richard M. Nixon, 'Asia After Viet Nam', *Foreign Affairs*, vol. 46, no. 1, October 1967, pp. 111–25.

4. See, for example, Simei Qing, *From Allies to Enemies: Visions of Modernity, Identity, and U.S.–China Diplomacy, 1945–1960* (Cambridge, MA: Harvard University Press, 2007), pp. 96–102.

5. Unnamed staffer quoted in Margaret Macmillan, *Nixon and Mao: The Week that Changed the World* (New York: Random House, 2007), p. 273.

6. Quoted in Douglas Brinkley and Luke A. Nichter (eds), *The Nixon Tapes, 1971–1972* (Boston, MA: Houghton Mifflin Harcourt, 2014), p. 358.

7. Quoted in Harper, *The Cold War*, p. 170.

8. 'Joint Communiqué Between the United States and China', 27 February 1972, Wilson Center Digital Archive, https://digitalarchive.wilsoncenter.org/document/121325.

9. The issue came to a head in 1982, when the Chinese insisted that the US set a date for the end of arms sales. See James Mann, *About Face: A History of America's Curious Relationship with China, from Nixon to Clinton* (New York: Alfred A. Knopf, 1999), chapter 7.

10. Richard Nixon, *RN: The Memoirs of Richard Nixon* (New York: Simon & Schuster, 1990), pp. 558–9.

11. *Ibid.*, p. 572.

12. See Brinkley and Nichter (eds), *The Nixon Tapes, 1971–1972*, p. 400.

13. Quoted in *ibid.*, p. 498.

Copyright © 2022 The International Institute for Strategic Studies

Noteworthy

War against Ukraine

'It is a fact that over the past 30 years we have been patiently trying to come to an agreement with the leading NATO countries regarding the principles of equal and indivisible security in Europe. In response to our proposals, we invariably faced either cynical deception and lies or attempts at pressure and blackmail, while the North Atlantic alliance continued to expand despite our protests and concerns. Its military machine is moving and, as I said, is approaching our very border.

Why is this happening? Where did this insolent manner of talking down from the height of their exceptionalism, infallibility and all-permissiveness come from? What is the explanation for this contemptuous and disdainful attitude to our interests and absolutely legitimate demands?

The answer is simple. Everything is clear and obvious. In the late 1980s, the Soviet Union grew weaker and subsequently broke apart. That experience should serve as a good lesson for us, because it has shown us that the paralysis of power and will is the first step towards complete degradation and oblivion. We lost confidence for only one moment, but it was enough to disrupt the balance of forces in the world.

As a result, the old treaties and agreements are no longer effective. Entreaties and requests do not help. Anything that does not suit the dominant state, the powers that be, is denounced as archaic, obsolete and useless. At the same time, everything it regards as useful is presented as the ultimate truth and forced on others regardless of the cost, abusively and by any means available. Those who refuse to comply are subjected to strong-arm tactics.

[…]

In this context, in accordance with Article 51 (Chapter VII) of the UN Charter, with permission of Russia's Federation Council, and in execution of the treaties of friendship and mutual assistance with the Donetsk People's Republic and the Lugansk People's Republic, ratified by the Federal Assembly on February 22, I made a decision to carry out a 'special military operation'.

The purpose of this operation is to protect people who, for eight years now, have been facing humiliation and genocide perpetrated by the Kiev [sic] regime. To this end, we will seek to demilitarise and denazify Ukraine, as well as bring to trial those who perpetrated numerous bloody crimes against civilians, including against citizens of the Russian Federation.

[…]

I would now like to say something very important for those who may be tempted to interfere in these developments from the outside. No matter who tries to stand in our way or all the more so create threats for our country and our people, they must know that Russia will respond immediately, and the consequences will be such as you have never seen in your entire history. No matter how the events unfold, we are ready. All the necessary decisions in this regard have been taken. I hope that my words will be heard.'

Russian President Vladimir Putin speaks in Moscow on 24 February 2022 after ordering an invasion of Ukraine.[1]

Survival | vol. 64 no. 2 | April–May 2022 | pp. 52–54   https://doi.org/10.1080/00396338.2022.2055823

'Russian warship, go fuck yourself.'

A Ukrainian officer stationed on Snake Island responds to a demand to surrender from a Russian naval ship on 24 February.[2]

'We saw a staged political theatre in Moscow – outlandish and baseless claims that Ukraine was about to invade and launch a war against Russia, that Ukraine was prepared to use chemical weapons, that Ukraine committed a genocide – without any evidence.

We saw a flagrant violation of international law in attempting to unilaterally create two new so-called republics on sovereign Ukrainian territory.

And at the very moment that the United Nations Security Council was meeting to stand up for Ukraine's sovereignty to stave off invasion, Putin declared his war.

Within moments – moments, missile strikes began to fall on historic cities across Ukraine.

Then came in the air raids, followed by tanks and troops rolling in.

We've been transparent with the world. We've shared declassified evidence about Russia's plans and cyber attacks and false pretexts so that there can be no confusion or cover-up about what Putin was doing.

[…]

The next few weeks and months will be hard on the people of Ukraine. Putin has unleashed a great pain on them. But the Ukrainian people have known 30 years of independence, and they have repeatedly shown that they will not tolerate anyone who tries to take their country backwards.

This is a dangerous moment for all of Europe, for the freedom around the world. Putin has committed an assault on the very principles that uphold global peace.

But now the entire world sees clearly what Putin and his Kremlin – and his Kremlin allies – are really all about. This was never about genuine security concerns on their part. It was always about naked aggression, about Putin's desire for empire by any means necessary: by bullying Russia's neighbours through coercion and corruption; by changing borders by force; and, ultimately, by choosing a war without a cause.

Putin's actions betray his sinister vision for the future of our world – one where nations take what they want by force.

[…]

And Putin's aggression against Ukraine will end up costing Russia dearly – economically and strategically. We will make sure of that. Putin will be a pariah on the international stage. Any nation that countenances Russia's naked aggression against Ukraine will be stained by association.

When the history of this era is written, Putin's choice to make a totally unjustifiable war on Ukraine will have left Russia weaker and the rest of the world stronger.

Liberty, democracy, human dignity – these are the forces far more powerful than fear and oppression. They cannot be extinguished by tyrants like Putin and his armies. They cannot be erased by people – from people's hearts and hopes by any amount of violence and intimidation. They endure.'

US President Joe Biden speaks at the White House on 24 February.[3]

'We are all here. We are protecting our independence, our state. And we will continue to do so.'

> *Ukrainian President Volodymyr Zelensky releases a video on 25 February from the streets of Kyiv in response to reports that he had left the city.[4]*

'At the heart of the matter is the question of whether power can break the law. Whether we allow Putin to turn back the hands of time to the days of the great powers of the nineteenth century. Or whether we find it within ourselves to set limits on a warmonger like Putin.'

> *Addressing the Bundestag on 27 February, German Chancellor Olaf Scholz announces a major departure from Germany's long-standing defence policies, including a dramatic increase in defence spending.[5]*

'Ukraine [was not] looking to have this war. The [Ukrainians] have not been looking to become big, but they have become big over the days of this war. We are the country that [is] saving people despite having to fight one of the biggest armies in the world. We have to fight the helicopters, rockets.

[…]

And I would like to remind you of the words that the United Kingdom [has] already heard, which are important again. We will not give up and we will not lose.

We will fight until the end, at sea, in the air. We will continue fighting for our land, whatever the cost.

We will fight in the forests, in the fields, on the shores, in the streets.

I'd like to add that we will fight on the banks of different rivers and we're looking for your help, for the help of the civilised countries.'

> *Zelensky addresses the British House of Commons on 8 March.[6]*

Sources

1 Kremlin, 'Address by the President of the Russian Federation', 24 February 2022, http://en.kremlin.ru/events/president/news/67843.

2 Elias Visontay, 'Ukraine Soldiers Told Russian Officer "Go Fuck Yourself" Before They Died on Island', *Guardian*, 25 February 2022, https://www.theguardian.com/world/2022/feb/25/ukraine-soldiers-told-russians-to-go-fuck-yourself-before-black-sea-island-death.

3 White House, 'Remarks by President Biden on Russia's Unprovoked and Unjustified Attack on Ukraine', 24 February 2022, https://www.whitehouse.gov/briefing-room/speeches-remarks/2022/02/24/remarks-by-president-biden-on-russias-unprovoked-and-unjustified-attack-on-ukraine/.

4 Laurie Churchman, 'President Zelensky Posts Video from Kyiv Street and Reassures Ukraine He's Staying Put', *Independent*, 25 February 2022, https://www.independent.co.uk/news/long_reads/world/ukraine-president-zelensky-kyiv-russia-b2023627.html.

5 Melissa Eddy, 'In Foreign Policy U-Turn, Germany Ups Military Spending and Arms Ukraine', *New York Times*, 27 February 2022, https://www.nytimes.com/2022/02/27/world/europe/germany-ukraine-russia.html?searchResultPosition=1.

6 "Thirteen Days of Struggle": Zelenskiy's Speech to UK Parliament – Transcript', *Guardian*, 8 March 2022, https://www.theguardian.com/world/2022/mar/08/thirteen-days-of-struggle-volodymyr-zelenskiys-speech-to-uk-parliament-transcript.

Copyright © 2022 The International Institute for Strategic Studies

SALT 50 Years On: Strategic Theory and Arms Control

Lawrence Freedman

It was the conceit of arms control, as it emerged as a distinctive school of thought in the late 1950s and early 1960s, that it offered an enlightened means to help meet the core objectives of national security. In their landmark book, published in 1961, Thomas C. Schelling and Morton H. Halperin insisted that the 'aims of arms control and the aims of a national military strategy should be substantially the same'.[1] This perspective appeared to be vindicated when the Anti-Ballistic Missile (ABM) Treaty was signed in Moscow a decade later. Controls on defensive systems were not on the agenda until the mid-1960s, not least because the idea appeared counter-intuitive. Yet so compelling was the rationale developed for such controls that the administrations of Lyndon B. Johnson and Richard Nixon not only accepted them, but also were able to persuade the Soviet Union to take the same view. Schelling, a key figure in generating the ideas behind arms control, later described the 15 years from 1957 to 1972 as a 'remarkable story of intellectual achievement transformed into policy'.[2]

My argument in this article is that this achievement was exceptional, and, as we know, did not last. Ballistic-missile defence (BMD) was unusual in that it could be presented as a threat to strategic stability, yet one that was unlikely to be effective in practice. In principle it could support a first-strike capability, but the most likely consequence of deployment was that the adversary would simply build up offensive capabilities to overwhelm

Lawrence Freedman is Emeritus Professor of War Studies at King's College London.

Survival | vol. 64 no. 2 | April–May 2022 | pp. 55–80   https://doi.org/10.1080/00396338.2022.2055824

the radars and interceptors. BMD did not therefore appear to be a good investment. Robert McNamara, the US secretary of defense from 1961 to 1968, sought to convince the Soviet leadership of the value of joint restraint only after he had failed to convince the Joint Chiefs of Staff and Congress. In practice, even without arms control, BMD deployments would not have changed the strategic balance, although they would have led to much wasteful expenditure.

When Johnson and Nixon decided to make the deployments, they struggled to find a rationale that avoided the theoretical threat to strategic stability. McNamara tentatively opted for one based on a future Chinese threat. The Nixon administration constructed one based on the need to defend against a partial surprise attack directed against American intercontinental ballistic missiles (ICBMs). The problem with this was that when the negotiations succeeded and the investment stopped, the rationale remained. A problem had been identified for which there was now no obvious solution. At the same time, the parallel efforts to impose limits on offensive systems, which led to the interim agreement on offensive arms, also signed in Moscow in May 1972, had the effect of increasing the salience of numerical comparisons.

The combination of demands for rigid equality with the unsolved problem of ICBM vulnerability complicated subsequent efforts to agree on a treaty. Instead of arms-control negotiations implementing existing strategic theory, the negotiating process created a new strategic theory. This assumed that perceptual asymmetries mattered without any obvious empirical foundation. The measures proposed were too arcane and complicated in practice to influence international or even domestic opinion. In this respect, arms control did not so much apply good theory as encourage bad theory.

There are other benefits to arms control that might still make the effort worthwhile, including a degree of transparency and predictability when it comes to future force levels, as well as the value of the negotiating process itself in providing opportunities to engage in dialogue and to explore related security issues. But these benefits still depend on a favourable political context. With Russian President Vladimir Putin having gone to war to occupy and control Ukraine, the current context is as unfavourable as one might imagine. At some point, when he is gone from power, it will certainly be necessary to open discussions again about how best to manage the continuing dangers of the nuclear age. Whether the classical model of arms control will provide the best approach is less clear.

Arms control and disarmament

The close link between measures of arms control and national security was a key theme of what Jennifer Sims later called the Cambridge School of arms control.[3] The ideas were developed in a series of workshops and seminars around Harvard and MIT in the late 1950s, and set out in a volume edited by Donald Brennan, first for the journal *Daedalus* in 1960 and published, with some additional material, as a book the following year, and also in Schelling and Halperin's book.[4] Hedley Bull's *The Control of the Arms Race*, which came out at roughly the same time, was the outcome of a study group convened in London, but Bull was part of this intellectual community.[5] Their approach departed from more traditional and narrower approaches to national security by pointing to interests shared with the Soviet Union, including avoiding situations in which misapprehensions and miscalculations might lead to a rush into a catastrophic war. It was developed by many of the same figures who had been refining deterrence theory over the 1950s. Indeed, as Schelling later noted, they did not self-identify as arms controllers but largely saw themselves working on a broad range of foreign and security issues, especially those bound up with nuclear weapons.[6]

They were also careful not to dismiss possibilities for disarmament. Brennan noted that many disarmers thought that arms control was a 'wicked' doctrine because it served the status quo and reduced pressure for proper disarmament, so he insisted on a comprehensive definition of arms control, which included disarmament. Schelling and Halperin also offered an inclusive definition. The objectives of arms control were described as 'reducing the likelihood of war, its scope and violence if it occurs, and the political and economic costs of preparing for it'.[7] There was obvious value in saving money by removing surplus capacity.[8] Yet the Cambridge School could not see disarmament as an end in itself. If cuts went too far and force levels went too low, rash actions might no longer be deterred. There was a tension between deterrence and reducing the scope and violence of war should it occur. Deterrence depended on a war of fearful scope and violence. Without this prospect deterrence might fail.

At the time governments still routinely claimed to be seeking general and complete disarmament under international control, though without any confidence that much progress would be made. In 1961, Soviet negotiator Valerian Zorin and his American counterpart John J. McCloy agreed on a 'roadmap' for future negotiations with the eventual aim of abolishing war, envisaging that military establishments would be dismantled and disputes solved peacefully. It was backed enthusiastically by the United Nations General Assembly in December 1961.[9] The aspiration lives on in Article VI of the 1970 Treaty on the Non-Proliferation of Nuclear Weapons, which requires the nuclear-weapons states to work towards this wider objective, as well as nuclear disarmament specifically.[10]

Deterrence depended on a war of fearful scope

Those adopting such objectives could claim the moral high ground, but they were not operating in the realm of practical policy. The underlying theory appeared simplistic in the presumption that fewer arms meant more peace, and unrealistic given the unimpressive history of conferences undertaken in the name of disarmament during the interwar years. The most serious obstacle to any cooperative agreements at this time, whether labelled arms control or disarmament, was the Soviet refusal to accept American demands for inspections to verify compliance. Moscow saw inspections as a form of legalised espionage. This attitude cast a shadow over all negotiations, including those on a nuclear test ban, the most advanced at the time. The introduction of reconnaissance satellites at the start of the 1960s, which opened up superpower territory to intrusive surveillance, was in effect a necessary condition for the progress that eventually occurred.

The differences between past disarmament negotiations and prospective arms-control negotiations were also less substantial in practice than the surrounding rhetoric might have suggested. The Hague conferences of the late nineteenth century were the first international gatherings to address the impact of new types of weapons.[11] The aim at that stage was to keep war available as a political instrument by imposing limits on its destructiveness. They were more about damage limitation than crisis stability. After the First World War there were attempts to regulate armaments in the 1922 Washington Naval Conference and the 1932–33 Geneva Disarmament Conference.[12] The first was successful in agreeing ratios of 5:5:3:1.7:1.7 on capital ships for the United States, British Empire, Japan, France and Italy respectively. Politically, however, it probably did more harm than good, as it left the Japanese feeling slighted. The second was unsuccessful because Adolf Hitler was elected in Germany while it was ongoing. Both sets of talks showed up the tension between negotiability and strategic sense, between confirming an existing 'balance' and amending it, and between keeping matters simple and including all the factors that shaped military power.

At the 1932–33 disarmament conference there were attempts to develop more sophisticated approaches comparable to later ones to encourage stability in the nuclear balance. The negotiators struggled to capture the full range of strategic possibilities in comparative tabulations of military capabilities, but the real value of a set of military capabilities depended on the total force structure of the likely enemy. There were proposals to render aggressors impotent through the proscription of 'offensive' weapons, but whether weapons were offensive or defensive depended on circumstances. Was a professional army more inherently aggressive than a conscript army? Was it sufficient to consider only forces in being, or would the speed of national mobilisation need to be considered?[13]

After the war the lessons drawn from this earlier experience were largely about how unwise it was to trust aggressive states, how enthusiasm for disarmament risked being seen as a sign of weakness, and how, despite all the diplomatic efforts put into designing international structures and agreements to avoid another great confrontation, war nonetheless occurred. Less attention was paid to how much they demonstrated the difficulty of devising measures that would enable force structures to be compared in a way that was generally agreed and analytically useful.

In the late 1940s, efforts to prohibit the military uses of nuclear energy faltered, caught up in developing Cold War tensions, apparently confirming the ineffectuality of disarmament negotiations.[14] The issue was revived

during the 1950s because of concerns about the arms race. In his introduction to the 1960 *Daedalus* collection, Jerome Wiesner, who would soon
become John F. Kennedy's science advisor, observed 'a growing realization
among knowledgeable people that if the arms race is allowed to continue its
accelerating pace, our country will have less security, not more, with each
passing year'.[15]

At the time there was an erroneous impression that the United States
was falling behind in this race. The Soviet Union had tested the world's
first ICBM in summer 1957 and underlined the achievement by launching
the world's first artificial Earth satellite that October. American debates
began to exhibit a degree of panic about falling behind. This was the result
of limited intelligence on actual Soviet capabilities, a problem that was also
soon solved by the introduction of reconnaissance satellites. Soviet leader
Nikita Khrushchev had encouraged the impression of a substantial Soviet
lead by talking of missiles coming off assembly lines like 'sausages'.[16] As a
result of investigations conducted at the RAND Corporation into the vulnerability of US long-range bomber and ICBM bases, the possibility of being
caught by a surprise first strike that would remove any means of retaliation
and in effect spell defeat in a nuclear war became more salient. To build
up a second-strike capability that would allow the US to absorb a Soviet
first strike and still retaliate, the Eisenhower administration accelerated programmes to deploy ICBMs in protective silos and, most importantly, much
more survivable ballistic-missile-carrying submarines.

Assured destruction and anti-ballistic missiles

The idea that arms control might be one way to address the problem of
surprise attacks had been raised as early as January 1953 in a report
commissioned by the Truman administration. It was pessimistic on the
prospects of any agreement with the Soviet Union on disarmament, but it
did point out that the best approach to 'arms regulation' might be to set
narrow but valuable goals. It suggested reducing the 'size of stockpiles and
bombing fleets' so that neither side need fear a sudden knockout blow.[17]
Surprise attacks remained the focus of the work of Harold Stassen while he
was in charge of arms control for the Eisenhower administration. In 1958,

the US and the Soviet Union even got as far as holding a special conference of experts to consider surprise attacks, although the two countries had opposing views about where the danger came from. The Soviets worried about another conventional offensive launched from Germany, while the Americans fretted about first strikes and a 'nuclear Pearl Harbor'.[18] The effect of this exercise was to entrench the risk of an attack on US nuclear capabilities as a high-priority problem. Soon there was another anxiety about the danger not so much of being caught out by a deliberate surprise attack but of a dynamic series of apparently limited moves generating a process of escalation, fuelled by misapprehensions and miscalculations, that could get out of control.[19] This argued for improved forms of communication, as was eventually achieved with the 'hotline'.

Such worries assumed not only that the arms race was close but also that the Soviet Union was ahead. During 1961, the first year of the Kennedy administration, with the benefits of satellite imagery, perceptions of the Soviet programme began to shift. The early Soviet missiles were large and cumbersome, and few were produced. By autumn 1961 the Kennedy administration was confident that instead of there being a 'missile gap' in the Soviets' favour, it was the other way round. On 21 October, Roswell Gilpatric, the US deputy secretary of defense, delivered a speech in which he described American nuclear strength – 600 strategic bombers, six *Polaris* submarines, dozens of ICBMs – and then continued:

> The destructive power which the United States could bring to bear even after a Soviet surprise attack upon our forces would be as great as – perhaps greater than – the total undamaged forces which the enemy can threaten to launch against the United States in a first strike. In short, we have a second strike capability which is at least as extensive as what the Soviets can deliver by striking first.[20]

This was at a time of heightened tension between East and West over the status of West Berlin, although by this time the crisis had become more manageable because of the construction of the wall dividing East from West Berlin. As it would take time before the Soviets' ICBM production could catch up with America's, Khrushchev looked for short-term fixes to compensate for the Soviet inferiority in long-range systems. He authorised new atmospheric tests, emphasising the destructive power of his arsenal, including a 56-megaton shot, the largest explosion ever. Later he looked to create an 'ersatz' ICBM capability by putting medium- and intermediate-range missiles in Cuba, which led to the Cuban Missile Crisis in October 1962. None of these measures helped Khrushchev resolve either the Berlin or Cuban confrontations on favourable terms. The most relevant balance with respect to the missile crisis was conventional, and especially maritime, forces. In the United States' backyard, its superiority appeared overwhelming.[21]

Over the next few years there was therefore less pressure on the US to worry about controlling the arms race. This is one reason why the main arms-control effort during the Kennedy years was put into limiting nuclear tests, which led to a ban on atmospheric, though not underground, tests in 1963. The question of the level at which nuclear forces should be capped was seen as a matter for unilateral decision, taken with reference to Soviet capabilities but not as a result of formal negotiations.[22] To answer the question of how much was enough, Pentagon analysts developed the concept of 'assured destruction'. A level of destruction was set from which it would be impossible for the Soviet Union to recover.[23] They then asked whether American forces could inflict this damage even after the worst first strike that the Soviets could inflict upon the United States. The relative invulnerability of ballistic-missile submarines ensured that the US had an assured-destruction capability. Any attempted pre-emption would be pointless.

This meant that the US had a nuclear arsenal with numbers much higher than needed for purposes of deterrence. Although planned ICBM deployments were scaled down, Pentagon presentations to Congress made a point of showing the US well ahead quantitatively. McNamara pointed out that the US had three or four times as many bombers and long-range ballistic missiles available as the Soviets. This combination of factors ensured that until the mid-1960s there was no incentive on the US side to consider negotiations with the Soviet Union to regulate the arms race, as no meaningful race appeared to be under way.

By 1967 the situation had changed. Soviet numbers were catching up with those of the United States, which led McNamara to play down the importance of numerical comparisons. He could still point to multiple independently targeted re-entry vehicles (MIRVs) on missiles. They were not designed to make the US look good in comparison with the Soviet Union, but rather to provide more targeting options.[24] But they did help allay concerns about numbers of weapons.

They could also help maintain an assured-destruction capability as the Soviets developed an ABM system around Moscow. The ease with which offensive capabilities could be upgraded to swamp any defences, including with multiple warheads, was the main reason McNamara saw little point in vast expenditure on American ABMs. Not trying to defend against an attack, however, seemed reckless to many. There was a strong lobby in the military and Congress to go ahead, especially as the Soviets were moving ahead with their defences around Moscow.[25]

Not trying to defend against an attack seemed reckless

BMD had not loomed large up to this point because only limited progress had been made on the requisite technology, though in principle systems that might limit damage in a nuclear attack seemed to be a good thing. The idea that defensive systems could be destabilising gained currency in 1964, however. Jerome Wiesner and Herbert York, two figures with inside knowledge of weapons systems, argued that 'paradoxically, one of the potential destabilizing elements in the present nuclear standoff is the possibility that one of the rival powers might develop a successful antimissile defense'. This was because it might 'effectively nullify the deterrent force of the other, exposing the latter to a first attack against which it could not retaliate'.[26] Yet they also explained why a viable defence was unlikely. The standard of effectiveness would have to be extraordinarily high, with virtually no tolerance of failure; the defensive system itself would be vulnerable to attack; and the offensive side would still have the advantage of surprise and choice of targets. They therefore argued that BMD would not work; yet, at the same time, if one side attempted to build such a system this could stimulate an arms race.

The first part of this case was undermined in part by some technological advances, but more by evidence that the Soviet Union clearly thought differently about the value of these systems. McNamara was faced in 1966 with a recommendation from the Joint Chiefs of Staff for a full-scale ABM system.

As both superpowers were investing in systems that McNamara's rational analysis told him were pointless, his best hope of holding back on the American programme was to persuade the Soviets to hold back on their own. Johnson agreed that McNamara could explore the possibilities of stopping an ABM race. This was the judgement that eventually led to the Strategic Arms Limitation Talks (SALT).

At first, the effort did not get very far. On 23 June 1967, McNamara was given an opportunity to make his pitch to Soviet prime minister Alexei Kosygin, then meeting with Johnson in Glassboro, New Jersey. In the official account of the meeting, McNamara sought to explain 'the desirability of avoiding an ABM race between the two countries' and how this was 'an insane road to follow', adding that this would 'begin to dampen the expansion of nuclear arms – both offensive and defensive' and that this carried no implication of disarmament. McNamara 'considered complete disarmament to be beyond achievement at the present stage of world affairs'. Kosygin challenged the idea, previously expressed by McNamara in public, that ABM systems were somehow worse than offensive systems because the latter were cheaper to develop. This 'type of approach', which McNamara no doubt saw as simple cost–benefit analysis, Kosygin considered to 'be actually immoral' – a 'commercial approach to a moral problem which was by its very nature invalid'. His view, from which McNamara did not dissent, was that it was necessary to 'consider the entire complex of the arms race in offensive and defensive weapons'.

Kosygin stuck with his objections as McNamara tried to explain how the only consequence of the development of new defensive systems would be to stimulate new offensive systems.[27] Other notes indicate that on one philosophical point McNamara and Kosygin agreed. The secretary of defense observed that the two sides 'were engaged in an arms race advanced beyond any limit', adding, 'we react to you, and we must maintain a certain nuclear strength'. Kosygin then came in: 'And we react to you – so that is an agreed point.' McNamara responded: 'Yes, you are no different from us – you must react to us. What an insane road we are both following.' 'How well you speak!' exclaimed Kosygin. They agreed on the more general point, as McNamara put it, that the two sides should 'begin to dampen down the expansion of our nuclear arms … to put a lid or limit on weapons'.[28]

There was a basis for talks on all relevant systems, just not a specific agreement directed against missile defences. Without any prospect of such an agreement, the pressure to deploy a US ABM system became irresistible. McNamara equivocated about whether the purpose of the one he would announce would be to protect US cities against an incipient Chinese missile threat or US ICBMs against a Soviet missile threat. He opted for the Chinese rationale.[29] The announcement appeared as a discordant concluding note to a long speech in which McNamara explained that there was no possibility of 'an impenetrable shield over the United States', that the attempt to build one would simply lead the Soviets to increase their offensive capabilities, and that this showed how the two superpowers 'mutually influence one another's strategic plans'.[30]

The case for arms control, however, had now been made. That much Kosygin had accepted, and as the Soviets began to appreciate the significance of US MIRV capabilities they also began to see the merits of limitations on ABMs. In August 1968 the two sides were ready to announce the talks, but when the Soviet Union occupied Czechoslovakia the effort was postponed, to be picked up by a new administration.

SALT and the problem of ICBM vulnerability

When Nixon entered office in January 1969, he inherited plans for strategic arms-control talks with the Soviet Union and the construction of ballistic-missile defences around American cities. He accepted the need for the negotiations (which eventually began in November 1969) but his immediate problem was the construction work. The American people seemed less impressed by possible protection against an attack than concerned about drawing fire to their neighbourhoods.

If the coming negotiations were going to be about ABMs, then Nixon and his national security advisor, Henry Kissinger, were sure they needed an

American system, if only to be able to bargain it away. But if the system was really needed as a defence against Chinese missiles – McNamara's rationale – how could it be a bargaining chip? If this was a valid rationale, why should it be abandoned? Alternatively, if it was to protect against a Soviet attack, could a credible case be made?

The administration adopted McNamara's alternative rationale, based on a possible Soviet strike against US *Minuteman* ICBMs, and changed the name of the ABM system from *Sentinel* to *Safeguard*. The idea was to use ABMs to ensure that the ICBM leg of the 'triad' did not become vulnerable to a Soviet first strike. The two other legs – submarine-launched missiles and bombers – would still be able to retaliate. Instead of just saying it would be a prudent hedge to have three different types of delivery systems available, a construct was developed that turned the triad into a strategic imperative. According to the construct, if ICBMs were eliminated in a surprise Soviet attack, retaliation would be possible but it could not be in kind. As many Soviet ICBMs would have been used up in the attack, they would not be available as tit-for-tat targets. The submarine-launched *Poseidon* missiles lacked accuracy and so could only be used to attack cities. But, the argument continued, the president would be inhibited from launching them because it would then invite a Soviet response in kind against American cities.

There were several reasons why this scenario was far-fetched. Soviet strategists would know the risks with a partial first strike. They could not eliminate the possibility of retaliation or that the enemy would launch on warning. The collateral damage would still be enormous, so even an attack directed against ICBM silos and bomber bases would be experienced as a full nuclear attack with millions dead. The Soviets could not know for sure how an American president would respond to such a devastating attack. He or she might be paralysed with indecision or passionately decisive. In addition, to the extent that this was at all plausible as a scenario, it would only be for a limited period. Eventually, submarine-launched ballistic missiles (SLBMs) would receive accurate warheads and the issue would no longer arise. Until that time came, it was extremely expensive and difficult to find a way of protecting ICBMs against surprise attacks, as the US came to discover in the prolonged and eventually fruitless discussions about how best to base the new MX ICBM.[31]

The 1969 analysis had to assume that the large Soviet SS-9 missile was capable of a devastating first strike on US ICBMs. This was a single-warhead 25-megaton weapon that was being tested with a multiple warhead. It was not clear that its individual warheads would have the accuracy required for first-strike purposes. On this matter intelligence agencies were split. Yet the administration still talked up the Soviet programme to get the votes in Congress.[32] As it became apparent that Congress was unlikely to support *Safeguard* on its merits, Melvin Laird, Nixon's secretary of defense, argued that its value lay in providing an 'added incentive for productive arms control talks'. His deputy, David Packard, described it 'as a hedge against the failure of arms control'. The vote in the Senate on funding *Safeguard* on 6 August 1969 was tied, and the initiative passed only with the vice president's vote. Without the arms-control rationale, there might have been no funding.[33]

The ABM Treaty was signed at a summit meeting between Nixon and Soviet leader Leonid Brezhnev in Moscow in May 1972, limiting the number of ABM launchers to 200 for each side. This number was halved in 1974 and the US eventually mothballed its system. This diplomatic success, which was part of a more wide-ranging detente with the Soviet Union, left the Nixon administration with a paradoxical problem. The formal case for a US ABM system rested on a scenario in which, without such a system, *Minuteman* ICBMs would be left vulnerable to a developing Soviet threat which might destabilise the strategic balance. Having stressed the stabilisation role for the ABM, the administration was left with a supposedly big strategic problem for which there was now no solution.

This dilemma dominated US debates for the rest of the decade. When Paul Nitze, a leading opponent of SALT II, was asked why a comparative Soviet advantage in counterforce capabilities mattered when the US would still be able to destroy the Soviet Union, he replied that this would only be true if US retaliation was directed deliberately against counter-value rather than counterforce targets 'despite the desperate consequences to us and the world of doing so'.[34] Colin Gray wrote in 1978:

On current trends in the strategic balance, an American President should, prudently, be deterred from initiating strategic nuclear employment; should he proceed nonetheless, the war would very likely terminate after an almost wholly counter-military exchange (which the Soviet Union should win unequivocally) because the United States could not possibly secure an improved war outcome by initiating attacks against Soviet industry and (through re-location) population.[35]

Enormous funds were directed towards finding the most survivable basing mode for the new MX ICBM. Eventually, a commission headed by Brent Scowcroft killed off the debate, pointing out that:

The existence of several components of our strategic forces permits each to function as a hedge against possible Soviet successes in endangering any of the others … Although the survivability of our ICBMs is today a matter of concern (especially when that problem is viewed in isolation) it would be far more serious if we did not have a force of ballistic missiles, submarines at sea and a bomber force.[36]

Essential equivalence

A similar process occurred with offensive arms. Nixon had campaigned for the presidency in 1968 calling for clear US superiority. Studies by the National Security Council staff demonstrated that the US could not regain the sort of superiority it once enjoyed. As the effort to do so would probably lead to an expensive arms race, Nixon decided in office not to pursue superiority as a goal. But he was not happy with the idea of 'parity', which to him sounded too close to inferiority. He insisted that 'we're not settling for second place'. From a 'diplomatic standpoint this would be devastating to our policies all over the world and I do not intend to allow this to happen – whatever the political consequences may be'.[37]

The alternative chosen was 'sufficiency'. It did not fare well. It was described as consisting of four parts: a second-strike capability to deter an all-out surprise attack on US nuclear forces; forces to ensure that the Soviet

Union would have no incentive to strike first in a crisis; the ability to deny the Soviets the ability to inflict more damage on the US than they would suffer; and deploying defences to limit damage from small attacks or accidental launches. An additional criterion, which was the subject of some debate, was the capability to 'emerge in a position of relative advantage from any level of strategic nuclear warfare'.[38]

Sufficiency did not last long as a description of strategic objectives. It was not sharp enough to provide planning guidance. Packard dismissed 'sufficiency' as merely 'a good word to use in a speech. Beyond that it doesn't mean a God-damned thing.'[39]

The criteria did not make much difference in the actual negotiations on offensive arms. Michael Krepon has argued that the real need in the late 1960s was to limit MIRVs, because they constituted the innovation that was going to lead to a major increase in the nuclear capabilities of both sides. Some options for controlling warheads were discussed prior to the talks that were supposed to start in August 1968, but the delays in getting SALT going meant that the US programme was proceeding apace. There were other challenges to controlling MIRVs: numbers of warheads were hard to verify; there were no doubts about whether they would work; and the supposed value of these missiles for the Pentagon lay not only in their ability to overwhelm missile defences but also in allowing more targets to be added to nuclear war plans. Unlike ABMs, MIRVs therefore seemed like a better investment, and those in the administration and executive branch who might have been inclined to stop MIRVs decided to concentrate on the more vulnerable system.[40]

The offensive side of SALT therefore made very little difference to either side's plans. The interim agreement, also signed at the May 1972 Moscow summit, was to last for five years and put a freeze on numbers of missile launchers, with an allowance for the momentum in the Soviet construction programme. The US was allowed 1,054 ICBMs and 656 SLBMs, the Soviet Union 1,409 ICBMs and 950 SLBMs, with a sub-limit of 308 'heavy' ICBMs.[41] In November 1974, Gerald Ford, now president, and Brezhnev agreed on a framework for a new treaty. This would set ceilings of 2,400 strategic nuclear-delivery vehicles – that is, bombers and missiles – and deal with

MIRVs by counting not warheads but MIRVed missiles, for which a sub-ceiling of 1,320 was set.

The 1972 interim agreement was immediately criticised in the Senate for embedding Soviet superiority. Senator Henry Jackson got an amendment passed requesting the president to 'seek a future treaty that, *inter alia,* would not limit the United States to levels of intercontinental strategic forces inferior to the limits provided for the Soviet Union'.[42] This threw into sharp relief the issue of how to measure offensive forces in a way that could be reflected in an agreement. The difficulty this posed in terms of working out who was ahead and whether it mattered led to one of Kissinger's more famous outbursts, as he was trying to negotiate the next strategic arms treaty in 1974: 'And one of the questions which we have to ask ourselves as a country is what in the name of God is strategic superiority? What is the significance of it, politically, militarily, operationally, at these levels of numbers? What do you do with it?'[43]

There was no self-evident index of strategic nuclear power against which the two sides' force structures could be evaluated. Although with mutual assured destruction there might be symmetry in their effects, their composition was quite asymmetrical. On the one hand, the US had more bombers and their forces were MIRVed earlier. On the other, Soviet ICBMs were more numerous and larger. When all were MIRVed, they could carry more warheads of larger individual yield. The Soviets had a larger SLBM force, but it seemed to be of inferior quality and efficiency. There was a large Soviet force directed solely against European targets. US forces of compara-ble range based in Europe were smaller but could reach Soviet territory. The United Kingdom and France had their own missiles and bombers ranged against the Soviet Union. Soviet forces were also deployed to deter growing Chinese nuclear capabilities, of less interest to the US as a result of the rap-prochement with China. Thus, the nature of the balance created could be varied by focusing on, for example, delivery vehicles as against warheads, and whether the additional opponents faced by the Soviet Union – China, France and the UK – were taken into account.

The more analysts tried to account for factors that shaped force effectiveness – target structure, defences, reliability and tactics, as well as the accuracy, yield and numbers of warheads – the more complicated the analysis became, and the more unquantifiable factors had to be considered. Several measures were investigated.

Gross megatonnage was a measure of aggregate weapon yield. However, aggregate yield conveys little about destructive potential without some consideration about how this yield is to be divided and distributed.

Equivalent megatonnage acknowledged that destructive power did not grow proportionately with yield and indicated counter-city potential.

Throw-weight, referring to the weight of missile-delivery packages after the boost phase of the flight, was a measure of potential on the assumption that the larger the package the more that could be packed into it. The bomber equivalent for throw-weight was *payload*.

Lethality or counter-military force potential was measured by dividing the equivalent megatonnage by the circular error probable (CEP). CEP is a measure of accuracy.[44]

Straightforward measures of capability, such as numbers of missiles, could be readily understood by the general public. But these more complex measures were unlikely to make much sense to a non-specialist audience. It was hard to see how they could affect international perceptions.

In addition, the relationship between increments in military power and crisis behaviour remained hard to establish. The Pentagon sought to capture the general idea that asymmetries mattered through the concept of 'essential equivalence'. This term sought to describe the nuclear balance in a way that made some sense in strategic terms but could also serve as a negotiating objective as required by the Jackson Amendment. Essential equivalence required that neither side had a 'unilateral advantage'. Instead of simply trying to develop a rough-and-ready measure that could help in negotiations, however, they developed a strategic theory to back it up. According to James Schlesinger, the secretary of defense at the time, it was important 'for symbolic purposes, in large part because the strategic offensive forces have come to be seen by many – however regrettably – as important to the status and stature of a major power'. Lack of equality, he explained, could

> become a source of serious diplomatic and military miscalculation.
> Opponents may feel that they can exploit a favorable imbalance by means

of political pressure, as Hitler did so skillfully in the 1930s, particularly with Neville Chamberlain at Berchtesgaden. Friends may believe that a willingness on our part to accept less than equality indicates a lack of resolve to uphold our end of the competition and a certain deficiency in staying power. Our own citizens may doubt our capacity to guard the nation's interests.[45]

Harold Brown, his successor in the Carter administration, also subscribed to this concept. Essential equivalence, he said, guarded 'against any danger that the Soviets might be seen as superior – even if the perception is not technically justified'.[46] Schlesinger argued that it would be a mistake to allow any major asymmetry to develop between the United States and the Soviet Union in the 'basic technological and other factors that shape force effectiveness'.[47]

This theory was not empirically grounded. The core proposition was that an impression of inferiority, even if mistaken, might embolden adversaries, undermine allied confidence in guarantees and encourage the non-aligned to turn away. This might happen even though this apparent superiority could not be turned into a decisive strategic advantage. Yet in times of crisis it was never likely that big decisions on matters of war and peace were going to be taken on the basis of superficial impressions of a military balance.[48] Under the heading of 'Unnecessary Capability as an Indicator of Resolve', Robert Jervis later took apart claims that these perceptions were decisive, yet also noted that they could be 'self-perpetuating'. He cited work by Steven Kull, who found that those who believed that superiority mattered were often hard put to explain why, but resorted to the claim that it mattered to the Soviets.[49] As Jervis noted, it was unclear whether this view held that the Soviets saw real military advantages in superiority, that they simply had not thought matters through, or that superiority mattered to them because they thought it mattered to the United States.[50]

If military power was in the eyes of the beholder, then there could be no guarantee that it would be beheld in any particular way. However true it may be that additional missiles made little difference, one could not be certain that this would be universally realised. As Edward Luttwak observed: 'The political utility and military effectiveness of a given structure of armed forces exist in different worlds: one, the world of appearances, impressions, and the culturally determined value judgements of international politics; the other, the world of physical reality in actual warfare.'[51] He also noted that the Nixon administration had not paid much attention to this issue in force planning. Nixon specifically ruled out an increase in the numbers of ICBMs as a response to the Soviet build-up, preferring to strengthen quality rather than quantity.

The Soviet Union had been more concerned about appearances. In the early 1950s, the United States enjoyed a comfortable superiority in long-range bombers that could reach Soviet territory, while the few Soviet bombers could only mount attacks on a one-way mission. The Soviet leadership sought to exaggerate their actual strength. For example, during the Aviation Day parade in Moscow in July 1955 the impression was given that large numbers of the new *Bison* bomber had already been produced as first ten and then two flights of nine planes flew past the reviewing stand. These were in fact the same aircraft going round in circles.[52] Later, old missiles were rarely removed to make way for new ones. The United States, however, withdrew from service almost 1,000 ICBMs and more than 300 B-52 bombers between the early 1960s and the mid-1970s. If they had remained operational, a quite different image to the one that actually prevailed could have been presented. Even after the start of SALT, in which aggregate numbers were obviously going to be relevant, this policy of removal continued.[53]

What centrally mattered in practice were not the perceptions of the Soviet leadership in some hypothetical situation, but those of America's allies. The perceptions of others are tricky to manipulate. Some research suggested that in Europe, Japan and the Middle East there was no agreement on which superpower was ahead. Many respondents noted that the question was largely irrelevant because the two superpowers could destroy each other. There was no reason to suppose that there was much interest in marginal shifts in superpower capabilities or readiness to change political views as a result. If the US government regularly worried in public about the impact of perceptions, then the concern might become self-fulfilling. Perceptions did not develop independently, but were shaped largely by the pronouncements of authoritative Americans. Most Europeans relied on US sources for their information and ideas on the state of the strategic balance.

Even when NATO allies had concluded in the late 1950s that the Soviet Union was ahead in the arms race, they did not suddenly shift their allegiances.[54] These were founded in shared values and interests. It was appreciated, of course, that the shifting balance raised questions about the US nuclear guarantee to NATO. If the Soviet Union was always able to retaliate, would the US really put New York or Chicago at risk for Berlin or Paris? Unless a first-strike capability of some sort were developed that could eliminate the means of retaliation, that question was always going to gnaw away at the credibility of the guarantee. Variations in the numerical balance wouldn't change that reality.

Gerard Smith, Nixon's chief SALT negotiator, argued in a May 1969 meeting to discuss the US arms-control position that the Europeans were still reassured and the Soviets were still deterred. The situation was not that different from what it had bee, and he was 'disturbed to hear the implication that Europe [is] in greater danger today with regard to [the] U.S. nuclear umbrella'. The point was made that if anything, Europeans were more worried by the prospect of an American surge in building new nuclear weapons. Hal Sonnenfeldt observed that the Europeans would be alarmed if America either accepted inferiority or drove for superiority, as they considered parity conducive to international stability. Basically, they were content with the current situation.[55] Whether they should have been was another matter. Nixon observed in a February 1969 meeting, 'nuclear umbrella in NATO is a lot of crap. Don't have it!'[56]

What mattered was the political context. Although the Nixon years tend now to be remembered for SALT, some of the most important agreements coming under the broad heading of 'detente' of this period were those that helped manage broader political relations between East and West. They included the four-power agreement on Berlin, the development of formal relations between the Federal Republic of Germany and the Soviet Union and its satellite states, and the Conference on Security and Cooperation in Europe. Arguably these measures, especially those that addressed the role of Germany in the East–West conflict, had as much effect as any arms-control measures in reducing the risk of major war.

*   *   *

In 1985, Schelling lamented that the ABM Treaty was 'not merely the end point but the high point of successful arms control'. As evidence that it had gone 'off the tracks', he noted that to get arms control it had been necessary to demonstrate 'determination to match or exceed the Soviets in every category of weapons'. Schelling blamed this on the determination to have formal treaties that had come to focus on the number rather than the character of weapons. This, he said, was an unnecessary exercise because both sides could assure deterrence with 'economical and reliable retaliatory weapons'. There appeared to be an imperative behind arms control on offensive arms even though there was nothing constructive to be done. He therefore judged the 'negotiations on offensive weapons to have been mostly mindless', animated more by bureaucratic imperatives to keep negotiating and lacking a guiding philosophy.[57]

In terms of strategic relevance, Schelling's critique was compelling. The problem, as I have argued in this article, was that the logic of the negotiating process, including the need for bargaining chips, generated new and unconvincing theoretical constructs that argued for more rather than fewer arms. The SALT process began with the aim of stabilising the arms race by confirming the dominance of offensive systems. That was done by limiting and then banning missile defences, but even if this had not been done these defences would not have been a high priority for investment. The Reagan administration put a massive research effort into its Strategic Defense Initiative. In 2002, the Bush administration abandoned the ABM Treaty. The offence is still dominant.

There was no agreed theory capable of setting the optimum limits to offensive systems or explaining why one measure rather than another would make any strategic difference. The attempt to develop scenarios to justify positions taken in the context of SALT generated claims that 'ICBM vulnerability' and 'essential equivalence' represented real strategic imperatives. These positions then hindered efforts to reach agreements. Somehow a way had to be found to show that two comparable but asymmetrical force structures were essentially equal, or could be made to appear so with relatively minor adjustments.

An operational view of the 'strategic balance' in the nuclear age depended on an analysis of the threat the forces posed to each other rather than on whether they were essentially of the same size and composition. After a certain point numbers and variations in weapons systems became irrelevant. So long as the destruction of the other side could be assured there was no need to worry if the other side seemed to have acquired surplus capacity. By contrast, the more political approach resulting from Jackson's demand that only equal treaties be negotiated assumed that the size and composition of the respective arsenals made a real difference, especially if the agreed numbers implied that one side was in a superior position. Attempts to develop measures of capabilities that captured operational effectiveness acquired degrees of sophistication at odds with the idea that the problem was misperceptions. Unsurprisingly, the negotiators ended up with metrics that were understood – delivery vehicles and warheads.

To what extent nuclear weapons could dampen pressure towards conflict depended on the numbers deployed and the ease with which they could be used. The major powers learned to act cautiously in their presence. The search for ways to mount nuclear strikes that removed or reduced the risk of enemy retaliation proved futile. One of the few things widely understood about the nuclear age was that a few detonations could cause immense damage to a country and its people. In that light, strategic theory was as useful in explaining why arms control was not really necessary when it came to managing the US–Soviet nuclear relationship as it was in describing the path to pursue.

Does that mean that there was no value to the arms-control exercise at all? Once arms control was established as part of the routine of US–Soviet and then US–Russian relations it had value in providing a degree of transparency and predictability that might not otherwise have been present. The big summits organised around arms-control negotiations were opportunities for leaders to meet and get to know one another and explore ways to ease tensions. Most endorsements of actual agreements followed that of the US Joint Chiefs in 1979 when they described the SALT II Treaty, signed between Carter and Brezhnev but never ratified, as 'modest but useful'.[58]

There is one strategic arms-control agreement still in place: New START (for Strategic Arms Reduction Treaty), which was signed in 2010, entered into force in 2011 and was extended in 2021 for another five years.[59] It sets limits far lower than those of the original interim agreement of 1972 and covers warheads. The limits are 700 for deployed missiles and bombers and 1,550 for deployed warheads, and a separate limit of 800 for deployed and non-deployed launchers (missile tubes and bombers). This reflects the apparently more benign post-Cold War context and the lower salience of comparative missile numbers. It was possible to maintain strategic deterrence at lower numbers than before. When in March 2022 Putin made nuclear threats to warn NATO countries not to interfere in his attempted occupation of Ukraine, few paid much attention to the details of the nuclear balance. The big issue was the state of Putin's mind.[60]

Notes

[1] Thomas C. Schelling and Morton H. Halperin, *Strategy and Arms Control* (Washington DC: Pergamon-Brassey's, 1985 [1961]), p. 2.

[2] Thomas C. Schelling, 'What Went Wrong with Arms Control?', *Foreign Affairs*, vol. 64, no. 2, Winter 1985/86, pp. 219–33.

[3] See Jennifer E. Sims, *Icarus Restrained: An Intellectual History of American Arms Control, 1945–1960* (Boulder, CO: Westview, 1990).

[4] See Donald C. Brennan (ed.), *Arms Control, Disarmament, and National Security* (New York: George Braziller, 1961); and Schelling and Halperin, *Strategy and Arms Control*.

[5] See Hedley Bull, *The Control of the Arms Race* (London: Weidenfeld & Nicolson, 1961),

[6] See Thomas C. Schelling, 'The Thirtieth Year', *Daedalus*, vol. 120, no. 1, Winter 1991, pp. 21–31.

[7] Schelling and Halperin, *Strategy and Arms Control*, p. 3.

[8] See Bernard Brodie, 'On the Objectives of Arms Control', *International Security*, vol. 1, no. 1, Summer 1976, pp. 17–36.

[9] See 'McCloy–Zorin Accords', 20 September 1961, NuclearFiles.org, http://www.nuclearfiles.org/menu/key-issues/nuclear-weapons/issues/arms-control-disarmament/mccloy-zorin-accords_1961-09-20.htm.

[10] Article VI reads: 'Each of the Parties to the Treaty undertakes to pursue negotiations in good faith on effective measures relating to cessation of the nuclear arms race at an early date and to nuclear disarmament, and on a treaty on general and complete disarmament under strict and effective international control.'

[11] For more background, see Lawrence Freedman, 'Is "Old School" Nuclear Disarmament Dead?', in Bård Nikolas Vik Steen and Olav Njølstad (eds), *Nuclear Disarmament: A Critical Assessment* (London: Routledge, 2019).

[12] See Roger Dingman, *Power in the Pacific: The Origins of Naval Arms Limitation, 1914–1922* (Chicago, IL: University of Chicago Press: 1976);

B.J.C. McKercher (ed.), *Arms Limitation and Disarmament: Restraints on War 1899–1939* (Westport, CT: Praeger, 1992); and Stephen E. Pelz, *Race to Pearl Harbor: The Failure of the Second London Naval Conference and the Onset of World War II* (Cambridge, MA: Harvard University Press, 1974). For a sharp, classic critique of disarmament over this period, see Salvador de Madariaga, *Disarmament* (Port Washington, NY: Kennikat Press, 1967), originally published in 1929.

13 See US Senate Foreign Relations Committee, *Conference on the Limitation of Armament* (Washington DC: Government Printing Office, 1922), p. 270; and William B. Hale, 'Limitation of Armaments', *American Bar Association Journal*, vol. 18, no. 3, March 1932, pp. 195–204.

14 See David Lal, *The American Nuclear Disarmament Dilemma, 1945–1963* (New York: Syracuse University Press, 2008).

15 Jerome B. Wiesner, 'Foreword to the Issue "Arms Control"', *Daedalus*, vol. 89, no. 4, Fall 1960, p. 678.

16 Vladislav Zubok and Constantine Pleshakov, *Inside the Kremlin's Cold War: From Stalin to Khrushchev* (Cambridge, MA: Harvard University Press, 1996), p. 192.

17 'Report by the Panel of Consultants of the Department of State to the Secretary of State', January 1953, in Lisle A. Rose and Neal H. Peterson (eds), *Foreign Relations of the United States, 1952–1954*, vol. 2, Part 2, National Security Affairs (Washington DC: US Government Printing Office, 1984), doc. 67.

18 Jeremi Suri, 'America's Search for a Technological Solution to the Arms Race: The Surprise Attack Conference of 1958 and a Challenge for "Eisenhower Revisionists"', *Diplomatic History*, vol. 21, no. 3, Summer 1997, pp. 417–51.

19 This was discussed in Thomas C. Schelling, 'Meteors, Mischief, and War', *Bulletin of the Atomic Scientists*, vol. 16, no. 7, September 1960, pp. 292–300.

20 Quoted in Michael Beschloss, *The Crisis Years: Kennedy and Khrushchev, 1960–1963* (New York: HarperCollins, 1991), pp. 329–30.

21 For an argument on the importance of nuclear superiority in such crises, see Matthew Kroenig, *The Logic of American Nuclear Strategy: Why Strategic Superiority Matters* (New York: Oxford University Press, 2018).

22 For further background, see Lawrence Freedman and Jeff Michaels, *The Evolution of Nuclear Strategy*, 4th ed. (London: Palgrave, 2019).

23 See Alain Enthoven and Wayne Smith, *How Much Is Enough? Shaping the Defense Program, 1961–69* (New York: Harper & Row, 1971).

24 See Ted Greenwood, *Making the MIRV: A Study in Defense Decision-making* (Cambridge, MA: Ballinger, 1975).

25 See Morton H. Halperin, 'The Decision to Deploy the ABM: Bureaucratic and Domestic Politics in the Johnson Administration', *World Politics*, vol. 25, no. 1, October 1972, pp. 62–95.

26 Jerome B. Wiesner and Herbert F. York, 'National Security and the Nuclear-test Ban', *Scientific American*, vol. 211, no. 4, October 1964, pp. 27–35.

27 'Memorandum of Conversation', Glassboro, New Jersey, 23 June 1967, in David C. Humphrey and Charles S. Sampson (eds), *Foreign Relations*

of the United States, 1964–1968, vol. 14, Soviet Union (Washington DC: US Government Printing Office). McNamara's own account was dramatic. Kosygin, he recalled, 'absolutely erupted. He became red in the face.' This is not supported by any other account. See Michael Charlton, *The Star Wars History – From Deterrence to Defence: The American Strategic Debate* (London: BBC, 1986); and Michael Krepon, *Winning and Losing the Nuclear Peace: The Rise, Demise, and Revival of Arms Control* (Stanford, CA: Stanford University Press, 2021), pp. 98–9.

28 'President's Daily Diary, 23 June 1967, Prepared by White House Secretary Marie Fehmer', available at National Security Archive, George Washington University, https://nsarchive.gwu.edu/briefing-book/nuclear-vault/2021-12-07/strategic-stability-during-middle-cold-war.

29 See Lawrence Freedman, *US Intelligence and the Soviet Strategic Threat* (London: Macmillan, 1977), chapter 7; Edward Randolph Jayne, *The ABM Debate: Strategic Defense and National Security* (Cambridge, MA: MIT Center for International Studies, 1969); and Halperin, 'The Decision to Deploy the ABM'.

30 Robert S. McNamara, 'The Dynamics of Nuclear Strategy', speech of 18 September 1967, reprinted in *Department of State Bulletin*, vol. 52, 9 October 1967, p. 446. Morton Halperin drafted the speech.

31 This issue is addressed in Freedman and Michaels, *The Evolution of Nuclear Strategy*, especially chapter 32.

32 See Freedman, *US Intelligence and*

the Soviet Strategic Threat; and John Prados, *The Soviet Estimate: U.S. Intelligence and Soviet Strategic Forces* (Princeton, NJ: Princeton University Press, 1986).

33 See Krepon, *Winning and Losing the Nuclear Peace*, pp. 117–19.

34 Paul H. Nitze, 'Assuring Strategic Stability in an Era of Détente', *Foreign Affairs*, vol. 54, no. 2, January 1976, pp. 207–32.

35 Colin S. Gray, 'The Strategic Force Triad: End of the Road?', *Foreign Affairs*, vol. 56, no. 4, July 1978, p. 775.

36 'Report of the President's Commission on Strategic Forces', April 1983, http://web.mit.edu/chemistry/deutch/policy/1983-ReportPresCommStrategic.pdf. See also R. James Woolsey, 'The Politics of Vulnerability: 1980–83', *Foreign Affairs*, vol. 62, no. 4, Spring 1984, pp. 805–19. On the ICBM vulnerability issue, see David Dunn, *The Politics of Threat: Minuteman Vulnerability in American National Security Policy* (London: Palgrave, 1997).

37 Richard Nixon, *RN: The Memoirs of Richard Nixon* (London: Sidgwick and Jackson, 1978), p. 415.

38 See 'National Security Decision Memorandum 16 – Subject: Criteria for Strategic Sufficiency', 24 June 1969, https://irp.fas.org/offdocs/nsdm-nixon/nsdm-16.pdf.

39 Quoted in Desmond Ball, 'Déjà Vu: The Return to Counterforce in the Nixon Administration', California Seminar on Arms Control and Foreign Policy, 1974, p. 8.

40 See Krepon, *Winning and Losing the Nuclear Peace*, pp. 119–23.

41 To make way for the extra SLBMs,

the Soviet Union had to dismantle 209 old ICBMs. On SALT I, see John Newhouse, *Cold Dawn: The Story of SALT* (New York: Holt, Rinehart & Winston, 1973).

42 Office of the Federal Register, 'United States Statutes at Large', vol. 86, Public Law 92-448, 30 September 1972, p. 747.

43 'Press Conference by the US Secretary of State Dr Henry A. Kissinger, 3 July 1974', reprinted in *Survival*, vol. 16, no. 5, September/ October 1974, pp. 239–46.

44 In ballistics, CEP is the radius of a circle, centred on the mean, whose boundary is expected to include the landing points of 50% of the rounds. This formula has the unfortunate property of producing a lethality equivalent to infinity when the CEP is zero. See Fred A. Payne, 'The Strategic Nuclear Balance: A New Measure', *Survival,* vol. 20, no. 3, May/June 1977, pp. 107–10.

45 James R. Schlesinger, 'Annual Defense Department Report, Fiscal Year 1976 and 1977', 5 February 1975, p. II-7.

46 Harold Brown, 'Department of Defense Annual Report, Fiscal Year 1979', 2 February 1978, p. 5.

47 Schlesinger, 'Annual Defense Report FY 1976 and 1977', p. II-7.

48 Even with the obvious example of Munich, it was the balance of alliances as much as that of forces that was most pertinent. See P.E. Caquet, 'The Balance of Forces on the Eve of Munich', *International History Review*, vol. 40, no. 1, January 2018, pp. 20–40.

49 See Steven Kull, *Minds at War: Nuclear Reality and the Inner Conflicts of*

Defense Policymakers (New York: Basic Books, 1988).

50 Robert Jervis, *The Meaning of the Nuclear Revolution: Statecraft and the Prospect of Armageddon* (Ithaca, NY: Cornell University Press, 1989), p. 199.

51 Edward N. Luttwak, 'The Missing Dimension of US Defense Policy: Force, Perceptions and Power', in Donald C. Daniel (ed.), *International Perceptions of the Superpower Military Balance* (New York: Praeger, 1978), p. 28.

52 Freedman, *US Intelligence and the Soviet Strategic Threat*, p. 66.

53 *Ibid.*, pp. 21–3.

54 See Gabriel A. Almond, 'Public Opinion and the Development of Space Technology: 1957–60', in Joseph M. Goldsen (ed.), *Outer Space in World Politics* (London: Pall Mall Press, 1963), pp. 71–96.

55 See 'Minutes of Review Group Meeting, Washington', 29 May 1969, in M. Todd Bennett (ed.), *Foreign Relations of the United States, 1969– 1976,* vol. 34, National Security Policy, 1969–1972 (Washington DC: US Government Printing Office, 2011).

56 'Minutes of National Security Council Meeting', 19 February 1969, in *ibid.*, p. 25.

57 Schelling, 'What Went Wrong with Arms Control?'

58 Quoted in Charles Mohr, 'Arms-pact Debate: A New Script Has Both Sides Winning', *New York Times*, 30 July 1979.

59 On the negotiations, see Rose Gottemoeller, *Negotiating the New START Treaty* (Amherst, NY: Cambria Press, 2021).

60 See Lawrence Freedman, 'Would Putin Dare Drop the Bomb?', *Sunday Times*, 6 March 2022.

Copyright © 2022 The International Institute for Strategic Studies

Restraining an Arms Race in Outer Space

Paul Meyer

The Russian invasion of Ukraine has galvanised a Western response to an act of naked aggression that many had thought would never again darken the European continent. These actions may well rekindle a hotter and more complicated version of the Cold War that shaped the international security order for more than 70 years. At the same time, the interests of both states and their societies suggest that realms of restraint and cooperation should be preserved. One such realm is that of outer space.

Beauty, it is said, is in the eye of the beholder. Must the same be said of 'responsible behaviour', or might a common understanding of the term be achieved? The question has clear implications for space security and the prospect of outer space remaining free from human-devised threats. The number of satellites orbiting the Earth has grown exponentially in recent years, providing global society with a wide array of services on which it has become increasingly dependent. In 2020 there were roughly 2,000 active satellites; the following year that number had increased to some 4,800, and there are plans to launch another 35,000 over the next five years.[1] These satellites pose new challenges for the safety and security of operations in an increasingly congested orbital environment. Largely driven by the private sector, these developments also serve to highlight the limits of existing

Paul Meyer is Adjunct Professor of International Studies at Simon Fraser University in Vancouver and a founding Fellow of the Outer Space Institute. Previously, he had a 35-year career in Canada's Foreign Service including serving as Canada's Ambassador to the UN and the Conference on Disarmament in Geneva (2003–07). His ORCID designation is http://orcid.org/0000-0002-9199-165X.

Survival | vol. 64 no. 2 | April–May 2022 | pp. 81–94   https://doi.org/10.1080/00396338.2022.2055825

global governance and the fragile nature of the policy consensus among leading space powers.

Judging solely by the declaratory policy of states, space security appears relatively unproblematic. For some 40 years, a resolution adopted annually at the United Nations General Assembly entitled 'The Prevention of an Arms Race in Outer Space' (PAROS) has outlined global space policy. This resolution seems to have been embraced almost universally by UN member states – only the United States and Israel have regularly dissented, alternating between 'no' votes and abstentions, and even they joined the consensus in 2021.

The resolution stresses the need to avoid an arms race in space and to prevent its weaponisation. It urges states to 'consolidate and reinforce' the existing legal regime for outer space and to 'enhance its effectiveness'.[2] Yet this strong expression of intent has not been matched by state efforts to implement the resolution's putative goals. Voting annually for PAROS has become something of a ritualised act by states, signalling their support for the resolution's aims but not spurring them to take any particular diplomatic action.

PAROS's failure to launch has been exacerbated by the prolonged paralysis of the 65-nation Conference on Disarmament (CD) in Geneva. Ostensibly the UN's sole forum for the negotiation of multilateral arms-control and disarmament agreements, the body has been unable to initiate any official work on the PAROS goal. This failure is due to the wider dysfunction of the CD, whereby its insistence on consensus decision-making, the differing priorities of its members and negative linkage politics (whereby states decline to support the preferred negotiation of other states unless they receive support for their own priority negotiation) have prevented it from agreeing on a programme of work for 25 years. This disappointing state of affairs seems to have been tolerated by states for decades, in part because there was no sign of an arms race in outer space.

The return of anti-satellite weapons

This comfortable situation was rudely disrupted in 2007, however, by China's January test of an anti-satellite weapon (ASAT) at a high altitude (860 kilometres), which destroyed one of China's own satellites, producing thousands of pieces of debris. The test was in contravention of the 1967 Outer Space Treaty, which precludes actions that would constitute 'harmful interference' with the space operations of other states and which requires prior consultation with states that might be affected by any unilateral action. The 2007 ASAT test compounded an existing space-debris problem: there are almost 30,000 pieces of trackable debris (measuring more than 10 centimetres) in space, and nearly a million more smaller pieces.[3] The high speeds of such orbital debris mean that even a small piece can carry a huge kinetic impact. The growth of space debris is already a cause of concern for the safety of space operations, especially in the relatively congested low-Earth orbits in which most satellites can be found, without adding destructive ASATs into the mixture.

Although many Western states decried the Chinese test, the United States followed suit in February 2008 with a demonstration of the ASAT capability of its *Aegis* missile-defence interceptors. The operation was presented as necessary for public safety because the targeted re-entering satellite contained toxic fuel, and the demonstration was conducted at a low altitude to avoid the creation of long-lasting debris. In an apparent effort to avoid being left behind by the ASAT club, India conducted its own ASAT test using a direct-ascent missile in March 2019 at an altitude of 300 km, claiming that this produced no significant debris (a claim challenged by civilian experts).[4] In November 2021, Russia, which has developed both direct-ascent-missile and co-orbital ASATs but had until then avoided destructive testing, surprised many observers by conducting a kinetic ASAT test against a target satellite at an altitude of 480 km, producing an estimated 1,500 pieces of trackable debris.[5]

While both the United States and the Soviet Union had ASAT programmes during the Cold War, tests of such weapons had been subject to a tacit moratorium as of the mid-1980s that had held for almost a quarter-century. There was even an effort in 1979 under the Carter administration to negotiate a US–Soviet agreement banning ASAT tests, but the accord was never concluded, falling victim to, inter alia, the chilling effect on bilateral relations of the Soviet invasion of Afghanistan. The advent of the Reagan administration and concerns that agreed constraints on ASATs could hamper the development of the president's signature Strategic Defense Initiative led the United States to abandon this arms-control initiative.[6]

The reappearance of destructive ASAT tests shattered the complacency that had settled in with respect to space security. No longer could it be taken for granted that the 'peaceful purposes' stipulation of the Outer Space Treaty would continue to be respected by spacefaring powers. The revival of what has been called great-power rivalry – notably signalled by Russia's annexation of Crimea in 2014; the Trump administration's creation of a Space Force and its official characterisation of outer space as a 'warfighting domain';[7] and an increasingly assertive Chinese approach to outer space – has fuelled fears that the relatively benign environment of outer space could be suddenly turned into a battleground, with devastating effect.

Even as concerns over the security of outer space have grown, there has been a rapid increase in space activity, largely led by the private sector. Well-resourced companies such as SpaceX, OneWeb, Amazon's Project Kuiper and China's StarNet have advanced plans for 'mega constellations' comprising tens of thousands of satellites – already, SpaceX's Starlink constellation accounts for almost one-third of all active satellites in orbit. Commercial launches are proceeding at pace, but it is clear that the risks to companies' business models would become overwhelming if inter-state armed conflict were to break out in outer space.[8]

A new tack from the UK

One country has not allowed diplomatic lethargy, the spread of 'counter-space' capabilities, the bellicose rhetoric of leading space powers or the rapid growth of civilian space activity to deter it from championing a new diplomatic initiative in the spirit of PAROS. Boldly going where no one has gone before, the United Kingdom introduced a resolution at the UN General Assembly's First Committee (Disarmament and International Security) in 2020 entitled 'Reducing Space Threats Through Norms, Rules and Principles of Responsible Behaviours'. The chief purpose of the resolution was to encourage states to submit their views to the UN secretary-general on what they perceived as threats and what might be done to reduce them. The resolution's focus on delineating 'responsible' and 'irresponsible' behaviour in outer space, and its call for states to enumerate examples of both, were particularly noteworthy.[9] One of the authors of the resolution was Aidan Liddle, the UK's ambassador to the CD, who explained that the British government had proposed the resolution 'because we believe that coming to a common understanding of responsible behaviour can help avoid miscalculations and escalation that could lead to conflict ... and to address the factors that could drive an arms race in outer space'.[10]

The resolution was adopted by a wide majority, and some 30 states (plus the European Union and nine non-governmental organisations) provided substantive submissions by the May 2021 deadline. In August, the UN secretary-general released a report containing a compendium of the national views received.[11] The UK's innovative delineation between responsible and irresponsible behaviour was reflected in several of the national responses. Many suggested that restraint measures were more likely to be effective if they focused on behaviours rather than weapons systems, which would be difficult to define given the dual-use nature of space objects – anything in orbit could potentially be used as a weapon against another space object. As the German submission put it:

> In view of such dual-use concerns, threats in outer space cannot be deduced from objects or capabilities alone, but from a combination of capabilities and behaviour, or from the observation of actual actions, operations and activities. As a consequence, traditional arms control approaches, such as prohibiting specific types of objects in outer space, are inadequate and do not solve the security problem.[12]

Norms versus law

The resolution's emphasis on 'norms, rules and principles', which are of a political character, is contested by those states which favour legally binding measures. The governments of China and Russia – as well as Brazil, India and Mexico – have supported a new legal instrument, whereas the US and many other Western states have preferred non-binding transparency and confidence-building measures. The argument against relying on political norms was articulated by Li Song, China's ambassador to the CD, at a PAROS-related discussion in June 2021:

> The formulation of norms, rules and principles on responsible behavior is by its very nature a transparency and confidence-building measure. While it has a positive role to play, such a measure is not legally binding and cannot fill the loopholes in existing international legal instruments on outer space or replace negotiations on an arms-control treaty on outer space. Given the complex nature of [the] outer space security issue, the binary distinction between 'responsible' and 'irresponsible' behaviors in outer space is too simplistic, and subjective, and is open to political manipulation.[13]

While not rejecting the normative approach, China clearly sees it as inferior to legally binding measures, which it believes should be supported by all states genuinely committed to PAROS. In China's submission to the secretary-general, it asserted that 'whether a country has the political will to participate in such a negotiation [of a legally binding agreement] is the touchstone for its sincerity in terms of behaving responsibly'. The Chinese submission also observed that a 'space war cannot be won and should never be fought'.[14]

Russia is likewise unconvinced by the normative approach, and its submission contained a thinly veiled critique of the United States and its more militarised positions regarding outer space:

> Steps towards using outer space for military operations (both 'defensive' and 'offensive' operations, including preventive activities) are motivated by the pursuit of military dominance. They are detrimental to international peace and security and could result in severe instability and an arms race in outer space, which would completely undermine the prospects for arms limitation and reduction in general.[15]

Both China and Russia refer in their statements to their draft Treaty on Prevention of the Placement of Weapons in Outer Space and of the Threat or Use of Force Against Outer Space Objects (better known by its acronym PPWT). This treaty, which was first introduced at the CD in 2008 (a revised version was tabled in 2014), would as its title suggests ban placing weapons in outer space and the threat or use of force against a space object. The US has been highly critical of the proposal, noting its lack of definitions of key terms (such as 'space weapon') and of verification provisions, as well as its focus on weapons in space as opposed to terrestrial-based threats to space objects (such as ASATs). The two co-sponsors have repeatedly stated in response to this criticism that they are open to discussing and modifying the draft treaty, but their insistence that consideration of the treaty be confined to the CD despite this forum's gridlock has meant that it has not received sustained attention.[16]

Escaping the deadlock?

While China and Russia are not alone in wanting to see action on PAROS at the CD, the national submissions reveal greater flexibility as to the forum in which the envisaged work on norms, rules and principles might take place. Several submissions supported the establishment of an Open-ended Working Group (OEWG) or a Group of Governmental Experts as the appropriate diplomatic vehicles to advance this work. Both of these mechanisms have been employed productively by the UN in the past, notably on cyber security, although the OEWG is the more open and inclusive of the two. Importantly, both mechanisms are established by the UN General Assembly, which operates on the basis of majority vote rather than by consensus as at the CD, where each member state effectively wields a veto. General Assembly-mandated negotiations are responsible for all recent multilateral arms-control and disarmament agreements (including the 2013 Arms Trade Treaty and the 2017 Treaty on the Prohibition of Nuclear Weapons), whereas the last agreement concluded at the CD (the Comprehensive Test-Ban Treaty) dates back to 1996.

The UK moved swiftly to capitalise on the momentum generated by its 2020 resolution by introducing at the 2021 session of the General Assembly a resolution authorising the establishment of an OEWG to make further progress on norms development.[17] The resolution was adopted in December 2021 with a vote of 150 in favour, eight opposed and seven abstentions.[18] Although Russia and China were opposed, and India, a significant spacefaring state, abstained, all states are expected to participate in the new OEWG, which is to meet in Geneva for two one-week sessions in both 2022 and 2023, and to report to the autumn 2023 session of the General Assembly if the participating states can agree on the report's contents.

What kind of measures can be expected to emerge from the OEWG's proceedings? The national submissions in the secretary-general's report contained a variety of proposals, but they reflected a convergence of interest in two potential measures – a ban on debris-creating ASAT tests, and rules to govern so-called proximity and rendezvous operations in which a satellite manoeuvres to be close to another space object. A prohibition on debris-causing ASAT tests has been proposed many times, but an increase in enduring debris, coupled with the increased number of satellites in orbit, would seem to make such a measure, which would benefit all space operators, a compelling option. Similarly, the development of space objects capable of close-proximity operations (to accomplish on-orbit servicing and other beneficial functions, but with potential ASAT capabilities) would make agreement on standards for these operations an appealing arrangement for all space users.

What role for the US?

Any agreement on significant restraint measures in space would require support from the leading spacefaring powers. This support seems unlikely to be forthcoming, however, given the ongoing criticism being exchanged between China and Russia on the one hand and the United States on the other. Much will ultimately depend on the position taken by Washington. Unlike the provocative stance of the Trump administration, whose Space Force was given a mission of dominance, the Biden administration may well steer a more moderate course, with a greater emphasis on diplomacy in sustaining a safe and secure outer space. The US submission refers to the Biden administration's interim National Security Strategy and affirms that the 'United States will lead in promoting shared norms and forge new agreements on outer space'.[19]

The US has not toned down its critique of the Sino-Russian PPWT, nor its accusations of duplicity and malign intent behind the space-security policies of China and Russia. In a recent statement to the CD, US Ambassador Robert Wood affirmed that the PPWT contained 'fundamental flaws' and failed to meet the criteria required for a credible arms-control proposal for space. He further stated that

> the two countries that authored the draft Treaty [PPWT] have turned space into a warfighting domain. The People's Republic of China continues to field new destructive and non-destructive ground- and space-based anti-satellite weapons … Russia, for its part, continues to field ground-based anti-satellite missiles intended to destroy satellites in low Earth orbit and ground-based anti-satellite lasers probably intended to blind or damage sensitive space-based optical sensors on low Earth orbit satellites.[20]

In making the case for pursuing voluntary norms instead of a new legal instrument, Ambassador Wood observed that a 'focus on voluntary, non-legally binding norms of responsible behaviour has multiple advantages, including the ability to adapt quickly to changing circumstances or technologies (and to avoid the problem of spending years negotiating legally binding instruments that may be outpaced by technological developments)'.[21]

Alongside the US State Department's position, the US Department of Defense has recently articulated its support for a set of norms ('tenets') of responsible state behaviour to govern its own activity in outer space and to demonstrate global leadership. A July 2021 memorandum from Secretary of Defense Lloyd J. Austin III enumerated five such tenets: 1) operate in, from, to, and through space with due regard to others and in a professional manner; 2) limit the generation of long-lived debris; 3) avoid the creation of harmful interference; 4) maintain safe separation and safe trajectory; and 5) communicate and make notifications to enhance the safety and stability of the domain.[22]

The references to 'due regard to others' and the avoidance of 'harmful interference' echo provisions from Article IX of the Outer Space Treaty and suggest a more cooperative approach rooted in acknowledged international legal restraints on space activity. This change in tone from the unilateralism and pugnacious language of the Trump administration will be welcomed by the international community. The Biden administration issued a 'United States Space Priorities Framework' in December 2021, which, while preserving the institutions created by its predecessor (notably the National Space Council and the military's Space Force), returned to a more cooperative declaratory policy. The framework called for the US to transition to a 'more resilient national security space posture' and to 'strengthen its ability to detect and attribute hostile acts', while also affirming that the US 'will engage diplomatically with strategic competitors in order to enhance stability in outer space … Finally, U.S. national security space operations will continue to comply with applicable international law and demonstrate leadership in both the responsible use of space and stewardship of the space environment.'[23]

Sceptics will flag the 'unless otherwise directed' caveat of the Defense Department memorandum and the absence of any acknowledged restraint on ASATs beyond the commitment to 'limit the generation of long-lived debris'. It should be noted that no agreed definition exists of the term 'long-lasting' – this would presumably be one of the points requiring clarification if proposals for a test ban on kinetic (debris-causing) ASATs are to advance.

Recent reports suggest that the United States may soon unveil an ASAT of its own, presumably one that does not create debris.[24] The use of lasers, directed-energy weapons or electronic-warfare systems could all be capable of disrupting the normal functioning of a space object. Unveiling its own ASAT will deprive Washington of the moral high ground with respect to China and Russia, which it has long accused of 'weaponising' outer space through their development of ASAT capabilities. Beyond contributing to an emerging arms race in outer space, such a step by the United States could also provide an impetus to space arms-control efforts. The history of arms-control agreements demonstrates that it is usually only after a weapons system is deployed that serious negotiations get under way to control it. Whether the presumptive parties to such a negotiation would be content with a stand-alone 'norm of responsible state behaviour', or insist on a more binding and verifiable accord, remains to be seen. Another key question for the parties to decide is whether it would be necessary to conduct negotiations on a multilateral basis given the growing number of states with space capabilities, or on a more restricted bilateral or trilateral basis.

A 'responsible' way forward?

The apparent popularity of a ban on destructive ASAT testing and the related but less demanding goal of establishing rules for proximity operations could yield real substance from the new OEWG process if the participating parties are prepared to produce tangible results. Yet Russia and China have expressed reservations about this new forum and may take steps to disrupt it. Moving beyond an exchange of views to an actual negotiation is not often a straightforward process, and there are already signs of disagreement among participating states. The organisational meeting for the OEWG that took place on 7 and 9 February 2022 did not agree to hold the OEWG's first substantive meeting that same month, so this was pushed back to mid-May.

Despite these birthing pains, the OEWG on 'Reducing Space Threats' appears to be the most promising diplomatic avenue for progress in preventing an arms race and reducing the danger of actual armed conflict in outer space. The OEWG, as a functioning diplomatic process, has at long last provided a forum to discuss and take action on space security free from the straitjacket that the CD has imposed on this subject.

That said, a functional negotiating forum is a necessary but not a sufficient condition to ensure real progress. While much will depend on whether leading space powers opt for cooperation concerning space-security norms, it will also be important for other states and interested parties to advocate for negotiations on cooperative security measures. Civil-society organisations are becoming increasingly vocal on space security: in October 2021, a 'Joint Statement on Outer Space' prepared by civil-society actors called upon states 'not to deliberately disrupt, damage or destroy space assets' and urged them to consider an open letter signed by scores of former politicians, officials and civilian space experts exhorting the UN General Assembly to begin work on a treaty banning debris-causing ASAT tests.[25]

If and when serious negotiations on space security get under way, there will be a need for flexibility on the part of participating states as to whether the product of any negotiations will be legally binding. Given the long-standing differences among states on this issue, it might be prudent to set the status of any agreed measures to one side, to be determined at a later stage of negotiations. Establishing common ground on how to define and assess threats to space security will be necessary for the OEWG (or any other process) to succeed. In the absence of common understandings of what constitutes a threat to space operations or any collective commitment to reduce such threats, debates over defining 'responsible' behaviours in outer space may not yield meaningful results.

Notes

1   Victoria Samson, 'The Complicating Role of the Private Sector in Space', *Bulletin of the Atomic Scientists*, vol. 78, no. 1, 2022, p. 6.

2   UN General Assembly, Resolution A/RES/76/22, 'Prevention of an Arms Race in Outer Space', adopted 16 December 2021 without a vote.

3   European Space Agency, 'Space Debris by the Numbers', updated 3 March 2022, https://www.esa.int/Safety_Security/Space_Debris/Space_debris_by_the_numbers.

4   For a comprehensive account of these ASAT tests and other 'counter-space capabilities', see Brian Weeden and Victoria Samson (eds), 'Global Counterspace Capabilities: An Open Source Assessment', Secure World Foundation, April 2021, https://swfound.org/media/207162/swf_global_counterspace_capabilities_2021.pdf.

5   Shannon Borgos, 'Russian ASAT Test Creates Massive Debris', Arms Control Association, December 2021, https://www.armscontrol.org/act/2021-12/news/russian-asat-test-creates-massive-debris.

6   See Aaron Bateman, 'Mutually Assured Surveillance at Risk: Anti-satellite Weapons and Cold War Arms Control', *Journal of Strategic Studies*, January 2021, https://www.tandfonline.com/doi/abs/10.1080/01402390.2021.2019022.

7   White House, 'President Donald J. Trump Is Unveiling an America First National Space Strategy', 23 March 2018, https://trumpwhitehouse.archives.gov/briefings-statements/president-donald-j-trump-unveiling-america-first-national-space-strategy/; and White House, 'President Donald J. Trump Is Launching America's Space Force', 23 October 2018, https://trumpwhitehouse.archives.gov/briefings-statements/president-donald-j-trump-launching-americas-space-force/.

8   See Samson, 'The Complicating Role of the Private Sector in Space', p. 9.

9   UN General Assembly, Resolution A/RES/75/36, 'Reducing Space Threats Through Norms: Rules and Principles of Responsible Behaviours', adopted 7 December 2020.

10 Conference on Disarmament, 'Final Record of the One Thousand Five Hundred and Seventy-seventh Plenary Meeting', CD/PV.1577, 1 June 2021, p. 3.

11 UN General Assembly, 'Reducing Space Threats Through Norms, Rules and Principles of Responsible Behaviours: Report of the Secretary General', A/76/77, 13 July 2021,

https://www.un.org/disarmament/topics/outerspace-sg-report-outer-space-2021/.

12 *Ibid.*, p. 47.

13 'Remarks by H.E. Ambassador Li Song on the Prevention of an Arms Race in Outer Space at the Thematic Debate of the Conference on Disarmament', 1 June 2021, https://documents.unoda.org/wp-content/uploads/2021/06/20210601Remarks-by-Ambassador-LI-Song-on-PAROS-at-CD-Thematic-Debate_OK-for-web-.pdf.

14 UN General Assembly, 'Reducing Space Threats Through Norms, Rules and Principles of Responsible Behaviours: Report of the Secretary-General', pp. 32, 34.

15 *Ibid.*, p. 79.

16 For the most recent text of the Sino-Russian treaty, see 'Letter Dated 10 June 2014 from the Permanent Representative of the Russian Federation and the Permanent Representative of China to the Conference on Disarmament', Conference on Disarmament, CD/1985, 12 June 2014. For the US critique, see 'Letter Dated 19 August 2008 from the Permanent Representative of the United States of America', Conference on Disarmament, CD/1847, 26 August 2008. For the Sino-Russian rebuttal, see 'Letter Dated 18 August 2009 from the Permanent Representative of China and the Permanent Representative of the Russian Federation', Conference on Disarmament, CD/1872, 18 August 2009.

17 See Aidan Liddle, 'Responsible Behaviours in Outer Space: Towards UNGA 76', 8 June 2021, https://blogs.fcdo.gov.uk/aidanliddle/2021/06/08/reducing-space-threats-towards-unga-76/.

18 UN General Assembly, Resolution A/RES/76/231, 'Reducing Space Threats Through Norms, Rules and Principles of Responsible Behaviours', adopted 24 December 2021.

19 UN General Assembly, 'Reducing Space Threats Through Norms, Rules and Principles of Responsible Behaviours: Report of the Secretary-General', p. 95.

20 Conference on Disarmament, 'Final Record of One Thousand Five Hundred and Seventy-sixth Plenary Meeting', CD/PV/1576, 1 June 2021, p. 17.

21 *Ibid.*, p. 18.

22 Lloyd J. Austin, 'Tenets of Responsible Space Operations', memorandum, 7 July 2021, https://media.defense.gov/2021/Jul/23/2002809598/-1/-1/0/TENETS-OF-RESPONSIBLE-BEHAVIOR-IN-SPACE.PDF.

23 White House, 'United States Space Priorities Framework', December 2021, p. 6, https://www.whitehouse.gov/wp-content/uploads/2021/12/United-States-Space-Priorities-Framework-_-December-1-2021.pdf.

24 See Theresa Hitchens, 'Pentagon Poised to Unveil, Demonstrate Classified Space Weapon', *Breaking Defense*, 20 August 2021, https://breakingdefense.com/2021/08/pentagon-posed-to-unveil-classified-space-weapon/.

25 See 'First Committee Exchange with Civil Society: Joint Statement on Outer Space 2021', available at Reaching Critical Will, https://reachingcriticalwill.org/images/documents/Disarmament-fora/1com/1com21/statements/8Oct_outerspace.pdf;

and Outer Space Institute, 'Re: Kinetic ASAT Test Ban Treaty', letter dated 2 September 2021, http://outerspaceinstitute.ca/docs/OSI_International_Open_Letter_ASATs_PUBLIC.pdf.

Copyright © 2022 The International Institute for Strategic Studies

Four Circles: Comprehending the China Challenge

David C. Gompert

China is a revisionist superpower. Its regime views the United States as the main obstacle to achieving its goals. It follows that the US will continually be confronted with challenges and choices involving China. Given the stakes and risks involved for America, conceptual clarity and deliberate policy are essential. Yet Sino-US relations are bewilderingly complex, involving geopolitical manoeuvring, military dangers, technological rivalry, economic interdependence, ad hoc collaboration and third-party interests. Perhaps understandably, clarity of purpose has eluded American leaders and professional China-watchers who advise them. Here is an analytic model that might help.

This is hardly the first such model. Before Chinese President Xi Jinping came to power, Western policymakers and pundits figured that China would become a 'responsible stakeholder' internationally that would reform internally as it prospered from integration in the global economy – sort of a contented giant. Chinese conduct under Xi has revealed the naivety of that theory. Then came the idea of the Thucydides Trap – with America as Sparta and, ironically, China as Athens – whereby the established hegemon is forced to react to a wannabe. On inspection, this notion fails to take account of Sino-US economic interdependence, the benefits of cooperation on certain global problems and the extreme harm conflict would do to both nations.

David C. Gompert is on the faculty of the US Naval Academy and senior advisor to Ultratech Capital Partners. He has been Principal Deputy and Acting Director of National Intelligence, Special Assistant to President George H.W. Bush and Secretary of State Henry A. Kissinger, a senior officer of the RAND Corporation and a business executive. He has published many books and articles, including several in *Survival*.

Survival | vol. 64 no. 2 | April–May 2022 | pp. 95–110   https://doi.org/10.1080/00396338.2022.2055826

Lately, 'new cold war' has become shorthand for the Sino-US relationship. Wrong again. The Sino-US relationship bears no resemblance to the old Cold War. In likening China to the Soviet Union – a bygone, isolated and stagnant superpower – it is misguided and hazardous. Most folks who use this simplistic analogy know better.

With no model to understand the sum of China's challenges, we are left with a hodgepodge of US interests and instincts. This exposes policy to political currents, which presently flow in the direction of confrontation. The fact that US responses to China enjoy bipartisan support is better than partisan paralysis, but it does not satisfy the need for coherence.

To fill this conceptual vacuum, it is useful to start by recognising that the Beijing regime places highest priority on control. For Xi and company, control is not a mere goal but an ideology. This is borne out by unrelenting efforts to quash domestic dissent. It also leaps out from official maps that depict Taiwan as the same colour as the rest of China and feature the 'nine-dash line' that implies Chinese sovereignty over the South China Sea. Beijing's obsessive-compulsive need for control is consistent with Mao Zedong's dictum that only the Chinese Communist Party (CCP) can lay down the 'general policy' and his insistence that revolution must have a commander-in-chief. Today's CCP is less serious about communism than about the elimination of threats to itself. Xi's consolidation of power clearly reflects his attachment to control as the preferred means of getting everyone on the same page and silencing dissent.

With the urge to control as the premise, the model offered here suggests four concentric circles for understanding Chinese policies and formulating US responses. The first circle, in the centre, indicates the unshakeable commitment of the state, on behalf of the party, to control China's polity and society within its present boundaries. The second circle reflects China's resolute intention to extend sovereignty over lost territories that were torn away by foreign powers when China was weak. The third circle represents China's intention to become the supreme Asia-Pacific power and arbiter of East Asian affairs. The outermost circle is the Chinese aspiration to supersede the US-led liberal world order with an authoritarian one with China as its template.

The strength of China's determination to exercise control in these concentric circles varies in proportion to its ability to do so. This implies a need
to overcome resistance by force or inducement. This compulsion is unconditional in the first circle and nearly so in the second. Beyond their sovereign
claims, the Chinese know that dominating the region may not be easy or
come early, but must be pursued by combining charm and assertiveness.
Chinese plans to revise the global order to serve China's interests are pre-
tentious and grandiose, yet nonetheless important to examine.

US capabilities to deny Chinese control are negligible in the innermost
circle, shrinking in the next one, substantial in the third one and ample in
the outermost one. This suggests that thwarting China's attempts to control
lost territory and the region as a whole – that is, circles two and three –
deserve the priority attention of American policymakers, which comes as no
surprise. But we are getting ahead of ourselves.

The first circle

State and party control in China today faces numerous challenges, but none
it cannot handle. Tibetan separatism, compounded by religious identification, predates communist victory by two centuries. While there is no chance
of, and no international support for, actual Tibetan secession, Beijing's fixa-
tion on the Dalai Lama and his foreign travels is as intense as ever. More
threatening and more brutally suppressed are the Uighurs, which are ethni-
cally more Turkic than Sinitic. The Uighurs are anathema to the state not just
by being religious but especially by being Muslim, with a tradition of rejecting external control. 'Splittist' movements present in Inner Mongolia and
Manchuria, with some 65 million inhabitants combined, pose no danger of
secession. Yet they add to Beijing's worries about holding China together
and concomitant urge to suppress dissent.

Hong Kong presents the opposite problem: it is not trying to escape
Beijing's gravitational force but instead to resist getting pulled into it.
Despite the risk of stoking militancy in Hong Kong and condemnation
abroad, China has reneged on its pledge to allow Hong Kong to keep its
separate, quasi-democratic identity. Expectations that Xi would tread
lightly in this 'Special Administrative Region' lest it alarm the people of

Taiwan proved to underestimate his impulse to control. There is no better or more bitter evidence of Beijing's top priority than its head-cracking in the streets of Hong Kong.

Who needs to crack heads with clubs when one can recognise faces with artificial intelligence (AI)? China's impressive challenge to US leadership in emerging technologies is motivated as much by the aim of crushing domestic dissent as by the need to target American forces in the Western Pacific in circles two and three. The Digital Age hope that freely flowing information and the availability of networked communities would tame, if not topple, autocracies has been replaced by fear that their tech-savvy manipulation of data and media will empower them. China is the prime example.

Beijing's keenness on new technology, especially information technology, has shown an ugly face lately. For much of Xi's reign, the Chinese approach to developing key technologies could be seen as 'state capitalism' combining government resources, market-based capital allocation and private innovation. That changed abruptly about two years ago, as the state started reeling in high-tech corporations and the tycoons who ran them. Xi perceived Alibaba co-founder Jack Ma as a dangerously independent source of influence and ideas that smacked of globalism. Before long, he was out of sight. Others in the information and entertainment fields are feeling the heel of the state. The accountants who come to audit the books are the infantry, while the party provides command and control.

Xi and the party have explained that their aim is to point the nation and economy back towards socialism. Yet one can see that they intend to yoke China's high-tech industry tightly to the state's agenda, be it monitoring the people or competing with the United States in military technology. Even if the Chinese economy suffers from too much state and too little capitalism, Xi believes it is a price worth paying. If state and national interests converged during the 2010s, the state is now putting itself before nation – further evidence of the paramount importance of control.

How should the United States respond to Xi coming down hard on Uighur unrest, Hong Kong resistance, sundry separatist movements and unruly corporations? Obviously, the Chinese state's campaign to tighten control insults US values far more than it harms US national interests.

American stakes in the innermost circle are essentially humanitarian, with a tinge of domestic political concern. In any case, the ability of the United States to challenge state control of China's domestic affairs is close to zero. Like it or not, US policymakers should limit themselves to rhetorical outrage over Beijing's tightening internal grip.

In response to alleged genocide against the Uighur population in Xinjiang and human-rights abuses in Hong Kong and Tibet, the United States has applied sanctions and visa restrictions against certain Chinese officials. Surely the US government knows that such wrist-slapping will have no substantial effect on Beijing's treatment of groups considered to threaten China's tranquillity and cohesion. Conversely, the severity and breadth of US sanctions that might – repeat, might – influence China's policies in the first circle would necessarily inflict major pain on the Chinese economy, with a tsunami effect on economies throughout the Pacific, including the United States'.

Xi's effort to corral rambunctious enterprises is one of several factors that could retard Chinese economic growth. Others include the decline in working-age persons in proportion to elderly ones in need of support; the hangover from excessive real-estate investment and associated unserviceable debt; the impact of a return to a state-controlled economy and concomitant redistribution in the name of socialism; and discouragement of foreign investment. Still, given the regime's predilection for control, it is unlikely that a sagging economy would convince Xi to ease internal repression. Anyway, Chinese economic woes would not necessarily advance US interests, considering the consistently strong correlation between Chinese and US economic growth.

There is nothing the US government can do to weaken the Chinese state's internal control short of supporting separatists and dissidents, which would backfire, or economic war, which would have no winner.

The second circle

What the United States and others regard as expansionism in waters and islands off China's coasts, the Chinese regard as righting historical wrongs. What others consider disputed territory, the Chinese consider to be indisputably Chinese. Of greatest significance to Beijing are Taiwan and the

South China Sea – the former as a renegade province, the latter as sovereign waters of huge economic value. China has engaged in escalating attempts to intimidate Taiwan, in addition to its shoal-by-shoal, island-by-island efforts to secure de facto control of the South China Sea. The Chinese also define parts of the East China Sea as Chinese but are less vehement about retaking them, perhaps because Japan is internationally recognised as having administrative jurisdiction over the Senkaku islands, and the United States is on record that they are covered by the US–Japan defence treaty.

It must be assumed that the Chinese would use or threaten force to regain control of what they believe is organic to China. The pledge not to do so in return for the United States' long-standing acceptance in principle that Taiwan is part of China – the 'one China' policy – carries little weight in Beijing's present calculus. Chinese decisions about how to proceed depend mainly on expectations of US responses, particularly military ones. International disapproval is unlikely to impress the Chinese when it comes to matters of sovereignty. Beijing also will not be deterred by its poor approval ratings among the Taiwanese. Given Beijing's recent measures to take control of Taiwan and the South China Sea, the adage that the Chinese 'take the long view' offers little comfort. As Xi completes his work to consolidate control in China as it is, he is naturally turning to China as it was and must be. Control over these territories now appears to be China's highest priority.[1]

The 'one China' policy carries little weight

The requirement to take back lost territory largely explains China's heavy investment in anti-access/area-denial (A2/AD) military capabilities. Of highest priority are attack submarines, theatre-range conventional missiles, extended-range sensors and command and control, and air defence – basically, an aircraft-carrier-killer package. These are defensive in operational terms, but offensive in purpose. A2/AD functions as a shield to deflect US intervention, behind which the Chinese would use tactical airpower, amphibious forces, naval assets and shorter-range missiles and rockets to take back territories that were and must again be under Chinese control.

China's commitment to develop and apply advanced technologies, while useful in domestic control, can also be explained mainly by the operational military advantages these offer the side that has them first. AI can enhance sensing and command and control dramatically; quantum computing can break encryption; quantum communications can be unhackable; autonomous systems can make airborne, seaborne and submerged drones more lethal and effective. Although the United States has an advantage in private-sector innovation, the Chinese state has more resources to commit than does the US government. The jury is out on which side is winning and will win this race.[2]

While US acquiescence to China's harsh domestic policies is practically unavoidable, the United States has strong and abiding interests in preventing the Chinese from seizing Taiwan or the South China Sea. In the case of the South China Sea, these interests are, or at least border on, what can be considered strategic, as roughly one-third of global maritime shipping passes through these waters.[3]

Taiwan is an important cog in regional and world trade, especially in semiconductors and other advanced microelectronics. Moreover, adding Taiwan's $700 billion annual GDP to China's $16 trillion GDP would narrow the gap between China's and the United States' $22trn GDP. But the political and strategic stakes are even larger. Seizure of Taiwan would bring China one giant step closer to dominating the Western Pacific. If the United States did not try to rescue Taiwan or failed in an attempt to do so, the geopolitical swing in China's favour would be even greater. Operationally, for China to be relieved of the burden of maintaining a major force posture opposite Taiwan and able to stage forces out of Taiwan would alter the correlation of forces in the region.

Can the United States do anything to reduce this risk? Yes, but. China's capabilities to attack and invade Taiwan are progressing faster than those of the United States to deter or defeat them. Yet, if taking Taiwan means having to go to war with the US so close to China, the Chinese would likely choose to wait for a more auspicious time. I recently directed a crisis-management tabletop game at the US Naval Academy. It suggested that even as the odds favouring China improved, the Chinese were not ready to engage in hostilities with US forces in attempting to gain control of Taiwan. Perhaps Beijing could coerce the Taiwan authorities to negotiate terms and timing of reunification; but that too might fail if the United States reassured Taiwan of American intervention.

Accordingly, although China's determination to effect reunification is strong, it is not unqualified. Whether and when Beijing attempts such a feat depends on US military capabilities and will; in turn, US will depends on US capabilities. There are serious efforts afoot in important rings of the Pentagon to leapfrog China's A2/AD capabilities by reducing reliance on the surface fleet, especially aircraft carriers, that have long been the point of the US spear in the Western Pacific. The United States is moving towards more dispersed, diverse, elusive and uninhabited forces for US Indo-Pacific Command. These will confront Chinese forces with a different and much harder targeting challenge than they have been working to meet. The beating heart of this emerging force will be an information system to guide and integrate operations across all armed services and war-fighting domains: the Joint All-Domain Command and Control system. While managing capabilities in all domains, the system itself will be space-based, supported by surveillance drones.

Joint All-Domain Command and Control is vital for military success vis-à-vis China, and there is no higher development priority in US national defence. However, it will take years to complete this system and new platforms to exploit it. Meanwhile, China's capabilities to seize Taiwan even with US intervention are improving steadily. In the near term, the best hope for the United States to maintain operational superiority may be new-found Japanese willingness to join in the defence of Taiwan. The Japanese government is poised to break free of 75 years of pacifism and restrictions on the missions of the Japan Self-Defense Forces. The security of Taiwan and the South China Sea, as well as China's threat to Japan's claims in the East China Sea, have prompted this significant departure on Tokyo's part.

Even with a degree of ambiguity in the US commitment to defend Taiwan, China has to assume that the United States and Japan would go to war rather than allow China to force Taiwan's reunification. With Indian forces perched in the Himalayas, and Australian forces inter-operable with US ones, even China's increasingly robust A2/AD is probably not enough to support a decision by Xi to strike – again, probably.

As for the South China Sea, US naval preponderance is gradually diminishing. Moreover, China's strategy of taking control through repeated small steps appears to be working below the threshold of US and allied armed opposition. Even if China is deterred from attacking Taiwan, it has a reasonable chance of gradually gaining substantial control of this vital waterway.

With China bent on taking control of wayward territories and able to determine the timing and location of its military moves, the second circle is increasingly dangerous. Again, no surprise. US interests might be slightly less precious than China's off its coasts, and US capabilities are not improving fast enough to keep pace with China's.

The third circle

An Englishman named Halford Mackinder argued in the beginning of the twentieth century that whoever controlled the 'Heartland' (Central Asia) could control the 'World Island' (Eurasia), and whoever controlled the World Island could control the world. In that century, history proved Mackinder wrong. But here's an intriguing hypothesis for the twenty-first century: whoever controls East Asia could control the Asia-Pacific, and whoever controls the Asia-Pacific could control the world. While Mackinder was mistaken about the importance of the steppes, a case can be made that East Asia is the world's most productive and dynamic region.

Sure enough, China aspires to be the sun in the Asia-Pacific solar system. The antecedent for this goes back 3,000 years, when the Chinese believed that China was the only civilisation in a world of barbarians. The belief in China's centrality made it all the more painful for it to be molested by colonial powers for a century before Mao took power. Japan's atrocious treatment of China prior to the Second World War, its subordination to the Soviet Union until 1972 and American pre-eminence in East Asia during and after the Cold War have reinforced the Chinese determination to reclaim the mantle of regional leadership. The region's stunning economic performance, originating with Japan and moving on to South Korea, Taiwan and Southeast Asia, has given the Chinese an additional reason to stand atop it.

China sees regional leadership as both historically natural and practically key to access vast resources, markets and talent. Being the most important power in the world's most important region would put China on a par with the United States in global importance. More concretely, China wants to keep Japan in check, arbitrate Korean affairs, realign the states of Southeast Asia and control key choke points in the Pacific and Indian oceans. For the United States to hold sway in the Asia-Pacific, let alone Japan and America together, sticks in Beijing's craw. China also wants sufficient strategic depth not to be threatened again, which domination of the third circle would provide. Discouraging East Asian states from defence cooperation with the United States and from hosting US forces would be a Chinese achievement of major proportions.

At last count, there were 35m Chinese expatriates living in East Asia, with especially large populations in Indonesia, Thailand, Malaysia and Singapore. Yet, to their credit, the Chinese have not attempted to activate these populations, much less to annex their lands, as Russia has with respect to the 20m ethnic Russians living in Ukraine and other former Soviet republics. Should Xi's 'rejuvenation' of China lead to a rise in Chinese patriotism outside of China, how Beijing responds will be important. If any attempt is made to rally the Chinese of Southeast Asia to advance China's agenda, it would likely backfire.

That aside, pursuit of regional domination requires China to achieve success in three domains. Firstly, China aims to be the hub of the world's healthiest economic region. It already enjoys extensive trade, investment, supply-chain and technology relationships. To illustrate, total Chinese trade with Association of Southeast Asian Nations (ASEAN) countries grew from $30bn in 2000 to $685bn in 2020, whereas US trade with ASEAN countries grew during that period from $135bn (about four times China's) to $362bn (about half of China's).[4] The best thing the United States can do to prevent Chinese control of the region's economies is to maintain investment ties throughout East Asia, which makes the US decision to pass on the Trans-Pacific Partnership Agreement especially unfortunate.

Secondly, China wants to win friends and increase its popularity throughout the greater region, from Central Asia to Indonesia. On this score, China's clumsiness and perceived aggressiveness have worked against it. To illustrate, South Korea was until recently deferential to China because of their robust economic relationship and the belief that China could deliver peninsular reunification. No more. Seoul is counting as much as ever on US leadership. Vietnam is openly hostile to China. Other ASEAN states are troubled by China's effort to settle South China Sea disputes by force or pressure. After toying with the idea of dialogue with China, Australia has strengthened its alliance with the United States and joined Japan and India in the US-led Quadrilateral Security Dialogue (the 'Quad').

Thirdly, China seeks military superiority in the Asia-Pacific. Its military priorities in this circle are the same in kind as those needed to gain control of Taiwan and the South China Sea, albeit with greater range. They encompass attack submarines, missiles and extended-range targeting, empowered by the technologies China is vying with the United States to dominate: AI, quantum, autonomous systems and cyber. To be sure, controlling the waters off China's coasts, around Taiwan and in the South China Sea, is a smaller challenge than targeting and striking US forces 1,000 miles or more from China. A high Chinese military pri-

China's perceived aggressiveness has worked against it

ority will be in the use of space, including anti-satellite capabilities. Still, US development and deployment of more dispersed, elusive, submerged and uninhabited forces in the Pacific, networked by the Joint All-Domain Command and Control system, should be enough to perpetuate US operational advantages in the Pacific writ large, even if not enough to prevent China's seizure of Taiwan and waters it considers sovereign.

On balance, China is making economic and military progress towards pre-eminence in the third circle. Moreover, achieving control in the second circle would go some distance towards supplanting the United States as kingpin of the Pacific. The greatest impediment to China's regional supremacy is the icy reception it receives for its efforts to expand its influence, nowhere more so than in Japan. A critical issue is whether the United States can transform its regional military posture faster than China takes to extend its strike range. Compared to the second circle, the United States has greater interests in, and capabilities for, denying China dominion in the larger region.

In the long run, being of the region, China might have a leg up on the United States. However, the Chinese impulse to control is sure to generate resistance. A simple tally of Chinese 'friends' in East Asia suggests that it is already materialising. North Korea? Myanmar? Any others? Empirically, though paradoxically, the farther China tries to extend its influence, the less eager others are to entertain it.

The fourth circle

Xi Jinping and other Chinese leaders are speaking with increased clarity and confidence about a 'new world order' patterned after China's own authoritarian, state-centric system. In one version, a rejuvenated China emerges as the world's leading economy and pre-eminent Asia-Pacific power, with the United States a mere Atlantic power with waning influence in international institutions. If that is Xi's vision, he and his team are pursuing it with the same preoccupation with control that they manifest in the three smaller circles. As Elizabeth Economy has explained convincingly, many of China's initiatives on the international stage have produced backlash.[5]

Three factors work against China's realisation of Xi's vision. Firstly, the vision is not especially inspiring to other societies and states, except certain autocratic ones. Becoming anti-democratic is not exactly a motivational bumper sticker. Secondly, China benefits greatly from the liberal order it purportedly loathes. Indeed, the Chinese want the best of both worlds: continued prosperity through active trade and investment, with other states beholden to China for their economic health. Thirdly, as Economy has detailed, Chinese attempts to gain international influence have foundered because China uses its relationships for selfish purposes: securing privileged access to resources; weakening diplomatic support for Taiwan; launching the Belt and Road Initiative to increase China's economic and political clout; and saddling developing countries with concessional but excessive debt.

As Xi proclaimed the rejuvenation of China, his party published a report saying that he had brought China 'closer to the center of the world stage than it has ever been'.[6] The Chinese are either uninformed about what other societies seek or cynical in promising them what turns out to be best for China but not them. The Beijing regime seems to be following a 'China First' script.

In the era following the Second World War, the United States sacrificed to build and sustain an international order that served the interests of all who joined, including the losers of that war. In doing so, it projected its own image on the screen of the Free World. Just as it had its own enormous stake in the strength of this system, it sought to give Japan and West Germany a stake as well, and did so. As globalisation progressed, the United States endeavoured to instil in other states and institutions the values of open trade, free flow of capital and aid conditioned on reform. In the aftermath of the Cold War, the United States led the way in inviting former Soviet satellites to join the West and its liberal order. Again, this was not altruism but rather enlightened self-interest.

When it comes to this outermost circle, China seems unable to shed the preference for control in the broad sense that everyone knows who calls the shots. If China cannot persuade the leaders and people of Taiwan or, it appears, the youth of Hong Kong to accept control, attempting to exert it in the region and larger world is likely to flop.

In addition, the invasion of Ukraine by Russia – China's would-be ally – has probably dampened Xi's prospects for attracting other societies to his alternative version of world order. At least for now, Russia's belligerence makes the notion that an authoritarian, state-centric model would bring stability and peace hard to defend. Moreover, the decisive and united response to the invasion on the part of the democratic community, led by the United States, suggests that the liberal order has retained some value and strength. This is further indication that China's progress in its fourth circle faces serious impediments.

What if?

Admittedly, these four circles do not encompass every contingency. Three factors lying outside them that come to mind are a strong Sino-Russian alliance, an attempt by China to achieve nuclear parity with the United States (and Russia) and protracted American isolationism.

There are concerns in some quarters that an alliance of two unfriendly peers will make the United States and its allies vulnerable to two-pronged aggressiveness. However, Russia is not a peer of either the United States or

China. Its GDP is the equivalent of South Korea's, smaller than Canada's, 30% of Japan's, 12% of China's and 7% of the United States'. Its military budget is roughly the same as the United Kingdom's, 25% of China's and 8% of the United States'.[7] Russia does possess a large strategic nuclear arsenal and a plethora of intercontinental delivery systems. But it maintains such a force and invests in new delivery systems, including hypersonic missiles, out of concern that the US combination of offensive nuclear weapons, global conventional-strike systems and improving missile defences will jeopardise Russia's retaliatory capability in the far-fetched case of a disarming American strike.

An even more compelling reason China should not depend on Russia, if push comes to shove, is Russian President Vladimir Putin's extreme reckless-ness, on full display in Ukraine. While the Chinese might see opportunity – for instance, vis-à-vis Taiwan – if Russia ensnarled NATO in a war on its borders, they must worry that Russia might also get itself and its Chinese 'ally' into conflicts that serve no Chinese interest. Moreover, the Chinese know that Putin and friends are widely seen as gangsters. Such reserva-tions, combined with long-standing mutual suspicions between Russia and China, would seem to limit how closely Xi would want to associate with Putin. In any case, the United States, NATO and the Quad should be alert to intelligence pointing towards simultaneous and possibly coordinated moves in Ukraine and Taiwan.

What if China shovelled greater resources into large and sophisticated offensive nuclear forces? What the Chinese are doing to increase their nuclear arsenal and develop new delivery systems – for instance, orbital hypersonic vehicles – appears to be motivated by concerns about the erosion of confidence in and credibility of China's retaliatory deterrent. Like the Russians – though arguably with more cause for concern – the Chinese worry about a suite of US strategic capabilities including extremely accurate offensive nuclear and non-nuclear forces, as well as missile defence. China may not feel that a few hundred ballistic missiles are enough to maintain mutual deterrence with the United States. Yet the US does not necessarily have to be concerned about China's nuclear investments beyond its tradi-tional 'minimal deterrence' posture.

What if China decided to discard its long-standing no-first-use doctrine? That would send ripples through US war planning towards China. But it would make little strategic sense for China to stress the option of first use, and there appears to be no serious thought of doing so in China.

Lastly, for the United States to turn isolationist would obviously change everything in the second, third and fourth circles of Chinese aspirations. Taiwan would be toast. China could gain something close to control of its region. And there would be no US-led liberal world order to constrain China. Enough said.

*   *   *

The United States has the means and presumably the will to prevent China from dominating the Asia-Pacific or replacing the rules-based liberal international order, though preventing the former will take much greater effort and focus than the latter. The Chinese regime's control of what China is today is unshakeable, which is unfortunate from a humanitarian standpoint but not deleterious to US interests. It is in the second circle – Chinese sovereignty over all that China once was – that Chinese determination and US interests are both strong. Thus, defence of Taiwan and the South China Sea by the United States and its allies, especially Japan, is the foremost and most difficult challenge. This conclusion comes as no surprise, though it stands out as a subject ripe for intense systematic analysis.

To this end, military capabilities matter crucially. The US military and intelligence services should press strenuously towards a fundamentally new, less targetable posture. This makes it imperative that the United States, with its free-enterprise system and advanced allies, lead in the development of key emerging technologies: AI, quantum, autonomous platforms, cyber (offence and defence) and new satellite constellations.

As for Chinese political initiatives and inroads in the Asia-Pacific and its periphery, given the blowback from the Chinese regime's impulse to control, the United States should remain true to its values and confident in the wider order that it has created.

Notes

[1] See Elizabeth Economy, 'Xi Jinping's New World Order: Can China Remake the International System?', *Foreign Affairs*, January/February 2022, https://www.foreignaffairs.com/articles/china/2021-12-09/xi-jinpings-new-world-order.

[2] See David C. Gompert, 'Spin-on: How the US Can Meet China's Technological Challenge', *Survival*, vol. 62, no. 3, June–July 2020, pp. 115–30.

[3] See 'How Much Trade Transits the South China Sea?', *ChinaPower*, Center for Strategic and International Studies, 2 August 2017 (updated 25 January 2021), https://chinapower.csis.org/much-trade-transits-south-china-sea/.

[4] See Kishore Mahbubani, 'In Asia, China's Long Game Beats America's Short Game', *Foreign Policy*, 12 December 2021, https://foreignpolicy.com/2021/12/12/china-us-asean-trade-geopolitics/.

[5] See Economy, 'Xi Jinping's New World Order'.

[6] Quoted in *ibid*.

[7] See, for example, Caleb Silver, 'The Top 25 Economies in the World', Investopedia, updated 3 February 2022, https://www.investopedia.com/insights/worlds-top-economies/.

Copyright © 2022 The International Institute for Strategic Studies

A New Israeli Approach to Iran?

Dalia Dassa Kaye

Since Israeli Prime Minister Naftali Bennett ousted Israel's longest-serving prime minister, Benjamin Netanyahu, in June 2021, Bennett has gone out of his way to project a different governing style. He and his cabinet have actively engaged with Biden administration officials and have largely avoided publicly criticising US policies, including the chronically contentious one on Iran. To be sure, Bennett has forcefully stated that Israel would not 'be bound' by a revival of the Joint Comprehensive Plan of Action (JCPOA) – that is, the Iran nuclear agreement.[1] Addressing reports that negotiations to revive the nuclear deal were making significant progress, Bennett warned that a new agreement would be 'shorter and weaker', and that Israel was preparing for the day after 'in all dimensions'.[2] It is no secret that many other Israeli officials are not enamoured with the deal.[3] But Bennett maintained a relatively muted posture during the JCPOA negotiating rounds in Vienna, in contrast to Netanyahu's active and public campaign to derail the original agreement in 2015. Bennett's government has preferred to air differences with Washington largely behind the scenes.

The Biden administration has been equally eager to avoid public spats and has been solicitous of Israeli concerns despite its interest in returning to the JCPOA. Senior US officials have offered regular strategic dialogue with

Dalia Dassa Kaye is a senior fellow at the UCLA Burkle Center for International Relations and an adjunct political scientist at the RAND Corporation, where she previously served as the director of the Center for Middle East Public Policy.

Survival | vol. 64 no. 2 | April–May 2022 | pp. 111–124   https://doi.org/10.1080/00396338.2022.2055830

top Israeli national-security officials and made frequent official visits. US President Joe Biden warmly hosted Reuven Rivlin, then Israeli president, shortly after the Israeli election in June, asserting that 'Iran will never get a nuclear weapon under my watch'.[4] Biden hosted his first meeting with the new prime minister in late August 2021 in the midst of the crisis surrounding the US withdrawal from Afghanistan, promising an 'unshakable partnership'.[5] High-level visits by Israeli and American officials continued at a steady pace throughout 2021. When nuclear talks appeared to be floundering, senior American and Israeli officials even began discussing 'plan B' options.[6] Indeed, dimming prospects for success in Vienna gave Israel and the United States less to disagree about, though Israeli expectations for a renewed deal had increased by early 2022.[7] Russia's demand for guarantees that Western sanctions imposed following its invasion of Ukraine would not impact its dealings with Iran forced an unexpected pause in the talks just as they appeared to be reaching a conclusion.[8]

Do Bennett's friendly relations with the Biden administration, lower-key approach and allowance of more criticism of Netanyahu's handling of the nuclear issue signify a new approach on Iran? The short answer is no. For all the cordiality between the Bennett and Biden administrations, Bennett's Iran policies have not substantively changed from Netanyahu's. Credible voices from Israel's defence and intelligence establishment challenging the Israeli government's previous Iran policies are notable, but ultimately such positions are retrospective and are not likely to significantly impact current policy. While the new prime minister is unlikely to create or encourage overt friction in Israeli–American relations, if Israeli leaders do not view Iran's nuclear programme as contained, there is little reason to expect a less confrontational Israeli approach to Iran under Bennett.

Bennett's inheritance

During the presidential transition in the United States, it appeared that Israel and the incoming Biden administration were on a collision course with respect to Iran policy.[9] As a candidate, Biden had forcefully expressed his commitment to return to the JCPOA and bring humanitarian relief to the Iranian people, arguing that Trump's decision to withdraw from the nuclear agreement had not brought about a better deal but rather had yielded a more expansive Iranian nuclear programme and more aggressive regional activity.[10] Returning to the Iran nuclear deal was among Biden's top priorities in the Middle East, even as he and his advisers sought to reduce American engagement in the region as they turned their attention to China. The Biden team promised to build on a revived agreement to strengthen the nuclear terms of the original accord and address other issues of regional concern, such as missiles and Iran-aligned militias. But Biden made it clear that containing Iran's nuclear programme through the JCPOA was a critical prerequisite to such a 'longer and stronger' follow-up agreement.

Israel had different ideas. Less than a month after Biden's election victory, top Iranian nuclear scientist Mohsen Fakhrizadeh was assassinated in an operation widely attributed to Israel. Many viewed the assassination as a message to the incoming Biden administration that Israel would oppose an American return to the agreement. Indeed, Netanyahu explicitly expressed his opposition to a US return, stating that 'there can be no going back to the previous nuclear agreement. We must stick to an uncompromising policy of ensuring that Iran will not develop nuclear weapons.'[11] Lieutenant General Aviv Kochavi, chief of staff of the Israel Defense Forces (IDF), publicly opposed a US return to the nuclear deal just as Biden took office, arguing that 'anything similar to the current agreement or even an improved agreement would be unacceptable and should not be allowed'.[12] Although some Israeli military and intelligence officials had assessed that Trump's withdrawal from the JCPOA would have negative impacts, Israeli officials across the political spectrum largely backed Netanyahu's approach. Reports citing government sources suggested there was 'no daylight' between Netanyahu and political rivals such as Benny Gantz (who also served as defense minister under the previous government) on continued support for 'maximum pressure' policies.[13]

Influential former military officials such as Amos Yadlin, who was head of the IDF Military Intelligence Directorate, argued against a US return to the original agreement, suggesting that issues such as missiles, extended sunset clauses, stronger inspections and Iran's nuclear research needed to be addressed in new discussions.[14] Israeli officials and analysts also argued against the Biden administration's immediate return to the negotiating table with the Iranians, making the case that the United States and the West had sufficient leverage over Iran to extract concessions that extended beyond the restrictions in the original agreement.[15]

In light of such widely held views in Israel, had Biden decided to quickly rejoin the JCPOA in his first weeks in office, as some pro-agreement Americans expected, a crisis with Israel might have been difficult to avoid. But, as it turned out, Biden administration appointees signalled early on that the White House would not rush to return to the deal. Several stated that while they supported rejoining the deal, they were 'a long way' from that point and said it would 'take time', promising consultations with regional partners prior to any US decision.[16] The Biden administration restored a working group with Israeli national-security counterparts to consult on Iran, and US National Security Advisor Jake Sullivan reportedly proposed the resumption of the strategic dialogue with Israel on his first call to Israeli national security adviser Meir Ben-Shabbat just a few days after Biden's inauguration.[17]

Despite suspected Israeli sabotage at Iran's nuclear facility in Natanz on the eve of negotiations in April 2021, the Biden administration supported diplomacy in Vienna while seeking to distance itself from the covert attack.[18] Six rounds of talks in Vienna produced some progress on the key issues of sanctions relief, nuclear rollbacks and the sequencing for the American and Iranian return to mutual compliance. Several Israeli and American analysts argued that there was no need for haste in returning to the deal despite concerns that the window of opportunity for an agreement might close after Iran's June 2021 presidential election if hardliners came into power.[19]

Hardliners did end up consolidating power in Tehran with the orchestrated victory of Ebrahim Raisi. The new Iranian leadership put nuclear negotiations on hold, signalling that they also were not in any hurry either, and returned to negotiations in Vienna only after a five-month pause. They also reportedly submitted proposals that went beyond what the Americans and Europeans thought had been agreed in the previous rounds.[20] The new Iranian leadership thus appeared intent on making negotiations even more fraught than they were previously, when mistrust among the parties was already high.

Bennett, though presumptively a better interlocutor than Netanyahu from the Biden administration's standpoint, entered office facing a more complicated Iranian nuclear situation. After the Trump administration's withdrawal from the JCPOA, Iran's enrichment activities had expanded beyond the agreement's constraints as its nuclear programme moved closer to a nuclear-threshold state. Suddenly, it seemed, Iran's civilian nuclear programme could be converted to a weapons programme, should Iran decide to do so, in a much shorter time frame than the one imposed by the JCPOA, under which the breakout time was estimated to be one year. Iran's research and development activities after the US withdrawal also produced institutional knowledge that is likely irreversible, creating new obstacles to restoring the original agreement.

A new style and renewed debate

Despite the growing Iran challenge, Bennett and his coalition partners made a concerted effort to be more accommodating to the new US administration. In his first meeting with Biden at the White House in late August 2021, Bennett said he would not launch a public campaign against the JCPOA, even though he opposed a US return to the original agreement. According to an Israeli official present at the meeting, Bennett told the president that 'regardless of policy differences he wants to work according to rules of honesty and decency', in contrast to Netanyahu's public address to the US Congress in 2015 that sought to undercut a sitting American president, Barack Obama, on the then-prospective Iran deal.[21]

Instead, Bennett preferred to discuss differences in private and to repair relations with the Democratic Party that were severely strained during Netanyahu's tenure. Further coordination with US officials followed, including the establishment of a joint team at the National Security Council level to contain Iran.[22] As Bennett explained, 'I oppose the JCPOA … but I understand where America stands.'[23]

Another shift under Bennett has been the emergence of more debate on and criticism of previous Israeli policies on Iran, particularly the approach of Netanyahu and Trump. Many experts in Israel's security establishment are increasingly sceptical of the maximum-pressure policy, assessing that it has only led Iran to expand its nuclear capabilities. Some analysts even believe that the Israeli defence establishment sees Israel's opposition to a deal as mere posturing, secretly wanting a deal if it imposes significant limits on Iran's programme and thus slows Iran's advance towards nuclear-weapons capability.[24] Several former high-level Israeli officials have openly indicated that they consider Trump's withdrawal from the JCPOA and Netanyahu's encouragement of that step to have been strategic errors.

Former IDF chief of staff Gadi Eisenkot said the defence establishment was 'kept in the dark' about Trump's decision to withdraw from the nuclear deal, which he called a 'strategic mistake', especially since the deal would have enabled Israel to redirect significant resources to missions in Lebanon and Gaza.[25] Danny Citrinowicz, the former head of the Iran branch in Israel's military-intelligence division, has called Israel's Iran policies and opposition to the JCPOA a 'failure', noting that many defence and intelligence officials considered the nuclear agreement important and opposed Netanyahu's support for Trump's withdrawal from it with no alternative in place, but did not believe they could air their views publicly. Citrinowicz, like other former officials, also called the maximum-pressure policy a 'catastrophe'.[26]

Reports that some current officials may support a deal have also emerged, though any such support is usually caveated with the condition that it be a 'good' deal on the basis of criteria that are unspecified but largely understood to be infeasible. Positions of this kind also surfaced when the prevailing assessment in Israel was that the negotiations probably would not succeed, making it easier to offer qualified support. For example, in December 2021, Foreign Minister Yair Lapid told the *New York Times* that 'we have no problem with a deal' and 'a good deal is a good thing', but added that a 'bad' deal would be the worst outcome and that the original JCPOA 'was not a good enough deal'.[27] Defense Minister Gantz said Israel could live with a new Iran nuclear deal, though he also advocated preparations for a 'serious demonstration of power' should negotiations fail.[28]

In early January 2022, leaks emerged from a high-level security-cabinet meeting that the head of Israeli military intelligence preferred a deal to failed negotiations, arguing that an agreement would give Israel more time to prepare for escalatory scenarios with Iran. But at the same meeting, the head of Mossad, Israel's national intelligence agency, reportedly expressed his opposition to a restored deal and argued there was more time to influence the Americans to insert additional conditions into the talks.[29] Accordingly, recent statements of accommodation from former officials, or even current ones, should not be considered clear indications of official Israeli policy.

During Netanyahu's tenure, internal debates ultimately did not affect Israel's official stance. In the years before the JCPOA, there was a vibrant debate among Israel's security establishment about the merits of a diplomatic solution to the Iranian challenge and influential voices opposed Netanyahu's approach.[30] Indeed, Israel's security establishment has always been more supportive of the Iran deal than Israel's political leaders. Leaders of Israel's security services – including former IDF chiefs of staff Eisenkot, Gantz and Gabriel Ashkenazi, as well as former Mossad heads Meir Dagan and Tamir Pardo and former Shin Bet chief Yuval Diskin – were also key opponents of a military-strike option. But such voices failed to impede Netanyahu's campaign against the original agreement or his drive to have the deal scuttled once Trump was elected. And when Trump ultimately withdrew from the deal, domestic debate in Israel dissipated as a consensus emerged in support of the maximum-pressure approach.[31]

Biden's alternative approach on Iran – combined with Bennett's new style and evidence that maximum pressure was not working – reopened the debate. Analysts and former officials renewed their critique of Netanyahu's Iran policies and expressed additional concerns about the negative impacts of the US withdrawal. But if past is prologue, such debates are unlikely to alter Israel's positions on Iran and opposition to a revived nuclear pact.

No new strategy

Notwithstanding reinvigorated debate and improved atmospherics, official Israeli policy remains essentially unchanged from the Netanyahu era. Even before becoming prime minister, Bennett expressed views on Iran that were not dissimilar to Netanyahu's – for instance, espousing the 'octopus doctrine' whereby the head of the octopus (Iran), and not just its tentacles (Iranian-aligned groups in Syria and Iraq), must be cut off.[32] His public statements on Iran since becoming prime minister have echoed his previous positions.

Bennett has made clear that Israel maintains its 'freedom to act' whether or not there is an agreement in Vienna, and has expressed concerns about a deal that were common in the Netanyahu era, arguing, for example, that a 'deal that will send tens of billions of dollars to this rotten and weak regime will be a mistake because this money will go to terror against IDF soldiers and Americans in the region'.[33] Fear of what havoc sanctions relief might enable Iran to wreak in the region now outweigh Israel's concern that Iran is becoming a nuclear-threshold state, which Israel assesses is at this point a fait accompli in any case.[34] Bennett reportedly asked Biden not to sign a renewed JCPOA in a February 2022 call, arguing 'nothing will happen if you don't sign it'.[35]

Bennett sees negotiations as a form of blackmail by Iran to force Western concessions and prefers continued economic and diplomatic pressure.[36] A common perception among Israeli leaders is that Iran has limited leverage given its domestic preoccupations, and that the West should not buy into what they view as Iran's strategy to use the negotiations, or even a revived deal, merely to buy time. Israeli officials also worry that a revived deal will leave Iran just months away from acquiring enough fissile material to produce a nuclear weapon given Iran's technical advances after Trump's withdrawal from the agreement.[37]

Moreover, Israel's conflict with Iran extends beyond the nuclear realm, with Israeli strikes in Syria against Iranian-aligned interests ongoing.[38] The Israeli–Iranian conflict has also expanded to the maritime arena, and Israel maintains a close watch on the activities of Iranian-aligned groups throughout the region, particularly Hizbullah.[39] Statements by Gantz arguing that Iran's hegemonic and nuclear ambitions pose the 'biggest threat to global and regional peace and stability' and 'an existential threat to Israel' are nearly indistinguishable from typical Netanyahu proclamations.[40]

Conventional military options remain on the table, even if Israel may not have the capability to destroy Iran's nuclear facilities that it had a decade ago.[41] As negotiations were resuming in Vienna in December 2021 amid reports that Israel's military may not be prepared to strike Iran, incoming Israeli Air Force commander Tomer Bar asserted that Israel could destroy Iran's nuclear sites 'tomorrow', noting that 'we are not starting from zero.

We equipped ourselves with F-35s ... We procured thousands of Iron Dome interceptors for multi-layer defense.'[42] The Israeli Air Force reportedly drilled for a 'massive attack' against Iran's nuclear facilities in January 2022, with a US Air Force officer participating in the exercise as an observer.[43] While Israeli leaders would no doubt be wary of a direct conflict with Iran given the economic and pandemic-related pressures at home, they still consider military responses, including limited ones, viable options.

On balance, while former Israeli leaders may be questioning the wisdom of maximum-pressure measures and the American withdrawal from the JCPOA, current leaders are offering no alternatives to continued pressure, whether or not diplomacy in Vienna succeeds.

Looking ahead

There is probably no nuclear deal that Israel, even under the Bennett government, would consider a good deal. That said, unlike the Netanyahu government, Bennett's probably will not publicly and actively oppose a revived agreement in Washington. It will also allow more room for criticism of Trump's policies insofar as such criticism would by extension disparage Netanyahu's approach. Indeed, an anti-Netanyahu stance is the common denominator that enabled the coalition parties to form Bennett's government in the first place. But these factors do not mean Israel will embrace a new agreement.

The more likely Israeli response is what emerged when Netanyahu failed to kill the original agreement: a pragmatic adjustment to the new reality whereby Israel ultimately accepts the deal but does not admit to doing so. Once the original deal became a reality in 2015, even Israeli leaders who opposed it grudgingly came to accept it.[44] At the same time, Israel increased its pressure on Iran and Hizbullah in the Levant, particularly in Syria. That pattern too would probably continue. Israel would also be likely to actively monitor any agreement and publicly showcase perceived violations, as it has in the past, seeking to maintain American and international pressure to deter and respond to Iranian transgressions.

Israel's assassination and sabotage operations subsided after the 2015 agreement and resumed only after the US withdrawal.[45] This time, however, the shadow war that intensified after Trump left the nuclear agreement might continue even after a revival of the JCPOA because of uncertainty about its staying power and the reduced breakout time a new deal would inevitably allow.

If there is no revival of the JCPOA, Israel's shadow war against Iran could expand as well as intensify due to Israel's enhanced security ties and broader normalisation of relations with Arab Gulf states. Although Israel would try to avoid military entanglements with Iran and Iranian-aligned groups in conflict zones such as Iraq or Yemen, they could prove diplomatically difficult to avoid. And in the absence of an agreement, of course, Israel is more likely to consider conventional military options for targeting Iran's nuclear facilities.

$$* \qquad * \qquad *$$

Some analysts believe that Israel no longer has a viable military option given Iran's retaliatory capabilities and the impossibility of destroying all of Iran's nuclear assets through military strikes without American assistance. But the sober reality is that many current Israeli officials consider Israel's military options viable, as discussed earlier. They view more cautious assessments as underestimating Israel's risk tolerance as well as the moderating effects of Iran's own vulnerabilities and domestic pressures, pointing to Iran's relatively restrained responses to past attacks on Natanz and even to the assassination of the country's top nuclear scientist.[46] They argue that even limited strikes on Iran's nuclear facilities could set the programme back and buy time. The logic is not unlike that offered in support of Israel's periodic military campaigns against Hamas in Gaza.

Such calculations are highly risky, as they rest on assumptions that may not play out, potentially inviting greater military escalation than anticipated. Furthermore, the historical record has shown that military options have not resolved nuclear challenges; only diplomatic agreements have done so. With other global crises on his agenda, particularly the Ukraine war, Biden is unlikely to welcome Israeli military escalation with Iran. This would certainly be the case if Iran were abiding by a revived nuclear agreement, particularly as Israel has refrained from attacking Iran's nuclear capabilities after successful diplomacy in the past. Friction with the Biden administration would inevitably increase if Israel crossed this line because it believed the agreement was too weak and the timeline to constrain Iran too short. Whether the Biden administration's positive rapport with Bennett's government could prevent such escalation, or mitigate its effect, is uncertain. But the United States' willingness and ability to constrain Israel would be significantly reduced in the absence of a working nuclear agreement.

Notes

1 'Israel Not Bound by Any Nuclear Deal with Iran, Bennett Says', Reuters, 10 January 2022, https://www.reuters.com/world/middle-east/israels-wont-be-bound-by-any-nuclear-deal-with-iran-bennett-says-2022-01-10/.

2 Ministry of Foreign Affairs, Government of Israel, 'PM Bennett's Remarks at the Start of the Weekly Cabinet Meeting', press release, 20 February 2022, https://www.gov.il/en/departments/news/pm-bennett-s-remarks-at-the-start-of-the-weekly-cabinet-meeting-20-feb-2022.

3 See, for example, '"Turned Diplomacy into a Religion": Israel Officials Said to Lash Biden on Iran Deal', Times of Israel, 20 February 2022, https://www.timesofisrael.com/israeli-officials-lash-biden-for-meaningless-new-iran-nuclear-deal-report/.

4 'Biden Hosts Israeli President Ahead of Bennett Visit', France24, 28 June 2021, https://www.france24.com/en/live-news/20210628-biden-hosts-israeli-president-ahead-of-bennett-visit.

5 Annie Karni, 'Biden Vows "Unshakable Partnership" with Israel in Meeting with Bennett', New York Times, 27 August 2021, https://www.nytimes.com/2021/08/27/us/politics/biden-naftali-bennett-meeting.html.

6 See 'Israel, US Said to Discuss "Plan B" if Iran Nuclear Talks Don't Resume', Times of Israel, 22 September 2021, https://www.timesofisrael.com/israel-us-said-to-discuss-plan-b-if-iran-nuclear-talks-dont-resume/.

7 See Ben Caspit, 'Israeli Leaders Expect Iran Nuclear Deal in 2022', Al-Monitor, 4 January 2022, https://www.al-monitor.com/originals/2022/01/israeli-leaders-expect-iran-nuclear-deal-2022.

8 Steven Erlanger, 'Russian Demands to Ease Sanctions Halt Nuclear Talks with Iran', New York Times, 11 March 2022, https://www.nytimes.com/2022/03/11/world/europe/iran-nuclear-talks-russia.html.

9 See Neri Zilber, 'Israel Is the Wrench in Biden's Iran Policy', Foreign Policy, 30 November 2020, https://foreignpolicy.com/2020/11/30/israel-biden-iran-policy-netanyahu/.

10 See Joe Biden, 'Joe Biden: There's a Smarter Way to Be Tough on Iran', CNN, 13 September 2020, https://

www.cnn.com/2020/09/13/opinions/
smarter-way-to-be-tough-on-iran-joe-
biden/index.html.

11   Zilber, 'Israel Is the Wrench in Biden's
Iran Policy'.

12   Neri Zilber, 'Israel to Biden:
Tehran Can Wait', *New/Lines
Magazine*, 25 February 2021, https://
newlinesmag.com/reportage/
israel-to-biden-tehran-can-wait/.

13   Zilber, 'Israel Is the Wrench in Biden's
Iran Policy'.

14   *Ibid*.

15   The author participated in several
Track Two meetings with Israelis
during the presidential-transition process where such views were regularly
aired. See also Zilber, 'Israel to Biden'.

16   Kelsey Davenport and Julia
Masterson, 'Biden Officials
Express Support for Rejoining Iran
Deal', Arms Control Association,
28 January 2021, https://www.
armscontrol.org/blog/2021-01/
p4-1-iran-nuclear-deal-alert.

17   See Barak Ravid, 'Scoop: US and Israel
to Convene Strategic Forum on Iran',
Axios, 24 February 2021, https://www.
axios.com/us-israel-iran-working-
group-nuclear-deal-42340aa4-dc47-
4182-8de1-63318e817830.html.

18   See Laura Rozen, 'US, Disowning
Suspected Israeli Op at Iran's Natanz,
Stays Focused on Diplomacy',
Diplomatic, 12 April 2021, https://
diplomatic.substack.com/p/
us-disowning-suspected-israeli-op.

19   For an argument on why the United
States did not need to rush into nego-
tiations, see Ariane Tabatabai and
Henry Rome, 'For Iran, Negotiations
Aren't Optional', *Foreign Policy*, 15
September 2020, https://foreignpolicy.

com/2020/09/15/iran-negotiations-
deal-trump-biden-talks/.

20   See Stephanie Liechtenstein, 'Nuclear
Talks in Doubt Amid New Iranian
Demands', *Politico*, 3 December 2021,
https://www.politico.eu/article/
nuclear-talks-in-doubt-amid-new-
iranian-demands/.

21   See Barak Ravid, 'Israeli PM Tells
Biden He Won't Publicly Campaign
Against Iran Deal', *Axios*, 28 August
2021, https://www.axios.com/israeli-
pm-biden-behind-scenes-12949036-
3bcf-4f3d-9412-67101858010f.html.

22   See Ron Kampeas, 'Naftali Bennett
Says the US and Israel Have Set
Up Joint Team on Containing Iran',
Jewish Telegraphic Agency, 3 September
2021, https://www.jta.org/2021/09/03/
israel/naftali-bennett-says-the-us-
and-israel-have-set-up-joint-team-on-
containing-iran.

23   *Ibid*.

24   Author discussion with an Israeli
security analyst, 9 February 2022.

25   Anna Ahronheim, 'IDF Kept in the
Dark Over US Decision to Withdraw
from Iran Nuclear Deal – Eisenkot',
Jerusalem Post, 29 January 2022,
https://www.jpost.com/israel-news/
article-694901.

26   Jacob Magid, 'He Led IDF Intel
Gathering on Iran, Was Ignored
and Fears Israel Is Now Paying the
Price', *Times of Israel*, 30 November
2021, https://www.timesofisrael.com/
he-led-idf-intel-gathering-on-iran-
was-ignored-and-fears-israel-is-now-
paying-price/.

27   David E. Sanger and Patrick Kingsley,
'Lapid Says Israel Will Support Iran
Nuclear Pact, if It's "a Good Deal"',
New York Times, 23 December 2021,

https://www.nytimes.com/2021/12/23/world/middleeast/lapid-israel-nuclear-iran-palestinians.html.

28 Neri Zilber, 'Israel Can Live with a New Iran Nuclear Deal, Defense Minister Says', *Foreign Policy*, 14 September 2021, https://foreignpolicy.com/2021/09/14/israel-iran-nuclear-deal-defense-minister-gantz/.

29 'IDF Intel Chief Reportedly Says Restored Iran Nuke Deal Better Than Talks Failing', *Times of Israel*, 5 January 2022, https://www.timesofisrael.com/idf-intel-chief-reportedly-says-restored-iran-nuke-deal-better-than-talks-failing/.

30 See Dalia Dassa Kaye, 'A Different Israeli Take on Iran', *Los Angeles Times*, 12 November 2013, https://www.latimes.com/opinion/op-ed/la-oe-kaye-israel-iran-nuclear-20131112-story.html.

31 See Dalia Dassa Kaye and Shira Efron, 'Israel's Evolving Iran Policy', *Survival*, vol. 62, no. 4, August–September 2020, pp. 7–30.

32 See Naftali Bennett, address, Institute for National Security Studies, 12th Annual Conference, 30 January 2018, translated by the author from the original Hebrew.

33 Lahov Harkov, 'Bennett to "Post": Israel Will Continue Its Strategy to Stop Iran Even if There's a Deal', *Jerusalem Post*, 27 January 2022, https://www.jpost.com/arab-israeli-conflict/article-694773.

34 Author discussion with an Israeli security analyst, 9 February 2022.

35 See Barak Ravid, 'Inside the Biden–Bennett Call on Iran', *Axios*, 9 February 2022, https://www.axios.com/biden-bennett-call-iran-deal-vienna-talks-cb8240ef-a335-4cf7-92e6-7eeea33184fb.html.

36 See Lahav Harov and Tovah Lazaroff, 'Iran Nuclear Talks Must Be Halted, Bennett Tells Blinken', *Jerusalem Post*, 2 December 2021, https://www.jpost.com/breaking-news/bennett-calls-on-world-powers-to-halt-iran-nuclear-talks-687615.

37 See 'Israel Said to Fear Restored Iran Deal Will Leave Breakout Time of Only a Few Months', *Times of Israel*, 6 February 2022, https://www.timesofisrael.com/israel-said-to-fear-restored-iran-deal-will-leave-break-out-time-of-only-a-few-months/.

38 See Scott Lucas, 'Israel Strikes Assad Targets Near Damascus', *EA Worldview*, 3 September 2021, https://eaworldview.com/2021/09/israel-strikes-assad-targets-near-damascus/.

39 See Anchal Vohra, 'Iran and Israel's Naval War Is Expanding', *Foreign Policy*, 19 July 2021, https://foreignpolicy.com/2021/07/19/iran-and-israels-naval-war-is-expanding/.

40 See 'Israel's Gantz: "Iran Seeks to Destroy All Traces of Freedom"', i24 News, 9 December 2021, https://www.i24news.tv/en/news/israel/diplomacy/1639078778-israel-s-gantz-iran-seeks-to-destroy-all-traces-of-freedom.

41 On these respective points, see Judah Ari Gross, 'As Bennett Meets Biden, IDF Ramps Up Plans for Strike on Iran's Nuke Program', *Times of Israel*, 25 August 2021, https://www.timesofisrael.com/as-bennett-meets-biden-idf-ramps-up-plans-for-strike-on-irans-nuke-program/; and Amos Harel, 'An Israeli Strike on Iran Might Have Been Possible a Decade Ago.

Not Today', *Haaretz*, 12 December 2021, https://www.haaretz.com/israel-news/.premium.HIGHLIGHT-israel-strike-iran-nuclear-not-so-fast-trump-biden-1.10454480.

42 'Israel's Incoming Air Force Chief: "We Can Attack Iran Tomorrow if Needed"', *Jerusalem Post*, 22 December 2021, https://www.jpost.com/israel-news/article-689441.

43 'Israel Air Force Drilled "Massive Attack on Iran" in Presence of US Officer – Report', *Times of Israel*, 2 February 2022, https://www.timesofisrael.com/us-official-attended-israeli-air-force-drill-simulating-attack-on-iran-report/.

44 Regarding Israel's posture following the 2015 nuclear agreement, see Dalia Dassa Kaye, 'Israel's Iran Policies After the Nuclear Deal', Perspectives, RAND Corporation, 2016, https://www.rand.org/pubs/perspectives/PE207.html.

45 As one report documents, the first wave of Israeli attacks on Iran's nuclear programme occurred from 2010 to 2012, when nuclear negotiations began; the second wave occurred largely after Trump's withdrawal from the JCPOA in 2018. See 'Israeli Sabotage of Iran's Nuclear Program', Iran Primer, United States Institute of Peace, 12 April 2021, https://iranprimer.usip.org/blog/2021/apr/12/israeli-sabotage-iran's-nuclear-program. See also Dalia Dassa Kaye, 'Has Israel Been Sabotaging Iran? Here's What We Know', *Washington Post*, 15 July 2020, https://www.washingtonpost.com/politics/2020/07/15/has-israel-been-sabotaging-iran-heres-what-we-know/.

46 Such assessments were commonly aired during Track Two discussions attended by the author.

Orchestrating US Engagement with North Korea

Kelsey Davenport

Negotiations between former US president Donald Trump and North Korean leader Kim Jong-un failed to yield tangible results towards the denuclearisation of North Korea and the stabilisation of the Korean Peninsula. The process did, however, provide important insights into Pyongyang's priorities and its preferred negotiating approach that can be useful in crafting a more effective strategy for future engagement.

In talks with the Trump administration, Pyongyang made clear its opposition to any process that calls for dismantlement of North Korea's nuclear-weapons programme prior to receiving sanctions relief, and that a transformed relationship between Pyongyang and Washington would be necessary to make progress.[1] While the Biden administration has said little about the results of its North Korea policy review and attempts to communicate with Pyongyang, comments from US officials suggest that the White House is willing to accept the Singapore Summit declaration, signed in June 2018 by Trump and Kim, as a starting point for talks and to proceed in incremental stages towards those goals.[2] However, all outward signs suggest that negotiations with Pyongyang are not a priority for the United States – despite North Korea's growing nuclear-weapons programme and missile

Kelsey Davenport is the Director for Nonproliferation Policy at the Arms Control Association, where she focuses on the nuclear and missile programmes in Iran, North Korea, India and Pakistan, and on international efforts to prevent proliferation and nuclear terrorism. This article was written as part of an IISS project on North Korea's nuclear- and ballistic-missile capabilities, with generous support from the John D. and Catherine T. MacArthur Foundation.

Survival | vol. 64 no. 2 | April–May 2022 | pp. 125–140   https://doi.org/10.1080/00396338.2022.2055831

advances – and that US officials are continuing to draw on the same dual-track playbook of ratcheting up pressure while reiterating an openness for talks that has failed to lead to concrete results.[3]

With North Korea beginning to send signals that it may be interested in a resumption of diplomatic engagement with South Korea, the Biden administration has an opportunity to make clear to Pyongyang that the United States is interested in a more productive negotiating process. In particular, it could indicate that Washington is willing to negotiate dismantling the country's nuclear-weapons programme incrementally, while taking corresponding steps to address North Korea's security and economic concerns, including sanctions relief, early in the process. This would help demonstrate that the United States is genuinely interested in the new relationship between Washington and Pyongyang that Trump and Kim agreed to pursue in Singapore.[4]

Aligning goals and processes

In recent years, the United States has struggled in nuclear negotiations to align its negotiating processes with expectations as to what talks will produce. In negotiations with both Iran and North Korea, for instance, the US has pursued transactional bargains focused on exchanging nuclear restrictions for actions that roll back coercive measures (largely sanctions). While such approaches can reduce nuclear risk, the American expectation has been that what are rather limited bargains will produce transformational results that lead the country in question to modify its activities in other areas of policy. This misalignment has had a demonstrably negative impact on the success of negotiations and agreements.

The 2015 Joint Comprehensive Plan of Action (JCPOA), as the Iran nuclear deal is formally known, was successful in imposing strict limits on the country's nuclear programme and subjecting it to the most intrusive monitoring regime ever negotiated. Despite the agreement's success from a non-proliferation perspective, critics consistently described it as a failure because it did not alter provocative Iranian activities in the region that ran counter to US interests. Negotiators never intended for the nuclear deal to address broader regional security issues, but the constant drumbeat of criticism and overambitious promises for follow-up talks lent credence to the perception that the deal had failed simply because some Iranian threats remained. This imbalance between a transactional approach and transformational expectations contributed to Trump's decision to withdraw from the nuclear deal – despite Iran's compliance – and reimpose sanctions. In his May 2018 speech announcing those measures, Trump noted the deal did 'nothing to constrain Iran's destabilising activities, including its support for terrorism'.[5]

The damage caused by US misalignment between process and expectations does not have merely domestic ramifications. In the case of North Korea, Pyongyang's post-Singapore perception that the Trump administration was interested in a new relationship with North Korea – a fundamentally transformative objective – was undermined by the transactional approach that the US negotiating team took after the June 2018 summit. In follow-up talks and public messaging, the Trump administration focused on denuclearisation and repeatedly emphasised that North Korea had to take concrete steps towards that end prior to any US actions. The bar for sanctions relief – North Korea's primary objective – was even higher. In March 2019, Stephen Biegun, the US special representative for North Korea, stated that 'the lifting of sanctions will come with attaining' the goal of fully verified denuclearisation.[6] The United States also sought to tighten enforcement of United Nations sanctions on North Korea during the negotiating process.[7]

This pivot from a pledge to transform the US–North Korea relationship in the Singapore Summit declaration to transactional diplomacy focused heavily on denuclearisation clearly confounded the expectations of the Kim regime and degraded its confidence in the negotiating process. As Kim noted in an April 2019 address, the United States

> made much ado about improved relations and peace; on the other hand, it is resorting to all conceivable schemes in trying to prolong the economic sanctions, with the aim of preventing us from following the path of our own choice and disarming us first to create conditions for realising its ambition of overthrowing our social system.

He went on to say that 'if the US adopts a correct posture and comes forward for the third North Korea–US summit with a certain methodology that can be shared with us, we can think of holding one more round of talks'.[8] For the remainder of Trump's term, North Korea continued to push the United States to change its approach and commit to a step-by-step process that balanced actions by each side.

In fact, a step-by-step approach to a transformed relationship stands a greater chance of success than focusing too narrowly on denuclearisation, even though it will be more complex and time-consuming. A transformative approach will require addressing the root causes of North Korea's nuclear weapons and a range of security and economic issues that have contributed to tensions, mistrust and hostility between Washington and Pyongyang. The United States will need to put more on the table than a commitment to eventually waive or lift sanctions, and will need to think about how the US military presence in the region influences security perceptions as well as how to build economic and diplomatic ties with Pyongyang.

Addressing these root causes and embedding steps towards denuclearisation within a broader set of goals are more likely than a narrowly transactional approach to achieve the US goal of verifiably dismantling North Korea's nuclear-weapons programme. Kim has committed to denuclearisation, but his pledge remains largely untested, and there are legitimate reasons to doubt whether North Korea will ultimately be willing to give up what he calls his 'treasured sword'. Kim still views the country's nuclear weapons as integral to the security of his regime and to deterring an attack. Recent investments in shorter-range, more precise missiles suggest that Kim also seeks the capability to repel an attack should deterrence fail, and the ability to evade US missile defences.

This ongoing reliance on nuclear weapons suggests that only a transformative change in the relationship between the United States and North Korea is likely to alter Pyongyang's calculus regarding their necessity to North Korea's security. A transactional approach that trades nuclear restrictions for relief from coercive measures may reduce risks in the short term, but is unlikely to effect a transformative change in Pyongyang's threat perceptions and test Kim's commitment to denuclearise.

A mutually agreed framework

The United States and North Korea's shared commitment to negotiations based on the Singapore Summit declaration would indicate an interest by both sides in pursuing a transformative approach. But the goals of that declaration remain vague. The 'denuclearisation of the Korean Peninsula' and a 'lasting and stable peace regime on the Korean Peninsula' are open to a range of interpretations. Former US national security advisor John Bolton, for example, attempted to expand the definition in March 2019, asserting that the United States considers dismantlement of North Korea's chemical- and biological-weapons programmes to be an element of denuclearisation.[9] Bolton's interpretation appears to be an aberration. But early disagreements over the scope of the talks and whether the goals should be pursued sequentially or in tandem could be detrimental to the process. To maximise the chances of success, the United States and North Korea should establish a more specific framework outlining in greater detail the scope and goals of the negotiations.

US policy, for instance, defines denuclearisation as the 'complete, irreversible and verifiable dismantlement' of North Korea's nuclear weapons and nuclear-capable delivery systems.[10] The past several administrations, regardless of political party, have generally used this description, even though irreversibility is impossible at this point given the institutional knowledge North Korea has gained about nuclear-weapons production. Furthermore, Pyongyang's concept of denuclearisation focuses on more than just unilateral nuclear disarmament and encompasses the entire region. North Korea includes in its definition prohibitions on the deployment of US strategic assets in the region and the basing of US troops trained to use nuclear weapons in South Korea, as well as on US threats to use nuclear weapons. In December 2018, North Korea reiterated that denuclearisation means 'removing all elements of nuclear threats from the areas of both the north and the south of Korea and also from surrounding areas from where the Korean peninsula is targeted'.[11] North Korean officials typically describe these factors as a 'hostile policy' on the part of the US that necessitates Pyongyang's further development of nuclear weapons.

On both sides it is unclear if, or to what extent, civil nuclear activities, particularly uranium enrichment and reprocessing, would be allowed. North and South Korea agreed in the 1992 Joint Declaration of the Denuclearization of the Korean Peninsula not to 'possess nuclear reprocessing and uranium enrichment facilities' and not to 'test, manufacture, produce, receive, possess, store, deploy or use nuclear weapons'.[12] Pyongyang, however, declared in 2003 that it was no longer bound by that declaration.

Even less clear is how each side defines the Singapore Summit declaration commitment to pursue a 'lasting and stable peace regime on the Korean Peninsula'. The United States and North Korea should consider beginning talks by hashing out a more detailed understanding of the main elements of denuclearisation and a peace regime for the peninsula.

The 2013 Joint Plan of Action between Iran and the group of countries known as the P5+1 (China, France, Germany, Russia, the United Kingdom and the United States) provides a possible model. That document included baseline elements that all parties agreed would guide further negotiations and be reflected in a final deal. For instance, all parties recognised that Iran would continue certain civil nuclear activities after any final agreement, though its civil nuclear programme would be subject to limits and enhanced monitoring. The agreed elements also committed the parties to lift all nuclear-related sanctions imposed by the UN, the United States and others.[13] The broad parameters gave a sense of the final agreement's scope and provided assurances to all parties that their core concerns would be addressed. The JCPOA itself reflected the elements outlined in the 2013 text.

In the North Korean case, the two sides could agree on the general parameters for negotiations and the ideal end state, addressing in greater detail the main points agreed in the Singapore Summit declaration. In particular, they could clarify whether denuclearisation of the Korean Peninsula would include limitations on certain nuclear-capable missiles, as well as the verifiable dismantlement of North Korea's nuclear warheads and production infrastructure. The parameters could also call for North Korea's security concerns regarding US extended deterrence to be addressed in some way, perhaps through security guarantees or mutual inspections between North and South Korea to provide assurance of the absence of nuclear weapons on the peninsula. Possible future civil nuclear activities in North Korea could be referenced to indicate the scope of any future North Korean nuclear programme.

In addition, negotiators could consider noting that the parties would agree to the lifting of UN and certain US sanctions; pursuing a formal end to the Korean War; seeking to establish normal diplomatic relations; and perhaps mooting the possibility of a regional security dialogue on building peace and security in the region per the Singapore Summit declaration.

There is a risk that this preliminary definitional process could get bogged down and dim prospects for substantive talks. To demonstrate good faith in the diplomatic process and maintain momentum, Pyongyang and Washington could simultaneously pursue confidence-building measures (CBMs). Some of these could be traditional security CBMs, such as the re-establishment of regular military-to-military communications, and a commitment to pre-notifications of missile tests and military drills. Cultural exchanges, athletic events and humanitarian gestures could also be considered.[14]

Initial corresponding steps

Discussions about scope should go hand in hand with those about the negotiating process. The Biden administration's policy review reportedly settled on an incremental approach towards reaching the goals laid out in the Singapore Summit declaration. While a step-by-step process is clearly North Korea's preferred approach to negotiations, it may be challenging for the Biden administration to convince Pyongyang that it is sincere in wanting to move incrementally. During negotiations between Washington and Pyongyang after the Singapore Summit, it became clear that North Korea viewed the US approach as unbalanced in requiring Pyongyang to take concrete action upfront before the US would consider meaningful sanctions relief and security-related measures, and it refused to proceed on such terms.[15]

From the outset, it would be useful for the Biden administration to message consistently and publicly what benefits Pyongyang could receive early in the process. Without giving away the US negotiating position, the Biden administration could make clear that it would waive or modify certain sanctions and take steps to ease tensions if Pyongyang took tangible steps towards denuclearisation and peacebuilding.

Having established agreement on the end state and the process, the United States and North Korea could then contemplate initial corresponding steps towards meeting the agreed framework goals. Because these steps would not necessarily be the same for each, they should be cast as corresponding rather than reciprocal but also of equal worth for each side. Early steps should also focus on areas of pressing concern for both sides.

Negotiations between Trump and Kim post-Singapore suggest what each side may want to prioritise early in the process. After the Singapore Summit, Mike Pompeo, then US secretary of state, travelled to Pyongyang in pursuit of the Trump administration's first priority: a full declaration of North Korea's nuclear activities. While such a declaration would be beneficial in developing a verification regime and thinking through the sequencing and scope of dismantlement activities, Pyongyang understandably viewed it as tantamount to handing the United States a military target list.[16] In addition to being an unrealistic first step, such a declaration does little to reduce risk. A declaration will be necessary at some point in the process, but it could be deferred or provided in stages as North Korea gains confidence in the process and its own security.

A more reasonable starting point for corresponding steps would be a version of North Korea's offer at the February 2019 Hanoi Summit between Trump and Kim. According to North Korean foreign minister Ri Yong-ho, Kim proposed dismantling fissile-material production capabilities at Yongbyon under US monitoring, and formalising North Korea's voluntary moratorium on nuclear and long-range missile testing in exchange for relief from UN Security Council sanctions imposed in 2016 and 2017 that 'hamper the civilian economy and the livelihood of our people'.[17] US officials offered a slightly conflicting account. Biegun described the offer as one of 'partial denuclearisation for a full lifting of sanctions' with 'no subsequent commitments'.[18] In light of that understanding, it is unsurprising that the Trump administration declined the offer and unlikely that a future US administration would accept one that were similarly construed. However, the proposal does represent a starting point for negotiating a first round of corresponding steps and provides an indication of what North Korea might be willing to put on the table in a new round of negotiations.

Opponents of the dismantling of Yongbyon as a first step have argued that the facility has less value because it is a known entity. While it is true that North Korea's nuclear-weapons complex is geographically scattered and probably includes facilities not yet identified in open sources and perhaps not known to US intelligence, the Yongbyon complex is still a central element of the country's nuclear programme. The site houses North Korea's only means of plutonium and tritium production, useful for designing more advanced nuclear weapons. Dismantling and monitoring those production capabilities would reduce risk by preventing Pyongyang from producing and stockpiling those elements. Its verified and monitored dismantlement early in the process could afford Pyongyang assurances about how verification and monitoring procedures would function prior to disclosing the locations of covert uranium-enrichment and weaponisation sites, which US intelligence has confirmed exist. From the American perspective, as the site also includes a uranium-enrichment facility, Yongbyon's dismantlement would provide insights into North Korea's enrichment capabilities. Political feasibility is also a factor. US and international inspectors have been to Yongbyon in the past, and North Korea presumably would be more inclined to allow inspectors into a site with which they were already familiar.

Confidence-building measures could include mock inspections

CBMs that could encourage the parties to move forward would include mock inspections at a third-party site, technology demonstrations to give Pyongyang an understanding of the processes that might be employed, discussions about what information would be provided publicly, and scientist-to-scientist engagement. In return, the United States could consider a sanctions-relief package – North Korea's top priority – that would provide it with meaningful and immediate economic benefits, building momentum for subsequent steps.

Given that the Biden administration may face domestic opposition to the outright lifting of US sanctions, it could look at waiving or instituting caps on the import and export of certain materials currently subject to UN sanctions. If the United States is worried that North Korea will pocket the concessions and fail to follow through, the negotiators could include a time frame for implementation of the Yongbyon commitments, after which sanctions would be reimposed or automatically snapped back.

Relaxing sanctions early in the process would likely garner regional support. Russia and China have advocated lifting certain UN sanctions to get negotiations with North Korea back on track.[19] South Korea also appears to favour early sanctions relief, particularly if it facilitates inter-Korean economic projects. Regional support and coordination, particularly from China, could help ensure that North Korea gets meaningful relief promptly after sanctions are lifted, which proved problematic in the Iranian context when companies remained apprehensive about compliance.[20]

Provided an initial set of corresponding steps provides roughly equal benefit to both sides, there would be a reasonable chance of negotiating a second set that would further advance the process. This kind of intermediate progress might also help ensure that the process survives a presidential transition in the United States. Established talks yielding concrete results are a strong case for continuity in policy. Ideally, the second set of steps should continue to reduce risk and build stability on the peninsula and address key concerns on both sides.

Building on the Yongbyon step, the two sides could consider actions on North Korea's part such as:

- Verifiably closing North Korea's nuclear test site at Punggye-ri. To reinforce this step, North Korea could agree to sign the 1996 Comprehensive Test-Ban Treaty.
- Halting fissile-material production at sites outside of the Yongbyon complex. This could first be accomplished using remote monitoring if North Korea was still reluctant to allow inspectors on the ground at these sites. On-site monitoring and inspections could be introduced later.

- Accounting for and securing North Korea's stockpile of fissile material that has not yet been weaponised. This could include initially storing the materials in North Korea under seal and later disposing of them, either in-country or abroad.
- Allowing for international inspectors under the auspices of the International Atomic Energy Agency (IAEA) to begin applying safeguards and monitoring measures at certain locations. This could perhaps begin with Yongbyon itself if the initial dismantlement did not include an IAEA presence.
- Developing and agreeing on a procedure for verifiably dismantling North Korea's warheads and disposing of the fissile material.
- Determining which nuclear-capable ballistic missiles North Korea will forgo as part of the dismantlement process and procedures for verifiably dismantling those missile systems.

Later North Korean steps could include:
- Fully declaring North Korea's nuclear programme including nuclear infrastructure, materials and weapons, to be verified later by the IAEA. The guidelines and techniques established by the IAEA Model Additional Protocol for nuclear safeguards would provide a good foundation for verifying and monitoring the fuel-cycle portions of the declaration.
- Agreeing on a timeline for the verifiable dismantlement of North Korea's nuclear warheads and beginning that process.
- Allowing certain civil nuclear activities to commence or recommence under IAEA safeguards.
- North Korea's return to the Non-Proliferation Treaty as a non-nuclear-weapons state.

In return, corresponding US steps could include:
- Further lifting US and UN sanctions.
- Directly supporting certain mutually agreed-upon development projects in North Korea or as part of the North–South dialogue.

- Pledging to remove US strategic bombers from future joint military exercises with South Korea.
- Providing US security assurances not to use or threaten to use nuclear weapons against North Korea or to engage in preventive strikes.
- Committing to suspend further deployment of theatre-based missile defences in South Korea and to eventually remove them.
- Cooperating on nuclear issues of interest to North Korea, such as the inclusion of North Korean nuclear scientists in efforts related to radio-medicine, regional response and mitigation efforts in the event of a nuclear accident, and nuclear safety.

Later US steps could include:
- Terminating UN Security Council resolutions targeting North Korea's nuclear-weapons and ballistic-missile programmes.
- Fully lifting US sanctions on North Korea.
- Working with North and South Korea on possible options to allow Pyongyang to verify that there are no US nuclear weapons present in South Korea.

The process should also include actions that build peace and stability in the region, some of which would be undertaken jointly or reciprocally. These actions could include, for instance, negotiations on an end-of-war declaration and later a treaty formally ending the Korean War and the opening of diplomatic interest sections, and later embassies, in both countries. More ambitiously, the parties, along with other states in the region, could discuss establishing a regional security forum in which countries could raise and address security issues. These could include missile developments and deployments, since South Korea's missile posture would likely need to be addressed as part of any efforts to limit North Korea's nuclear-capable ballistic missiles. While longer-range systems may be better addressed in negotiations with the United States, any limits on short- and medium-range ballistic missiles, or verification measures to ensure such systems are geared towards conventional purposes, would be better negotiated as part of a regional dialogue.

*   *   *

Realising the goals of denuclearisation and peacebuilding on the Korean Peninsula is, in the best-case scenario, a complex, decades-long process. Negotiations will need to be durable and demonstrate tangible progress in risk reduction and stability-building to withstand changes in leadership in the United States – and possibly North Korea – and the machinations of spoilers. Setting up a process with a clear vision of end goals and swiftly demonstrating that each side will benefit through corresponding steps can help build confidence that the process will be truly transformational, and sustain its momentum.

Notes

1   See 'Kim Jong Un's 2019 New Year Address', National Committee on North Korea, 1 January 2019, https://www.ncnk.org/resources/publications/kimjongun_2019_new-yearaddress.pdf/file_view.

2   See John Hudson and Ellen Nakashima, 'Biden Administration Forges New Path on North Korea Crisis in Wake of Trump and Obama Failures', *Washington Post*, 30 April 2021, https://www.washingtonpost.com/national-security/biden-administration-forges-new-path-on-north-korea-crisis-in-wake-of-trump-and-obama-failures/2021/04/30/c8bef4f2-a9a9-11eb-b166-174b63ea6007_story.html.

3   See Doug Bandow, 'Korean Lesson Number One for Joe Biden: "Maximum Pressure" Is Over', CATO Institute, 11 February 2021, https://www.cato.org/commentary/korean-lesson-number-one-joe-biden-maximum-pressure-over; and 'Remarks by Ambassador Linda Thomas-Greenfield at the UN Security Council Stakeout on the DPRK', New York, 20 October 2021, https://www.youtube.com/watch?v=1-rPUVD4vkI.

4   See 'Joint Statement of President Donald J. Trump of the United States of America and Chairman Kim Jong Un of the Democratic People's Republic of Korea at the Singapore Summit', US Embassy and Consulate in Thailand, 12 June 2018, https://th.usembassy.gov/joint-statement-president-donald-j-trump-united-states-america-chairman-kim-jong-un-democratic-peoples-republic-korea-singapore-summit/.

5   White House, 'Remarks by President Trump on the Joint Comprehensive Plan of Action', 8 May 2018, https://trumpwhitehouse.archives.gov/briefings-statements/remarks-president-trump-joint-comprehensive-plan-action/.

6   'A Conversation with U.S. Special Representative Stephen Biegun', Carnegie Endowment for

International Peace, 2019 Carnegie International Nuclear Policy Conference, Washington DC, 11 March 2019, https://s3.amazonaws.com/ceipfiles/pdf/NPC19-SpecialRepresentativeBiegun.pdf.

[7] See 'Secretary Pompeo Remarks at a Meeting on the Democratic Republic of North Korea', US Embassy and Consulate in the Republic of Korea, 27 September 2018, https://kr.usembassy.gov/092718-secretary-pompeo-remarks-at-a-meeting-on-the-democratic-peoples-republic-of-korea/.

[8] 'On Socialist Construction and the Internal and External Policies of the Government of the Republic at the Present Stage', speech delivered by Kim Jong-un to the First Session of the 14th Supreme People's Assembly of the DPRK, National Committee on North Korea, 12 April 2019, https://www.ncnk.org/resources/publications/kju_april2019_policy_speech.pdf/file_view.

[9] See '"This Week" Transcript 5-13-18: President Trump's National Security Adviser John Bolton', ABC News, 13 March 2018, https://abcnews.go.com/Politics/week-transcript-13-18-president-trumps-national-security/story?id=55110238.

[10] See, for example, David Welna, '"Complete, Verifiable, Irreversible" A Tough Goal for North Korea Summit', National Public Radio, 6 June 2018, https://www.npr.org/2018/06/06/617619192/complete-verifiable-irreversible-a-tough-goal-for-north-korea-summit.

[11] Quoted in, for instance, Robert Carlin, 'DPRK Repeats Stance on Denuclearization', 38 North, 21 December 2018, https://www.38north.org/2018/12/rcarlin122118/.

[12] 'Joint Declaration of the Denuclearization of the Korean Peninsula', Bureau of Arms Control, US Department of State, 20 January 1992, https://2001-2009.state.gov/t/ac/rls/or/2004/31011.htm.

[13] See 'Joint Plan of Action', Geneva, 24 November 2013, https://www.armscontrol.org/files/Iran_P5_1_Nuclear_Deal_131123.pdf.

[14] US and North Korean actions surrounding the Singapore Summit process demonstrate the importance of negotiating reciprocal measures with perceived equal value. Ahead of the summit, Kim announced a unilateral moratorium on testing nuclear devices and long-range missiles, and took steps to dismantle North Korea's nuclear testing site. After the summit, Trump announced that the United States and South Korea would suspend joint military exercises as a demonstration of goodwill. These actions were traditional security-sector CBMs, but North Korea clearly did not perceive US actions as of equal value to its own moratoriums. Trump's focus on the cost savings of rolling back US–South Korean exercises and his general questioning of alliances may have contributed to North Korea's assessment that exercises were not suspended solely to address North Korea's security concerns.

[15] See, for example, Choe Sang-Hun, 'North Korea Threatens to Scuttle Talks with the U.S. and Resume Tests', New York Times, 15 March 2019, https://www.nytimes.com/2019/03/15/world/asia/north-korea-kim-jong-un-

nuclear.html.

16 See, for example, Edward Ifft, 'Lessons for Negotiating with North Korea', *Survival*, vol. 62, no. 1, February–March 2020, pp. 89–106.

17 Amy Held, 'In Rare News Conference, North Korea Offers Its Own Version of Summit Collapse', National Public Radio, 28 February 2019, https://www.npr.org/2019/02/28/699006894/in-rare-news-conference-north-korea-offers-its-own-version-of-summit-collapse.

18 'Negotiating with North Korea: An Interview with Former U.S. Deputy Secretary of State Stephen Biegun', *Arms Control Today*, June 2021, https://www.armscontrol.org/act/2021-06/interviews/negotiating-north-korea-interview-former-us-deputy-secretary-state-stephen.

19 See Michelle Nichols, 'China, Russia Say Lifting Some U.N. Sanctions on North Korea Could Help Break the Deadlock', Reuters, 17 December 2019, https://www.reuters.com/article/uk-northkorea-usa-un-china-idUKK-BN1YL0LN.

20 See Esfandyar Batmanghelidj and Mahsa Rouhi, 'The Iran Nuclear Deal and Sanctions Relief: Implications for US Policy', *Survival*, vol. 63, no. 4, August–September 2019, pp. 183–98.

Copyright © 2022 The International Institute for Strategic Studies

Swords and Emotions: The American Civil War and Society-centric Strategy

Jonathan (Yoni) Shimshoni

After eight years, France recently announced its intent to retreat from Mali, succumbing to the Islamic State (ISIS) and al-Qaeda. After spending some $2 trillion over 20 indecisive years of great human cost, the United States has left Afghanistan to the Taliban. Israel has been severely challenged by Hamas and Hizbullah, and lacks a satisfactory response to either. China has found ways short of direct kinetic engagement to coerce and often cow its neighbours near and far, and challenge the US strategically, while keeping its own homeland quite impenetrable. Russia, the weakest of the major powers, has been able to wield power and influence – in Belarus, Georgia, Kazakhstan, Syria and, even currently, in Ukraine – often thereby challenging European and American interests and values, even meddling directly in Europe and the United States. And, while China and Russia have not consistently bested their Western rivals and have not created positions of strategic superiority, all too often the US and its Western allies find themselves on their back feet, lacking a response that is effective commensurately with their preponderant resources and power.

The strategies for conflict of these nominally inferior rivals share one essential attribute: they are society-centric, focused on societal manipulation and impact. In response, stronger and wealthier Western states have largely remained focused on military operational and technological engagement, often with counterproductive and unwittingly escalatory results.[1] To

Jonathan (Yoni) Shimshoni is a Research Affiliate at the MIT Security Studies Program.

Survival | vol. 64 no. 2 | April–May 2022 | pp. 141–166   https://doi.org/10.1080/00396338.2022.2055832

be sure, these Western powers do sometimes pursue societal impact, by punishing civilians, imposing economic sanctions, adopting 'hearts and minds' counter-insurgency tactics, broadcasting propaganda and through social networks. But these measures are often applied in an ad hoc manner and do not reflect a full understanding of society-centric conflict.

A society-centric strategy involves attempts to coerce or steer the attitude and behaviour of a rival society by impacting and manipulating its collective emotions.[2] The tools of such coercion may include military force, economic pressure, rhetoric and threats, public diplomacy, propaganda and disinformation. Successfully executing such a strategy requires accurately predicting a rival society's emotional–behavioural reactions to coercion, which in turn demands a robust understanding of its collective psychological predispositions, such as long-standing sentiments, ideology, ethos and framing. Furthermore, effective application of coercive measures such as military force and economic pressure calls for a clear picture of a rival's ability to create, mobilise, sustain and marshal resources – its political culture and economy. Finally, a key element that must be accounted for in predicting behaviour is the universal psychological dynamics of war, such as the emotional–behavioural effects of the 'first shot' or leaders' frustrations.[3]

Although the American Civil War was a major war, spanning some 10,000 kinetic engagements, and militarily catastrophic, both the North and the South intended to prevail through societal impact, on all dimensions and with all available tools. Employing the general framework presented above, this essay marshals various historical accounts to explore the North's strategy towards the South, and the fate of its attempts to prevail through emotional–behavioural impact and manipulation.[4] In exploring Northern strategy, it adopts a unitary-actor perspective and is not concerned with the highly contested and emotionally invested motivations and visions across Northern society and polity. The analysis does consider differences within Southern society, as exploiting internal fault lines was central to Union strategy.

Union strategy and Southern society

Consistently failing to meet its goals, the Northern strategy climbed through four successive phases, each more aggressive in terms of society-focused coercion.[5] In the 'Secession Winter' of 1860–61, the goal was to *keep the peace*. As friction heated up around the issue of slavery and its potential expansion, Northern leaders pursued a stopgap compromise through frantic efforts to legislate the first Thirteenth Amendment, which would have guaranteed the protection of slavery where it existed, buttressed by Abraham Lincoln's commitment to that effect in his first 'we must be friends' inaugural address. Following the election of 1860, Northern politicians such as Stephen Douglas, considered credible and friendly to Southerners, travelled south to convince them that secession would drive the North to fight.[6] This combination of conciliation and political pressure was intended to allay the South's fear of the status quo, while heightening its fear of the violently disruptive consequences of secession. This effort was unsuccessful. In April 1861, the Confederacy declared independence and initiated war.

Win back characterises Union strategy from the Battle of Fort Sumter – generally considered the start of the Civil War – in April 1861 through mid-1862. The idea was to recreate the antebellum United States by building internal dissent from disunion and preventing the border states from seceding. The Union sought to achieve these ends through economic pressure in the form of a naval blockade and a clear demonstration of military superiority in defeating Southern armies, conquering territory and threatening symbols of Confederate power (most importantly Richmond), while applying a conciliatory policy that protected Southern civilians' lives and property – including slaves.[7] Operating in this manner was intended to coerce Southern compliance but defuse the perceived threat of impending social revolution and avoid humiliation, driving popular Southern anger towards Southern elites and away from the Union. In the event, while the border states did not secede, Confederate society only hardened in its commitment to secession and resistance.

By mid-1862, Northern leaders had come to understand that they faced a wholesale rebellion, not just an insurgency, and that Southern society could not be 'won back' but rather would have to be *beaten*. History would not be 'rolled back' but would have to be 'pushed forward': the Union would have to effect the collapse of the very structure and coherence of Southern society. At the same time, Northern leaders continued to believe that internal fissures could be created and exploited. Thus, in this second stage of the war, the Union sought to induce collective and personal fear, pessimism and anomie, and to undermine confidence in leadership, while providing hope for anyone who abstained from open hostility or, better yet, defected.

This new strategic paradigm involved several dramatic moves: the Emancipation Proclamation; the enlistment of black men in Union armies; and the abandonment of the conciliatory approach towards Southern civilians. The Emancipation Proclamation was to take effect in those areas still in rebellion by January 1863, and entailed an aggressive military policy of proactively enticing slaves to freedom.[8] This mixture of promise and threat was designed to help unravel the Confederacy by creating internal pressure within individual Southern states to abort the war and drive a wedge between border and Confederate states.[9]

With only spotty operational achievements, and facing vexing Southern guerrilla and broad societal resistance, Northern commanders began directly targeting non-combatants and their property.[10] They increased pressure with an ever-tightening naval blockade and a campaign of property destruction, escalating to 'foraging' – that is, organised pillaging.[11] Northern armies meted out collective punishment, bombarding and besieging towns and forcing migration. In occupied areas, Northern commanders applied a policy of 'directed severity' to erode social unity, punishing secessionists, treating peaceful bystanders leniently and rewarding unionists.[12]

To some extent, these policies had the desired emotional and behavioural effect. Economic pressure produced hunger and general want, leading soldiers to fear for their families, greatly increasing desertion rates and stoking anger against elites. Violent protests, often led by women, ensued, and white planters and yeomen became more apprehensive of slave uprisings and impending social collapse. In several rural areas – notably western North Carolina – the white social order began to disintegrate, and loss of faith in and indignation towards central-government policies regarding taxation and class-based preferences diminished sovereign control.[13] In occupied areas, some farmers defected in return for access to Northern commerce. In North Carolina, a bona fide peace movement arose. These are impressive results, but in net effect they fell short of being strategic. On balance, the collective reaction was even greater anger and rage, and an attitude of fight rather than flight. Southern leaders' ability to wage war did not crumble.

By autumn 1864 the Union had made tremendous military progress on the ground, but achieving the later-stage strategic goal of reunion without slavery seemed far off. Northern leaders – in particular, generals Ulysses S. Grant, William Tecumseh Sherman and Philip Sheridan – concluded that Southern society had to be not merely beaten but *crushed*. At the same time, the North needed to bring the war to a definitive conclusion, such that Southern resistance would not morph into persistent guerrilla warfare, and *seduce* Southern society into amicable reunion.

Southern society was to be overwhelmed – thrown into exhausted despair – through massive, simultaneous military campaigns. The main, traditional military action was Grant's Overland Campaign in Virginia. Its strategic purpose was to destroy Robert E. Lee's Army of Northern Virginia, Southern society's last remaining lifeline, en route to Richmond, the primary emblem of Confederacy sovereignty. Concurrently, the Union launched several large-scale incursions, including Sherman's March to the Sea and Sheridan's burning of the Shenandoah, aimed directly at Southern civilians, their property and their sustenance. As historian Mark Grimsley put it, 'the raids were intended to demonstrate two things to the Southern people – first that they could be hurt, and second, that the Confederate government was powerless to protect them'.[14]

Northern leaders concluded that the South had to be crushed

In parallel, the Union attempted seductive conciliation. The 'ten percent' amnesty plan sought to lure states to defect from the Confederacy by offering minimal thresholds of loyalty as conditions for readmission to the Union, reinforced by Lincoln's accommodating rhetoric as in the 'malice towards none' language of his second inaugural address. Except for a couple of marginal cases, this strategy fell flat. The North also differentiated among targets. Instructions were given to destroy the property of the elite, to demonstrate to the common people that the Union did not see them as the enemy. There is little evidence that this refinement had the intended effect. The conduct of the surrenders in the east was also designed to placate Southerners and encourage civil reconciliation. Grant at Appomattox and Sherman at Bennett House made concerted efforts to demonstrate respect, buttress Southern pride and, most importantly, extend terms that avoided humiliation.[15] The Southern armies did surrender and disperse, guerrilla warfare did not materialise, the war ended. But the Union failed to achieve its goal of amicable reunion, as the fraught Reconstruction period and the following century of segregation, discrimination, racial violence and Jim Crow would demonstrate.

At no stage did Northern strategy pan out as intended. The war dragged out and escalated to a ferocity of death, destruction and misery orders of magnitude beyond most Americans' pre-war imagination. Despite logistical advantages and operational successes, and the incredible pain it inflicted on the South, the Union at certain points considered throwing in the towel, while the weaker Confederacy, ground down by blockade, operational defeat, casualties, occupation, hunger and destitution, came uncannily close to victory.[16] Having lost the war and relinquished national independence and sovereignty, Southern society framed the South's effort and defeat in the Civil War as an honourable 'lost cause', and continued white racial dominance by other means.[17] Indeed, myth and cause persist even to this day, continuing to fuel contemporary right-wing movements in the United States. What went wrong?

Union misjudgement

The Union's ability to elicit intended emotional–behavioural reactions by Southern society suffered from three mutually reinforcing shortfalls: 1) a deficient understanding of the South's collective psychological and emotional world; 2) an underestimation of the Confederacy's ability to muster, organise and apply economic and military resources for societal resilience; and 3) an insufficient appreciation of the effects of universal psychological dynamics.

Despite decades of mostly cold but some hot war among civilians in Missouri and Kansas, and even violence in Congress, Northern leaders were surprised by the South's secession and turn to war. The failure of stopgap efforts to appease and coerce in winter 1861 highlights how badly the North misread Southern understanding of the crisis. While Northerners saw their 'American Project' threatened by slavery and potential Southern secession, white Southerners saw their own version of that project under attack, their social order facing revolution and they subjugation. The ultimate threat promised by Lincoln's election drove Southerners, extremely jealous of their way of life, to adopt an existentially defensive mindset, framing the required response as a pre-emptive counter-revolution.[18]

Through this cognitive lens, Southerners interpreted Northern actions of conciliatory intent as coercive and threatening. Thus, they perceived the proposed Thirteenth Amendment to be merely a trick to relax Southern vigilance and prevent the western expansion of slavery. Suggestions that secession would lead to war – even if not made by administration officials – were read as proof of Union belligerence. Southern sentiments of racial and cultural superiority, and contempt for Northern society and culture, provided the necessary confidence to act on these beliefs.

Through mid-1862, the notion that Southerners discreetly harboured unionist sentiment was an article of Northern faith, central to the North's strategic assessment and action. This helps explain Northern expectations that secession and war would not materialise and, once war started, that a 'win-back' strategy combining coercion and conciliation could be effective, especially if class-linked conflicting interests between slaveholding elites and the non-slaveholding population could be exploited.

In fact, secession was not a slam-dunk proposition in the South. In the months prior to Fort Sumter, secessionists had to fight hard (and often dirty) to overcome substantial political and popular opposition to disunion in nearly all the states that ultimately seceded, including South Carolina, the first to do so.[19] Furthermore, only after Fort Sumter did a critical mass of states secede, while the border states never did.

Northerners, however, conflated opposition to secession with affection for the North. For some Southerners, that opposition was simply a cynical 'bear hug' given in the belief that the South's remaining in the United States would ensure the constitutional protection of slavery.[20] Northerners were also poorly attuned to the growing sense of a unique and collective

Southern identity that crowded out the American attributes – language, race, historical and political heritage – that Southerners and Northerners shared.[21] Although slavery had been a burning political issue for decades, Northerners tended to take a somewhat transactional view of it, and did not fathom just how fundamental the institution was to white Southern ideology, identity, social order and status – shared across all classes, slave-holding and not.

As the war began, nationalism and religion took hold of the South, strengthening resilience in the face of coercion and undermining attempted conciliation. The very declaration of nationhood by way of the establishment of the Confederacy helped push patriotic sentiment into full and vibrant bloom. Southern elites rapidly endeavoured to upgrade collective identity from 'Southern' to 'Confederate', creating national institutions, adopting a constitution, establishing a national capital, raising national armies, minting a new currency, and designing and disseminating flags and other symbols. Southern intellectuals worked to develop a distinct Southern nationalist literature and educational curriculum, and the press amplified an us-versus-them divide. The newly created nation would become a singular source of collective confidence and pride, as well as a new object of identity and jealousy.[22]

Southern religious leaders defined their mission as a crusade

To boost society-wide mobilisation and stiffen resilience and resistance, Southern religious leaders – lay and clerical – defined their mission as a holy crusade, merging a strong secular ideology with faith in providential favour, destiny and control. In the process, Christianity became integral to Confederate national identity, forming a lens that shaped Southerners' appraisal of events and the inherent nature of Northerners.[23] Understanding themselves to be fighting a religious war against infidels, Southerners tended to understand hardships as God's punishment for national or personal impiety, signposts on the way to ultimate triumph. This mindset bolstered drive and resilience in the face of Northern coercion, leaving little psychological space for compromise or surrender in society at large, in the military or among political leaders. In sum, as historian Jason Phillips remarked, 'religion prolonged and intensified the conflict'.[24]

Northerners, understandably, did not foresee this Southern adoption of a collective religious framing of the war. Although mid-nineteenth-century American society was fairly religious, there was little tradition or precedent for religious intensity in war. America's earlier armed conflicts – the Revolutionary War, the War of 1812 and the Mexican War – were thoroughly secular and not cast as crusades. Indeed, military and political leadership in both sections and the basic ethos of the US military were solidly secular, and phenomena such as national days of fasting and thanksgiving became common only during the Civil War. Before the war, the clergy and religious press had avoided involvement in political issues, but as Harry Stout has noted, once the war began, 'in the blink of an eye all this would change, as war challenged ministers to privilege patriotism over spirituality'.[25]

Another aspect of Southern society confounded Northern expectations. Northerners considered the mostly rural-subsistence nature of Southern political economy primitive, and rated it a strategic liability. In certain respects, it was. But it also endowed Southern society with unexpected toughness. Northerners projected expectations onto the South born of the relative comfort they derived from a wealthy and rapidly industrialising and urbanising society, believing that material deprivation could readily sap Southern motivation. While growing hardship did lead to friction and tension on the home front and to significant desertions, Southerners overall exhibited resilience that only slowly and incompletely diminished under pressure.[26]

As we have seen, the Union attempted to impact Southern emotional–behavioural reactions through acts of conciliation in counterpoint to coercion. And like coercion, these were strategically ineffective. The soft-hand policies of the early years produced positive affect in certain locales, but as a rule met countervailing sentiments of hatred and jealousy and, in reaction to conquest and emancipation, anger and fear of humiliation, all against a background of contempt, hope and confidence. By 1864, as the tide of war turned against the South and despair inched in, conciliation enjoyed better fortune as more individuals, families, communities and at least one state succumbed to the promise of a better immediate future. But for Southern society writ large, the effect of such conciliation was washed over by anger and even rage, buttressed by religiously infused confidence or fatalism.

The final conciliatory moves of the war – Lincoln's appeasing rhetoric and honourable surrenders – could not motivate the amicable reunion the North desired. In Southern eyes, the war just ended had been an extended, vicious, unjust attack on Southern society that left it conquered, starved, ravaged, dispossessed and deeply humiliated, with its civilisation and vision destroyed. Deeply ingrained sentiments of shame, victimisation, humiliation and hate persisted for decades, for they could not be magically undone by kind words or a single act of conciliation, itself in the context of an unconditional surrender and not a peace agreement between societies.[27]

Northern leaders expected the material balance to weigh heavily in their favour and readily enable their application of military and economic coercive pressure. These were reasonable expectations, for they saw a foe relatively weak on most parameters of national power. Northern industrialisation was way ahead of the South's agricultural economy. The South accounted for only 16% of the United States' total industrial capacity, and the heavy industry required for ordnance manufacturing was extremely limited. Northern railroad tracks exceeded the South's by a factor of three, canal mileage by a factor of six. Southern shipping was nearly non-existent, while the North had a fair navy and a large commercial fleet. In population, the North outnumbered the South 20 million to 9m, of whom 4m were slaves. White illiteracy in the South was six times more prevalent than in the North. Northerners understood the slave-based political economy to be particularly inflexible and unamenable to economic development and industrialisation, and unlikely to meet the requirements of a major industrial war.[28]

Furthermore, in the years leading up to war, the South was a loose community of independent states, lacking national political or economic structure or apparatus, their political economy characterised by considerable interstate differences in economic interests. Southern states did share culture and ideology, but espoused decentralisation and states' rights. Southern white society's deep class-based cleavages appeared to render it particularly ill-suited for the mobilisation and unity of action and purpose that war might require. Thus, not only did the Southern resource base appear weak, but there was no apparent societal, cultural, ideological or institutional mechanism for converting resources to power. This was a reasonable assessment, but it was wrong.

The Union further skewed the material balance by blockade and, as the war progressed, through conquest, foraging and destruction. However, Southern disadvantages did not translate into ready defeat. Significantly, the South did not attempt to work around its disadvantages by adopting an asymmetric approach. Rather, it came together to overcome its political–organisational and material handicaps, and succeeded against all expectations, as Richard Bensel put it, to effect an 'almost futuristic mobilization of resources'. Contrary to the South's antebellum predilections for a minimal state, the Confederacy established the most extensive, intrusive and potent centralised bureaucratic state in American history – more so than the Union's – at lightning speed. In the process, it converted a laissez-faire, decentralised political economy into a corporatist, public–private partnership that generated an effective supply of ordnance deep into the war. Most telling was the Confederacy's ability to conscript an astounding one million soldiers, field large national armies and sustain an effective, intense and protracted struggle.[29] Innovative foreign sourcing and creative blockade-running yielded additional supplies, including small arms and ammunition.[30] In the maritime domain, the Confederacy made up for its numerical deficiencies by contracting for blockade-running services and purchasing a small number of warships from Britain, enabling its tiny navy to visit disproportionate damage on the North's commercial shipping fleet.

Three sets of factors explain the North's underestimation of the South – its misunderstanding of Southern psychological predispositions, as well as its material ability to wage and sustain war. The first is psychological: cultural ethnocentrism blinded Northerners to basic Southern attributes – such as identity, the role of slavery and threat perception – and allowed for the projection of Northern cultural sensitivities on a very different Southern society. Contempt motivated a gross underesti-mation of Southern capabilities and motivation.[31] And wishful thinking enabled Northerners to count on internal dissent to debilitate the South, while knowing that this did not hold true in the often-divided North. The second factor is analytical: as the war progressed, Union leaders and commanders saw that Southern resistance was only hardening under pres-sure. This did not lead them to analyse the Southern emotional ecosystem or dynamics that limited the effects of coercion and conciliation, nor did they consider the trade-offs between short-term and long-term emotional–behavioural impacts, thereby sowing despair and exhaustion, and reaping lasting humiliation and hate. The third and final factor is the confound-ing 'unknown unknown': critical elements of the Southern reaction and adjustment to war – such as the repositioning of religion or the revolu-tion in political organisation and economy – were unpredictable even to Southerners themselves. Echoing Charles Tilly: an unexpected state made war, and war made the state in unexpected ways.

Universal factors

In addition to erring with respect to the particular psychological land-scape of the South, the North failed to account for universal psychological dynamics of war. One such key dynamic is that of the first shot and self-entrapment. Prior to Confederate forces' firing on Fort Sumter in April 1861, the situation was fluid, war a distant prospect and consolidation of a critical mass of seceding states uncertain, even unlikely. The Confederacy consisted of seven states, while the other natural candidates – mostly in the Upper South, hence critical to both Union and Confederacy – remained internally divided over secession. The North itself was neither unified in support of war, nor gearing up for a violent contest.[32]

Fort Sumter had an immediate clarifying effect, highlighting the fault line and subordinating internal arguments. Both societies rallied around their respective flags, joined and exhorted by the clergy. Immediately fol-lowing Fort Sumter, Arkansas, North Carolina, Tennessee and Virginia, where secession had been most contentious, joined the Confederacy; Lincoln raised an army; war fever spread; and volunteerism bloomed north and south. The public and general media on both sides demanded action.[33] As Gerald Linderman notes:

> The South's terrible willingness to open fire on Fort Sumter and Abraham Lincoln's outrageous call for troops to be turned against the people of the South were actions so dramatic as to erase from the consciousness on either side any cognisance of antecedent moves and responses leading to them, and particularly of one's own side's contributions to the sequence.[34]

In other words, the war simply became a self-righteous fact, no questions asked.

As the war ground on, continued mobilisation and sacrifice required that the fighting spirit be nurtured by infinite certitude and mutual demonisation. Leaders framed the conflict as ideologically total and the threat from their respective rivals as existential.[35] Religion provided a moral shield. This concoction precluded retreat and almost guaranteed escalation.

The first shot and subsequent wagon-circling, flag-rallying and self-entrapping mechanisms drove another important phenomenon that was problematic for Northern strategy: they essentially insulated Southern society from effective Northern communication. Southern emotional predispositions were already distorting Northern messages, affording little appreciation for nuance and complexity. While the Confederacy tolerated internal criticism in the press, *de jure* war powers enabled Southern leadership to diminish receptivity and sensitivity to conciliatory messages and signals, and to internal debate and unrest – for example, through the suspension of habeas corpus.[36]

Frustration felt by leaders, commanders and soldiers was a powerful motivator of escalating violence against Southern civilians, undercutting the goal of post-war reconciliation and amicable reunion.[37] The most salient source of frustration was strategic shortfall. By mid-1862, it became clear that Northern society-oriented conciliatory policies were not panning out, and that major military operations were failing, George B. McClellan's Peninsular Campaign having proved a major debacle.[38] In 1861 and 1862, Congress passed the First and Second Confiscation Acts, which allowed the military to seize property and free slaves, initiating an escalatory process of targeting Southern society at its core. Lincoln had also basically abandoned conciliation by mid-1862, abjuring prosecution of the war 'with elderstalk squirts charged with rosewater'.[39] In the field, growing bitterness following operational defeat drove commanders to target civilians directly and soldiers to pillage, a prime example being Union General Ambrose Burnside's shelling and looting of Fredericksburg.[40]

Unable to pacify areas under their respective commands, two of Lincoln's generals moved way out ahead of Lincoln's emancipation policy and threatened to undermine it. In 1861, unable to control mayhem in Missouri, General John C. Frémont threatened emancipation to motivate slaveowners to stay in line. In 1862, General David Hunter declared blanket emancipation in Florida, Georgia and South Carolina. Border-state politicians and opinion leaders were 'apoplectic'.[41] In this respect, Southern guerrilla activity proved particularly exasperating for generals and small units alike, stimulating counterproductive cycles of collective punishment – burning, killing and banishment.[42] These reactions, and the unauthorised actions of small Union units and individual soldiers seeking retribution, also undermined Lincoln's strategic intent.[43]

By 1863, Northern leaders realised that the Southern people were resiliently arrayed against the Union, responding to neither coercion nor conciliation, while the Southern armies were intent on conducting major offensive actions northward. The Emancipation Proclamation and the enlistment of black soldiers followed.[44] By mid-1864, having tried coercion and conciliation, which failed, Grant, Sherman and Sheridan escalated to brutal military engagements and massive civilian targeting one last time, launching the devastating campaigns of 1864–65.[45]

The very passage of time was crucial to shaping attitudes, emotions, behaviour and strategy. One ramification was the inuring effect of repeated sights and experience, a process that made the unimaginable routine, ratcheting up the bounds of acceptable and expected violence, and enhancing the capacity of both sides to cause and endure pain and suffering. Of the brutalising effect of war Linderman wrote: 'In 1861 everyone assumed that the application of moral values to the struggle would determine both the forms and the results of the war. By 1865, those soldiers who survived had learned otherwise.'[46] Southern civilians experienced similar inurement over time, a process that blunted the effectiveness of Northern coercive measures. Remarkably, civilians in Southern cities enduring protracted siege, bombardment and starvation simply hunkered down into a new dystopian reality. And while their suffering did not expedite surrender, it guaranteed long-term sentiments of victimhood and humiliation.

As the war dragged on, it became divorced from its original motivations and strategies, driven to a large extent by its own internal dynamics. Aaron Sheehan-Dean notes that the 'propulsive demands of military conflict draw participants toward positions they never imagined taking', and that in the Civil War 'hate developed from what they did to each other, not because of who they were'.[47] Hate, in turn, drove a 'sunk cost' mindset that helped keep the war going.[48]

A certain estrangement between soldiers and society also developed over time, despite broad-based conscription and the close contact maintained between soldiers in the field and their communities throughout the war.[49] Armies gradually assumed their own sets of values, cultures and motivations, which to some extent put them at odds with the societies that had sent them to war. In particular, as disillusionment set in among the soldiers, they 'grew to resent unchanging civilian allegiance to the precepts with which the war began'.[50] This dynamic transformed the armies into political actors with the agency required to undermine or support national strategy. In the North, for example, soldiers and units initially reacted violently to the Emancipation Proclamation. By 1864, however, despite tens of thousands of casualties in the Overland Campaign, they had developed a strong allegiance to Lincoln that helped offset his loss of popularity within the Republican Party and among civilian voters.[51] Their support through the ballot box helped confirm Lincoln and Grant's mandate to continue the war to its conclusion.[52]

*　　*　　*

The Civil War demonstrates that in order to engender a strategically desired emotional and behavioural reaction, it is necessary to consider a rival's collective emotional ecosystem, which includes psychological predispositions – long-standing sentiments, ideology, ethos and framing – as well as other emotions already in play. Failing to do so will lead to undesired responses. For example, attempting to induce fear through coercion may engender so much anger and hatred as to stiffen resistance through collective rage, especially if it involves existential societal threat and abject humiliation.[53] In this connection, seeking total victory or unconditional surrender may come at a prohibitively high price. The war also demonstrates the complexity and severe limits of conciliation as a means to engender positive affect in a rival society, as the very same emotional ecosystem may neutralise or drown out its effects.

The war points to a number of discrete emotions that require vigilance, for once induced their effects can become dominant, undercut strategy and elude control. Humiliation stands out as particularly powerful, capable of galvanising violent collective action and lingering as a deep sentiment for decades. Hate can also become a long-lasting sentiment inimical to reconciliation, but even more pernicious is rage, which may be short-lived but can drive extreme collective violence not easily controlled. Also eluding control once in play, universal collective psychological dynamics, such as frustration and time, may undermine one's own strategy and drive unintended reactions and consequences. The Civil War directs us to account for these when formulating strategy and managing conflict.

The development of attitudes and collective emotional dynamics relevant to the Civil War were not confined to the boundaries set by the declaration of war at the beginning and the surrender and cessation of hostilities at the end. The Civil War sprang from practices, beliefs and attitudes that had endured for generations. Thus, the time frame for considering a strategy for societal conflict should reach back much farther than the proximate causes of armed hostilities. The Union's victory in the Civil War came at an exorbitant price that is still being exacted. It follows that the relevant strategic time frame should also extend well beyond the projected course of war and its immediate aftermath. Further to the insight that seeking total victory may be too costly and outright counterproductive, the upshot is that resolving society-centric conflict may call for a strategy that pursues long-term success as distinct from short-term victory. The bottom line here is that in society-centric conflicts it is imperative to devise strategy for a long-term relationship, not for a discrete war in the traditional sense. This is critical for success and is the *sine qua non* of long-term peace and reconciliation.

If society-centric strategy is about engineering emotional and behavioural reactions of a rival society, strategists need to be cognisant of three related limitations that come into play once a hot war begins. Firstly, a rival society tends to simplify its characterisation of hostile action. While the Union tried to create emotional fissures through differential treatment of Southern elites and common people, they all basically saw the Northern challenge as an attack on the South. Factions closed ranks and nuances were unheard or ignored. Secondly, even if fissures somehow emerge within a rival society, national leadership retains tremendous power to persist in war. The Confederacy suffered deep internal discord that rendered entire regions ungovernable, but they did not substantially impede the war effort until very late in the conflict.[54] Thirdly, once war begins a rival society may undergo revolutionary change in its ethos, collective sentiments and framing, as well as in its material capabilities. The South's rapid creation of a highly centralised bureaucratic state, the all-in mobilisation of religion and the sea change in its political economy were truly 'unknown unknowns' that derailed prior Union assessments and seriously undercut its strategy for emotional impact.

More comprehensive and systematic study of society-centric warfare is required. In particular, special effort is warranted to integrate expertise in national security and conflict with knowledge in the field of collective emotions.[55] In the meantime, this preliminary study of the American Civil War offers important lessons for society-centric strategy formulation and management. Taken together, they suggest that society-centric conflict may call for an approach that is more soft and slow than hard and fast. Less intense kinetic interaction and fruitful political conversation could afford space and opportunity to better assess a rival's collective emotional world, monitor its reactions and adjust strategy while avoiding the escalatory and often irreversible dynamics that lengthen war and root hostility which may persist long after the fighting is over.

Acknowledgements

I wish to thank the Woodrow Wilson International Center for Scholars and the MIT Security Studies Program for providing generous fellowships to support my study of society-centric warfare and the American Civil War. In trying to fast-track my way to a passable understanding of the Civil War, I was afforded patient guidance and feedback by several remarkable American historians, in particular James Broomall, Lorien Foote, Jason Phillips, George Rable and Michael Woods, as well as Michelle Krowl at the Library of Congress. Eran Halperin, Roger Petersen, Barry Posen and Stephen Van Evera provided critical input and feedback on emerging ideas and drafts. Finally, I am indebted to Ariel E. Levite. This essay continues to develop ideas and explore a path that we have staked out and navigated in concert over recent years.

Notes

1   This is not to argue that these challengers, including China and Russia, are infallible and never err in their strategic formulations and execution, for they too can and do get their society-centric strategies wrong. Hizbullah, for example, paid an enormous price for totally misreading Israel's likely response in 2006. And though too early to call or truly comprehend, the current Russian war of conquest and repression in Ukraine may turn out to have been a gross strategic error on Russia's part, based on a failure to correctly read Ukrainian society, Western societies and perhaps even its own. However, the overall record of recent decades is concerning and surely demands attention and consideration. For earlier discussions of society-centric warfare, see Ariel E. Levite and Jonathan (Yoni) Shimshoni, 'The Strategic Challenge of Society-centric Warfare', *Survival*, vol. 60, no. 6, December 2018–January 2019, pp. 91–118; and Jonathan (Yoni) Shimshoni and Ariel (Eli) Levite, 'Contemporary Society-centric Warfare: Lessons from the Israeli Experience', IRSEM, Report No. 69, September 2019, https://www.irsem.fr/data/files/irsem/documents/document/file/3206/Report%20No69%20Contemporary%20Society-centric%20Warfare%20Insights%20from%20the%20Israeli%20Experience.pdf.

2   Society-centric conflict naturally involves at least two societies, one's rival but also one's own, and may also involve third parties. To be fully successful, a society-centric strategy should address all of these. This article addresses the challenge of impacting a rival's society.

3   See Eran Halperin, *Emotions in Conflict: Inhibitors and Facilitators of Peace Making* (Abingdon: Routledge, 2016), Kindle file. The approach also draws on Roger D. Petersen, *Western Intervention in the Balkans: The Strategic Use of Emotion in Conflict* (Cambridge: Cambridge University Press, 2011). See also Daniel Bar-Tal, *Intractable Conflicts: Socio-psychological*

Foundations and Dynamics (Cambridge: Cambridge University Press, 2013). My notion of 'psychological predispositions' is similar to Bar-Tal's concept of 'socio-psychological infrastructure'.

4   Though touched on in many studies of the Civil War, the conflict from the explicit perspective of emotions has received only limited consideration. Examples include Robert E. Bonner, *Colors and Blood: Flag Passions of the Confederate South* (Princeton, NJ: Princeton University Press, 2002); James J. Broomall, *Private Confederacies: The Emotional Worlds of Southern Men as Citizens and Soldiers* (Chapel Hill, NC: University of North Carolina Press, 2019); and Michael Woods, *Emotional and Sectional Conflict in the Antebellum United States* (Cambridge: Cambridge University Press, 2014).

5   For purposes of this article, I present a somewhat stylised and 'broad-brush' periodisation of Union strategy. In practice, strategy developed with temporally overlapping policies and geographic variance.

6   See Daniel W. Crofts, *Lincoln and the Politics of Slavery: The Other Thirteenth Amendment and the Struggle to Save the Union* (Chapel Hill, NC: University of North Carolina Press, 2016), p. 91; Harold Holzer, *Lincoln and the Power of the Press* (New York: Simon & Schuster, 2014), pp. 260-1; and James McPherson, *Battle Cry of Freedom: The Civil War Era* (Oxford: Oxford University Press, 1988), pp. 231–2, 262–3.

7   See Mark Grimsley, *The Hard Hand of War: Union Military Policy Toward Southern Civilians* (Cambridge: Cambridge University Press, 1995),

chapters 1 and 2.

8   On the Emancipation Proclamation's turning the conflict into a truly revolutionary war and a 'conflict of societies', see Eric Foner, *A Short History of Reconstruction, 1863–1877* (New York: Harper Perennial, 2014), pp. 1, 3.

9   Note that the proclamation together with black enlistment did create a threatening and unsettling environment for the border states, in particular Kentucky, but by mid-1862 the threat of border-state defection had diminished substantially. See James Oakes, *Freedom National: The Destruction of Slavery in the United States, 1861–1865* (New York: W. W. Norton & Co., 2013), Kindle file, chapter 10.

10   Mark Grimsley argues that direct violent action against Southern civilians was not initially applied as a blunt tool to beat Southern society writ large into submission. Rather, it was to be applied in a 'pragmatic' manner, as necessary for military operations. See Grimsley, *The Hard Hand of War*, pp. 3–4 and chapter 5.

11   See Joan E. Cashin, *War Stuff: The Struggle for Human and Environmental Resources in the American Civil War* (Cambridge: Cambridge University Press, 2018), pp. 68–75; and Howard M. Hensel, *The Sword of the Union: Federal Objectives and Strategies During the American Civil War*, USAF Air Command and Staff College Military History Series 87-1 (Ann Arbor, MI: University of Michigan Press, 1989), chapter 4 and conclusion.

12   Foraging was also a mechanism to strengthen unionists by targeting

secessionists' properties. See Grimsley, *The Hard Hand of War*, pp. 100–2, 144. On Southern women as targets and in defiance, see Stephanie McCurry, *Confederate Reckoning: Power and Politics in the Civil War South* (Cambridge, MA: Harvard University Press, 2010), pp. 104–16; and Aaron Sheehan-Dean, *The Calculus of Violence: How Americans Fought the Civil War* (Cambridge, MA: Harvard University Press, 2018), pp. 111–14. On violence towards civilians, including a discussion of the Lieber Code, see Sheehan-Dean, *The Calculus of Violence*, chapter 5. Examples include the brutal and extended siege of Vicksburg, the ransacking and burning of Fredericksburg and General Charles Ewing's banishment of some 20,000 people in Missouri.

13 This effect of Northern strategy and operations was amplified by Confederate mismanagement in various arenas, such as commerce, taxation and agriculture.

14 Grimsley, *The Hard Hand of War*, p. 213.

15 In coaxing the surrender of General Joseph E. Johnston in North Carolina, Sherman overstepped the boundaries of his authority and of conciliation intended by the US government. See Jay Winik, *April 1865: The Month that Saved America* (New York: Harper, 2006), chapter 4 and pp. 293–7.

16 Grant wrote after the war that had the fighting been prolonged another year, the North 'might have abandoned the contest and agreed to separation'. Quoted in Russell F. Weigley, *The American Way of War: A History of United States Military Strategy and Policy* (New York: Macmillan, 1973), p. 128.

Jay Winik notes that by summer 1864, Northerners 'had grown weary of the war' and that 'in truth, the northern home front had nearly crumbled first'. Winik, *April 1865*, p. 153.

17 While white Southern men continued political and physical acts of defiance and violent racial domination through the Ku Klux Klan and similar organisations, white Southern women who had borne the brunt of society-wide suffering, dislocation and humiliation played a key role in perpetuating the emotional and ideological flame through such organisations as the Ladies' Memorial Associations and, later, the United Daughters of the Confederacy.

18 On Southern visions of America, see Mathew Pratt Guterl, *American Mediterranean: Southern Slaveholders in the Age of Emancipation* (Cambridge, MA: Harvard University Press, 2008); and McPherson, *Battle Cry of Freedom*, pp. 103–16. On the importance to both sections of western expansion, see Gary W. Gallagher, *The Union War* (Cambridge, MA: Harvard University Press, 2011), p. 79; and Megan Kate Nelson, *The Three-cornered War: The Union, the Confederacy, and Native Peoples in the Fight for the West* (New York: Scribner, 2020). On the economic imperative of Southern expansion westward, see Reid Mitchell, *Civil War Soldiers* (New York: Viking, 1988), p. 8. On the role and impact of jealousy in the South, see Woods, *Emotional and Sectional Conflict in the Antebellum United States*, chapters 3 and 6.

19 Joan Cashin notes that, in the elections of 1860, some 40% of Southerners voted against secession. See Cashin,

War Stuff, pp. 5, 28; and McCurry, *Confederate Reckoning*, chapter 2. On the difficult road to secession and establishing a unified Confederate state, see Emory M. Thomas, *The Confederate Nation, 1861–1865* (New York: Harper Perennial, 2011), chapter 3.

20 See Anne E. Marshall, *Creating a Confederate Kentucky: The Lost Cause and Civil War Memory in a Border State* (Chapel Hill, NC: University of North Carolina Press, 2010), p. 10; and Oakes, *Freedom National*, chapter 2.

21 James Broomall and George Rable have suggested that similarities and common heritage actually inhibited Northerners from seeking and identifying differences and unique attributes in each group.

22 On the rapid rise and intensive activities of Southern 'cultural nationalists', see Michael T. Bernath, *Confederate Minds: The Struggle for Intellectual Independence in the Civil War South* (Chapel Hill, NC: University of North Carolina Press, 2010). On the role of literature on both sides, see Alice Fahs, *The Imagined Civil War: Popular Literature of the North & South, 1861–1865* (Chapel Hill, NC: University of North Carolina Press, 2001). On the use of song, see Coleman Hutchison, *Apples and Ashes: Literature, Nationalism, and the Confederate States of America* (Athens, GA: University of Georgia Press, 2012), chapter 4. On the use and role of flags, see Bonner, *Colors and Blood*.

23 This discussion of the role of religion is based mostly on George C. Rable, *God's Almost Chosen Peoples: A Religious History of the American Civil War* (Chapel Hill, NC: University of North

Carolina Press, 2010); and Harry S. Stout, *Upon the Altar of the Nation: A Moral History of the Civil War* (New York: Penguin, 2007), Kindle file. The developments described here characterised both sections, though religion played a much more significant role in the Confederacy.

24 Jason Phillips, *Diehard Rebels: The Confederate Culture of Invincibility* (Athens, GA: University of Georgia Press, 2007), p. 10. On religion's role in extending the war, see Rable, *God's Almost Chosen Peoples*, p. 8. Of course, movements for compromise arose in both sections, in particular the Copperheads or Peace Democrats in the North and peace movements in North Carolina and other states in the South. Especially in the South, these never developed critical mass.

25 Stout, *Upon the Altar of the Nation*, chapter 3.

26 Though not a subject of this article, the contribution of Confederate mismanagement of domestic strategy to the erosion of internal resilience is critical to a complete understanding of the war's conduct. See Douglas B. Ball, *Financial Failure and Confederate Defeat* (Chicago, IL: University of Illinois Press, 1991); R. Douglas Hurt, *Agriculture and the Confederacy: Policy, Productivity, and Power in the Civil War South* (Chapel Hill, NC: University of North Carolina Press, 2015); and Daniel E. Sutherland, 'Guerrilla Warfare, Democracy, and the Fate of the Confederacy', *Journal of Southern History*, vol. 68, no. 2, May 2002, pp. 259–92. For a vivid portrayal of internal disintegration, see Lorien Foote, *The Yankee Plague: Escaped Union Prisoners*

and the Collapse of the Confederacy (Chapel Hill, NC: University of North Carolina Press, 2016).

27 The immediate counterproductive impact of humiliating action is illustrated well by the galvanised reaction of Southerners to General Benjamin Butler's 'Woman's Order' in New Orleans. See Amanda Foreman, *A World on Fire: Britain's Crucial Role in the American Civil War* (New York: Random House, 2010), p. 250. For a discussion of the various drivers of Southern humiliation, see Megan Kate Nelson, *Ruin Nation: Destruction and the American Civil War* (Athens, GA: University of Georgia Press, 2012). Nelson refers to sieges, domestic ruination and pillage, and most importantly the violation of private space (particularly 'gendered confrontations') as prime instigators of long-term memory and humiliation.

28 See Claudia D. Goldin and Frank D. Lewis, 'The Economic Cost of the American Civil War: Estimates and Implications', *Journal of Economic History*, vol. 35, no. 2, June 1975, pp. 299–326; Wayne Hsieh, 'The Strategy of Lincoln and Grant', in Williamson Murray and Richard Hart Sinnreich (eds), *Successful Strategies: Triumphing in War and Peace from Antiquity to the Present* (Cambridge: Cambridge University Press, 2014), p. 194; McPherson, *Battle Cry of Freedom*, pp. 91–100; and Mark G. Schmeller, *Invisible Sovereign: Imagining Public Opinion from the Revolution to Reconstruction* (Baltimore, MD: Johns Hopkins University Press, 2016), p. 159.

29 See Richard Franklin Bensel, *Yankee Leviathan: The Origins of Central State Authority in America, 1859–1877* (Cambridge: Cambridge University Press, 1990), pp. 97–8, 193; Michael Brem Bonner, *Confederate Political Economy: Creating and Managing a Southern Corporatist Nation* (Baton Rouge, LA: Louisiana State University Press, 2016); John Majewski, *Modernizing a Slave Economy: The Economic Vision of the Confederate Nation* (Chapel Hill, NC: University of North Carolina Press, 2009), chapter 5; McCurry, *Confederate Reckoning*, pp. 153–6; and Thomas, *Confederate Nation*, chapters 7 and 9.

30 On innovation and efforts in ordnance manufacturing, see James M. McPherson, *Embattled Rebel: Jefferson Davis as Commander in Chief* (New York: Penguin, 2014), pp. 163–4. Weigley argues that Confederate shortages did not determine a single Southern defeat in battle. See Weigley, *The American Way of War*, p. 132. See also Williamson Murray and Wayne Wei-siang Hsieh, *A Savage War: A Military History of the Civil War* (Princeton, NJ: Princeton University Press, 2016), p. 49.

31 Michael Woods has suggested that years of Northern criticism of slavery for its production of an economically backward, politically repressive and socially stratified society led to widely held and inaccurate assumptions about the Confederacy's inherent weaknesses.

32 Tellingly, the Union did not respond in kind to the pre-Fort Sumter mobilisation of a large Confederate army of some 100,000 soldiers. On the divergent interests and positions of states of the Upper South as opposed to the

lower states, see Majewski, *Modernizing a Slave Economy*, pp. 120–1.

33 One could argue that for Jefferson Davis, the firing on Fort Sumter was a purposeful move, and that he understood, foresaw and welcomed at least some aspects of the resulting dynamics, in particular the consolidation of a critical mass of seceding states. On Northern media and public pressure, see Holzer, *Lincoln and the Power of the Press*, pp. 304–5, 314; and Hsieh, 'The Strategy of Lincoln and Grant', p. 196. On Southern motivation to open fire, see Richard N. Current, 'The Confederates and the First Shot', *Civil War History*, vol. 7, no. 4, December 1961, pp. 357–69. On the pressures that pushed Lincoln to premature engagement at Bull Run, see Foreman, *A World on Fire*, pp. 123–4.

34 Gerald F. Linderman, *Embattled Courage: The Experience of Combat in the American Civil War* (New York: Free Press, 1987), pp. 80–1.

35 On the dynamics of demonisation, see George C. Rable, *Damn Yankees: Demonization & Defiance in the Confederate South* (Baton Rouge, LA: Louisiana State University Press, 2015). For a Northern perspective, see Edward J. Blum, '"The First Secessionist Was Satan": Secession and the Religious Politics of Evil in Civil War America', *Civil War History*, vol. 60, no. 3, September 2014, pp. 234–69.

36 Interestingly, the Confederacy did not resort to strong control of the press. Propaganda, support for the regime and suppression of internal opposition were pervasive and spontaneous, generated through local provost marshals, guerrillas, the press and the clergy.

The Confederacy did resort to various internal measures, such as suspension of habeas corpus. See McPherson, *Embattled Rebel*, p. 74.

37 This section owes much to Alexander B. Downes, *Targeting Civilians in War* (Ithaca, NY: Cornell University Press, 2008). Downes uses the term 'desperation'. I've chosen 'frustration' to suggest that a lower emotional threshold may suffice to drive targeting of civilians.

38 See Elizabeth R. Varon, *Armies of Deliverance: A New History of the Civil War* (Oxford: Oxford University Press, 2019), pp. 34–5.

39 Quoted in Grimsley, *The Hard Hand of War*, p. 87. Lincoln was pushed in this direction by his concern for political support for the war, a process in line with Downes's account of the heightened propensity in democratic states to escalate civilian targeting. See also Oakes, *Freedom National*, chapter 7.

40 See Linderman, *Embattled Courage*, p. 193; and Sheehan-Dean, *The Calculus of Violence*, pp. 126–31.

41 Varon, *Armies of Deliverance*, pp. 40–2, 108. In both cases, Lincoln acted quickly to neutralise the political and strategic damage. He sacked Frémont, and revoked Hunter's edict and reprimanded him. See also Daniel E. Sutherland, *A Savage Conflict: The Decisive Role of Guerrillas in the American Civil War* (Chapel Hill, NC: University of North Carolina Press, 2009), pp. 23–4.

42 See Grimsley, *The Hard Hand of War*, pp. 118–19; Mitchell, *Civil War Soldiers*, pp. 134–6; Sutherland, *A Savage Conflict*, p. 254; and Varon, *Armies of Deliverance*, pp. 294–5.

43 See Linderman, *Embattled Courage*, p. 196. Mark Grimsley's descriptions of the impact of one unit's behaviour in North Carolina, difficulties in controlling soldiers' foraging behaviour in the west and rank-and-file anti-civilian escalation in Jackson, Mississippi, are illustrative. See Grimsley, *The Hard Hand of War*, pp. 60–1, 98–104, 160. On how plundering undermined attempts to wage limited war, see Varon, *Armies of Deliverance*, pp. 97–8. On Union soldiers' inability to adhere to a conciliatory approach in northwest Virginia, see Sutherland, *A Savage Conflict*, chapter 2.

44 On the importance of black conscription to the Union order of battle, see Hsieh, 'The Strategy of Lincoln and Grant', p. 193. On extreme Southern reactions of frustration, humiliation and rage, leading to massacres of black troops, see Wayne E. Lee, *Barbarians and Brothers: Anglo-American Warfare, 1500–1865* (Oxford: Oxford University Press, 2011), pp. 237–41; and Rable, *Damn Yankees*, pp. 90–3, 111–12.

45 See Grimsley, *The Hard Hand of War*, pp. 162–3 and chapter 9. Strategic reasoning – including consideration of British attitudes – drove Lincoln to delay instituting the Emancipation Proclamation until he could show a significant battlefield success and thus avoid the perception that he was acting out of weakness and frustration. The Battle of Antietam in autumn 1862 provided just enough Union victory for the purpose.

46 Linderman, *Embattled Courage*, p. 3. For a general discussion of these effects, see *ibid.*, chapters 10 and 12.

On callousness growing with time, see Grimsley, *The Hard Hand of War*, p. 107. See also Mitchell, *Civil War Soldiers*, p. 64; and Phillips, *Diehard Rebels*, p. 87.

47 Sheehan-Dean, *The Calculus of Violence*, p. 72. See also Rable, *Damn Yankees*, p. 100.

48 See Gallagher, *The Union War*, p. 107.

49 The eastern Union armies daily received 45,000 letters and the western armies 90,000. Linderman, *Embattled Courage*, p. 94.

50 *Ibid.*, pp. 216–17. See also *ibid.*, chapter 11; Mitchell, *Civil War Soldiers*, pp. 38, 64–5; and Phillips, *Diehard Rebels*, p. 88.

51 Northern society was also willing to endure tens of thousands of casualties in a matter of weeks. This would not likely have been the case three years earlier.

52 This is not to say that the soldiers' vote determined the election results. But soldiers were significantly more supportive than civilians of the president and pro-Lincoln senators and representatives in several states, and, in Maryland, of the abolition of slavery. See McPherson, *Battle Cry of Freedom*, pp. 803–5.

53 For an analysis of rage, the drive for revenge and the impetus to wage war when it is otherwise irrational, see Rose McDermott, Anthony C. Lopez and Peter K. Hatemi, '"Blunt Not the Heart, Enrage It": The Psychology of Revenge and Deterrence', *Texas National Security Review*, vol. 1, no. 1, December 2017, https://tnsr.org/2017/11/blunt-not-heart-enrage-psychology-revenge-deterrence/.

54 Fissures developed along unexpected lines with implications for

Southern social cohesion. Through war Southern women arguably developed significant agency – to the point, argues Drew Gilpin Faust, that their ultimate withdrawal of support for the war doomed the Confederacy. It is not clear that, in all situations, leadership can continue despite internal strife. See Drew Gilpin Faust, 'Altars of Sacrifice: Confederate Women and the Narratives of War', *Journal of American History*, vol. 76, no. 4, March 1990, pp. 1,200–28; and McCurry, *Confederate Reckoning*.

55 On this point, see Halperin, *Emotions in Conflict*, p. 180.

Copyright © 2022 The International Institute for Strategic Studies

Review Essay

The End of the West?

Russell Crandall and Frederick Richardson

The Abandonment of the West: The History of an Idea in American Foreign Policy
Michael Kimmage. New York: Basic Books, 2020. $32.00. 384 pp.

In 1918, German historian Oswald Spengler published the first volume of *The Decline of the West*, in which he predicted the rise of Russia and the gradual decline of the West. Among those who rejected Spengler's thesis was University of Chicago history professor William H. McNeill, whose ambitious *The Rise of the West* (1963) covered thousands of years of Western history and concluded that the West – far from being in decline – was amid a 'great age' in which technology and reason were flourishing. However, published the very next year was James Burnham's *Suicide of the West* (1964), in which the conservative academic lambasted American liberalism and called for a return to 'Western' values. Burnham warned of a new enemy in the form of the American left, whose disdain of Western culture would, in his view, lead to the West's 'suicide'. With the cultural centre of Europe and its progeny in the United States cast adrift at the time, Burnham predicted that the unifying concept of 'the West' in American foreign policy would be replaced by a vague internationalism, and that the United States would likely lose the Cold War.

Russell Crandall is a professor of American foreign policy and international politics at Davidson College in North Carolina, and a contributing editor to *Survival*. His latest books are *Drugs and Thugs: The History and Future of America's War on Drugs* (Yale University Press, 2020) and, with Britta Crandall, *"Our Hemisphere"?: The United States in Latin American, from 1776 to the Twenty-first Century* (Yale University Press, 2021). **Frederick Richardson** is a master's student at Johns Hopkins University's School of Advanced International Studies (SAIS).

Survival | vol. 64 no. 2 | April–May 2022 | pp. 167–178   https://doi.org/10.1080/00396338.2022.2055833

History professor Michael Kimmage's *The Abandonment of the West* adds to these ruminations. Placing the idea of 'the West' under the lens of American culture and foreign policy, Kimmage highlights the importance of the crossroads at which America currently finds itself. Noting that the ability of Western institutions such as NATO and the European Union to act in an effective and unified manner is being called into question, while Americans re-evaluate their relationship with Western history and culture, Kimmage considers the concept of the West key to explaining the trajectory of American foreign policy. The author judiciously prefaces his study by acknowledging the challenge of defining 'the West': 'the label [Western] is so ubiquitous in the discussion of history, politics, culture, art, literature, philosophy and international affairs because it is so obligingly imprecise'

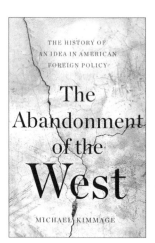

(p. 14). Consequently, he explains, the term has taken on simultaneous and often contradictory meanings; the domineering West of Edward Said's writings is starkly different from the heroic West of Ronald Reagan's speeches. Conscious of these difficulties, Kimmage adopts a narrower definition of a West that is 'embedded in a Euro-American narrative of self-government and liberty, a history of liberty, a project of building liberty, a future-oriented heritage of liberty' (p. 14). Throughout *The Abandonment of the West*, the author ties this idea of the West to American foreign policy, exploring how America's relationship with the West has changed over the centuries and documenting the United States' gradual drift from a Western-focused foreign policy. The result is a thought-provoking, innovative work that poses important questions about the future of American foreign policy.

'Columbian Republic'

Kimmage begins with the 1893 World's Columbian Exposition, which marked the 400th anniversary of Christopher Columbus's landing in the Americas. Set in motion by an act of Congress, the exposition featured replicas of the ships *Niña, Pinta* and *Santa Maria*; a statue of the explorer atop a chariot; and grand buildings designed in neoclassical style. As Kimmage points out, the fair was as much a nod to empire as it was a celebration of Western civilisation, but it also signified the Europhilia that had overtaken American institutions, particularly universities. With the Classics ingrained in many higher-education curriculums, students learned about the history of their civilisation and distilled essential truths from the ancients, including how to 'hold power in the right way' (p. 39). These lessons were not confined to the classroom: the architecture of the US Capitol, American universities (such as Columbia), and statues, archways and libraries across the country were also erected in the style of classical antiquity.

That first chapter is aptly titled 'The Columbian Republic, 1893–1919', establishing Kimmage's proclivity for examining the interplay between culture, power and policy. As he eloquently puts it later, 'culture and politics combine into story. The story evolves, and the story changes' (p. 322). In his estimation, the World's Columbian Exposition was just one 'appropriation of a classical past and of contemporary European idioms' through which the 'turn-of-the-century United States alluded to participation in a broadly European future' (p. 32). In laying its claim to antiquity, the US Romanised its origin story and moved itself closer to the European continent, its supposed progenitor.

America's Europeanisation could be problematic, especially in foreign policy. The relatively young United States' pursuit of empire alongside Europe through the 1898 Spanish–American War was hard to reconcile with America's past: while the United States had achieved independence from Britain, it was now ruling over Cuba and the Philippines. This contradiction was resolved by reframing imperialism as a civilising mission, in which the United States and Europe were responsible for 'beating back the black chaos of savagery and barbarism and eventually with translating barbarism into civilization' (p. 58). The US government used this justification in imitating its European counterparts despite the reaction of some Americans such as W.E.B. Du Bois, who fiercely attacked US imperialism in his 1903 *The Souls of Black Folk*. Everything changed with the First World War, when the Europe that had served as the blueprint for the 'Columbian Republic' became fractured and a political 'house of cards' (p. 66). The allure of participating in European imperialism had faded, and the next generation would chart a new course for American foreign policy.

Kimmage's second chapter, 'The Case for the West, 1919–1945', explores the interwar years and the later conflict between Western ideals and fascism and communism. Britain, France and the United States considered themselves the heirs to classical antiquity, and embraced Latin, Greek and the Enlightenment. Furthermore, 'they saw themselves as Western because they had inherited a practical understanding and a traditional love of liberty' (p. 72). But Adolf Hitler and Benito Mussolini also viewed their projects as descending from classical antiquity, as demonstrated by their obsession with classical architecture, European purity and painting themselves as contemporary Caesars. Their fascist version of the West was very different from the Anglo-Franco-American idea of liberty and freedom, and the resulting war was framed in terms of saving the West 'from the rabble-rousing totalitarian imposters' (p. 75). The West was also under threat from the Soviet project, which, despite rejecting capitalism, religion and personal liberty, still held some appeal with Europe's left. Karl Marx was born in the heart of Europe, and Leon Trotsky was well versed in the intellectual foundations of the West. Soviet architect Boris Iofan referenced Rome in his replanning of Moscow, while Pablo Picasso and Ernest Hemingway became cultural icons of France's left-wing Popular Front in the 1930s. Although the United States would come to see itself as the guardian of the West, it did not have a monopoly on Western culture.

President Franklin D. Roosevelt's upbringing and education gave him a particular admiration for Britain, which reinforced his strategic inclination to aid the country even before the United States' formal entry into the war after Japan attacked Pearl Harbor and Germany declared war on the United States. But while Germany and Italy were still part of 'the West', Japan was not. Its strike on Pearl Harbor constituted an attack on the West, one that would not go unpunished in the Pacific theatre. In Kimmage's view, the exacerbation of pre-existing American anti-Asian sentiment caused by the attack was reflected in the intensity of the United States' campaign in the Pacific theatre, along with its internment of around 110,000 Japanese

Americans (many of whom were US citizens). As in the American Indian Wars, racial bias influenced the treatment of the enemy such that Japan in the East suffered greater punishment than Germany in the West.

The Cold War years

After the Second World War, the new challenge for America was fighting the Soviet threat, and, once again, the solution was to marshal the Western ideals ingrained in the foreign policy of Thomas Jefferson and Woodrow Wilson. As Kimmage notes, Harry S. Truman and his advisers 'saw the United States as ordained to play a special role at mid-century, a messianic country tasked with remaking Europe and articulating the ideas around which historical change would unfold' (p. 121). Supporting Europe was key to defending the West against communism. With Europe lying in ruins, the United States thus became the steward of the West and assumed responsibility for countering Soviet incursions. Breaking with the tradition of avoiding European affairs, the US committed resources to its reconstruction and defence. To secure Congress's approval of the Marshall Plan, George C. Marshall, as secretary of state, invoked the idea of a civilisational battle in which Western liberty was pitted against the communist threat. The successful execution of the plan and the creation of NATO not only rejuvenated war-torn Europe but also strengthened transatlantic bonds. Now, the United States was not only the progeny of Europe but also its caretaker. Through its policy of containment, the United States fought wars globally in part to keep the European centre secure. As Dean Acheson, Truman's second secretary of state, noted, the battle lines between East and West might have been firmly established, but if the Soviets took an inch elsewhere, they could be empowered to expand in Europe.

In the third chapter, Kimmage documents the United States' ascendancy to the world stage. With the Truman Doctrine committing the US to the West's defence, Dwight D. Eisenhower's election in 1952 solidified the internationalist vein of American foreign policy. Eisenhower, flanked by the Dulles brothers, engaged the Soviet Union in a shadow war, combining covert action with foreign policy. As Kimmage observes, the cultural component of the war was integral to the conflict. The CIA secretly funded intellectuals and artists to try to win the hearts and minds of left-leaning Europeans. Cultural ties between the United States and Europe were also strengthened by the arrival of so-called 'refugee scholars' who had fled Germany; among them were Hannah Arendt and Leo Strauss, who incorporated ancient thought into modern political philosophy. But in fighting the Cold War, weapons and ideas were not enough. Fragile, underdeveloped countries were fertile environments for communist infiltration, so the United States also chose to assert the West's economic superiority. President John F. Kennedy appointed Walt Rostow as his director of policy planning at the State Department. Rostow, who had published *The Stages of Economic Growth: A Non-Communist Manifesto* in 1960, was a firm believer in the West's power to develop the Third World, seeing no reason that the rest of the world could not follow the West's successful model. The aim of Kennedy's foreign policy was to be more cosmopolitan, not only defending the West against communism but also, through the work of the Peace Corps and other organisations such as USAID, developing the rest of the world and thus bringing unaligned countries into the Western fold. The Bay of Pigs invasion and the Vietnam War compromised these ambitions, but the Kennedy administration did project not only American leadership in the West but also Western leadership across the world.

A beacon of liberty?

In the second part of the book, 'The Abandonment of the West', Kimmage traces the decline of the United States' pre-eminence. He begins with Malcolm X's observation in Washington DC that the neoclassical grandeur of the capital was juxtaposed with the neglected neighbourhoods just minutes away. The US Capitol was a microcosm of the country: behind the Europeanised legend of the United States lay an ugly past that complicated its origin story. America was not just Anglo-Saxon; it was also Irish, African, Asian and Indian, to name a few of many lineages. Kimmage asks, 'what was the relationship between the West, the neoclassical heritage, the alleged European patrimony of the United States and patterns of exclusion and prejudice in American life?' (p. 160).

Questions such as these gained greater importance as the twin shocks of the Civil Rights Movement and the Vietnam War cast doubt on the behaviour of the United States both at home and abroad. While decision-makers in Washington continued to adopt a Western-centred foreign policy, the universities that provided expertise to the government began to encounter resistance to their Western-focused curriculum. As Kimmage observes, 'universities were proudly beholden to the responsibilities of the West', but student bodies increasingly agitated against the Vietnam War and other perceived excesses of Cold War policy.

Moreover, many black Americans felt culturally isolated at such institutions owing to their focus on Western-orientated American history. The author describes the experience of African-American writer James Baldwin, who said he did not learn his own history but rather one that was imposed on him through the works of Aristotle, J.S. Bach, Rembrandt and William Shakespeare. Growing domestic activism against racism in the United States became a global political liability, as notable figures such as Louis Armstrong and Du Bois used their international platforms to draw attention to the discrimination in America – the former by cancelling a US-sponsored tour to the Soviet Union, and the latter by meeting with Chinese leader Mao Zedong and relocating to Ghana. Martin Luther King observed how young African-American men were sent to purportedly prop up democracy in Vietnam, yet were denied their constitutional rights at home. King and other black leaders such as Malcolm X and professional boxer Muhammad Ali were quick to point out the hypocrisy: how could the country be a beacon of freedom across the world when many of its own citizens were subject to racism? Such criticism both shaped and hindered the government's Cold War policies.

The Nixon and Ford administrations displayed substantial pragmatism in their respective foreign policies, primarily attributable to then-secretary of state Henry Kissinger. With trips to China, both Nixon and Ford gained leverage during the Cold War, but the loss in Vietnam and spread of communism in Africa and Latin America represented the 'semi-decline' of the West (p. 223). Against that trend, the neo-conservative movement – comprising former liberals who had abandoned the left – was gaining influence, with the magazine *Commentary* reminding Americans that 'the Soviet Union was an interventionist tyranny, and the United States was an arsenal of democracy' (p. 224). Through this lens, America still represented a beacon of liberty. If Richard Nixon seemed to have forgotten the American mission of projecting freedom across the world, neo-conservatives inspired Eastern European intellectuals such as Vaclav Havel and Adam Michnik, who had experienced the brutality of communism first-hand, to affirm that in the United States 'they still saw liberty in practice rather than a disturbing source of foreign-policy hubris, prejudice and error'. Reagan, a reader of *Commentary*, viewed communism as the principal enemy. Having witnessed anti-war protests while serving as governor of California, he believed the left intended to undermine US goals abroad. In Reagan's view, 'for the West to win the contest, Berkeley' – the California university campus famous for student demonstrations – 'would have to be defeated' (p. 227). The enervating trials of the Carter administration – including the Iranian hostage crisis, the energy crisis and the invasion of Afghanistan – only reinforced the views of the neo-conservatives.

The Reagan presidency represented a resurgence of the West, or at least Reagan's Judeo-Christian, capitalist version of it. He and British prime minister Margaret Thatcher saw themselves as a modern-day Roosevelt and Winston Churchill, respectively, working together to uphold Western values while pressuring the Soviet Union. Reagan believed the ageing USSR would not be able to defeat the West, with its free markets and religion, and 'honored the conservative movement by decrying stasis in the Cold War, having inherited a Cold War that he wanted to revolutionize, a Cold War stalled by Nixon's baby steps and Carter's malaise' (p. 229). Through aggressive military spending and covert operations, Reagan sought to roll back Soviet influence while diplomatically encouraging Soviet leader Mikhail Gorbachev to impose reforms that ended up hastening the Soviet Union's demise from within. In *The End of History and the Last Man* (1992), Francis Fukuyama framed the Soviet collapse and the West's victory in the Cold War in broad civilisational terms, arguing that liberal democracy constituted the culmination of ideological evolution, notwithstanding occasional regressions.

New divisions

Kimmage's final chapter, 'The Post-Columbian Republic, 1992–2016', begins with the planning of the quincentenary of Columbus's arrival in the Americas. McNeill, author of *The Rise of the West*, was part of the commemoration's planning team, but it soon became clear that there would be no grand monument to Columbus and the West like that of 1893, a popular and academic consensus having emerged that called for a halt to the celebration of a man now seen as the initiator of genocide against indigenous peoples. This re-evaluation was not confined to Columbus: the so-called 'culture wars' brought into question much of what had previously been celebrated in American society. As Kimmage notes:

> With culture and politics stalemated, the bipartisan foreign policy that had extended from Pearl Harbor to the assassination of John F. Kennedy was similarly a thing of the past. Reagan's West was already a partisan, conservative West. With the loss of the Soviet Union in 1991, the internal enmities advanced and bipartisanship receded. (p. 252)

In the Clinton and George W. Bush presidencies, Kimmage observes a significant evolution in American politics from some degree of political and ideological polarisation to the wholesale delegitimisation of the opposition. Bill Clinton faced staunch resistance while in office, culminating in his 1998 impeachment, and in 2001 Americans protested Bush's presidential victory following a disputed election. The Iraq War would further polarise the US population, as many questioned Bush's motives for invading the country. Then came Barack Obama, America's first black president, who had to contend with the vitriolic questioning of his citizenship and birthplace that could only be understood in the context of race. But for all its internal divisions, the United States remained the undisputed leader of the West.

For Clinton, Bush and Obama, of course, fighting communism was no longer the preoccupation. All three presidents focused on spreading liberty and self-determination, albeit through different means. But for all their efforts, Kimmage points out that 'from 1992 to 2016, the West was not universalised. The consensus on political economy and international affairs in Washington was supposed to blossom into a global consensus. This never came to pass' (p. 255). The author discusses at length the Iraq War, which he believes damaged the credibility of American leadership both at home and abroad, and tested the transatlantic relationship: 'Whether the United States was constructing an empire of liberty or behaving like an old-school empire lay in the eye of the European beholder' (p. 274). The war might have been fought in the name of democracy, but its aims did not make it just. Obama sought to repair the United States' reputation – for example, by working with the European Union on the Paris climate agreement and the Iran nuclear deal – but atoning for Bush's mistakes was no small task.

The rise of China and the re-emergence of Russia constituted the next challenges for the West. Russia did not (and still does not) abide by the rules of the liberal international order, while China, Kimmage says, was the 'most formidable enemy because it could be construed by some as an attractive alternative to this order. Illiberal China was growing in wealth and international clout, its rise both an affront and a challenge to an American-led liberal international order' (p. 291). Thus, Beijing posed a more credible threat than Moscow: while Vladimir Putin sought to merely undermine the international order, China could potentially displace the West as the global leader.

Alarming threats to the West also arrived in the form of internal divisions. In 2016, the United Kingdom voted to leave the EU, which signalled growing dissatisfaction with the body in other member states as well. Another blow was the 2016 US presidential victory of Donald Trump, who dismissed the international order and the foreign-policy ideals of his predecessors. His rejectionism reflected that of pundit Pat Buchanan, who had long railed against globalism, universalism and lax immigration policies. While criticising Obama, Bush and other internationalist presidents, Trump also managed to awaken America's greatest insecurities about its political foundations, its composition and arguably its very viability.

*   *   *

The Abandonment of the West is a thought-provoking book that exposes the contradictions inherent in the idea of the West while highlighting the reasons that America should not let it slip away. Kimmage does not idealise the West or its history, giving a voice to the many critics of Western civilisation who have pointed out examples of US hypocrisy. However, the West, especially in its heyday, accomplished great things, defeating fascism and countering the spread of communism. Now, as both the left and the right challenge the West, the author reminds us of its complicated legacy while cautioning against its wholesale abandonment. Beyond that, he fosters a better understanding of America's intellectual evolution, as well as the history and future of US foreign policy.

Copyright © 2022 The International Institute for Strategic Studies

Book Reviews

Culture and Society
Jeffrey Mazo

The Great Narrative: For a Better Future
Klaus Schwab and Thierry Malleret. Geneva: Forum Publishing,
2022. £14.99. 253 pp.

The Great Narrative is a sequel of sorts to the authors' *COVID-19: The Great Reset*, reviewed in *Survival* last year (vol. 63, no. 3, June–July 2021). That book identified the pandemic as a historic inflection point, and considered what the post-pandemic world might and should look like. *The Great Narrative* covers some of the same ground, but is mostly about how to actually achieve this more resilient, equitable and sustainable world. In the authors' words, *The Great Narrative* is a 'hybrid between an essay, a manifesto and a light academic précis' (p. 19).

The book rests on the premise – well-founded in the academic literature – that our species is *Homo narrans* as much as *Homo economicus*: 'we think, act and communicate in terms of narratives … Narratives shape our perceptions, which in turn form our realities and end up influencing our choices and actions' (p. 16). The 'Great Narrative' of the title is a central story the authors extract from 'a constellation of interrelated narratives that shed light on what's coming and what to do about it' (p. 17), mostly derived from interviews with 50 global thought leaders from a variety of backgrounds. The book is thus, by design, a broad and synthetic study, and by their nature such studies oversimplify. But the authors manage to thread the needle between the chaos of an interconnected world and a superficial, siloed account of our future.

Like *The Great Reset*, *The Great Narrative* divides global issues into five categories – economics, environment, geopolitics, society and technology – but stresses the complex and non-linear interactions between them. The authors also note that 'everything is happening much faster than it used to … and tends to take us by surprise' (pp. 28–9). Together, this complexity and velocity form the core of their conceptual framework. Klaus Schwab and Thierry Malleret discuss specific policy solutions to many of the trends and concerns they identify, but the theme that emerges as a common driver is one of collaboration, cooperation and hope. 'The first critical step is to replace the dominant narrative that "man is wolf to man" with a paradigm of empathy and sociality, through early education.' This is not, the authors say, 'a sentimental wishy-washy idea, but one grounded in science' (p. 97). But even if practical, this is a long-term solution. The immediate concern is to define and implement a minimum cooperative framework to address critical issues, which requires deep engagement between, especially, the United States and China.

More broadly, the great narrative tells of a world driven by social and local inclusivity; imaginative and innovative thinking; convergence of particular values and moral constructs affecting vital issues; sustainability and resilience; and a shift from shareholder to stakeholder value. Ultimately, the narrative is founded on hope, based on humanity's innate capacity for ingenuity and adapt-ability, the speed of innovation and the role of the younger generation.

These aspirations may seem amorphous, but Schwab and Malleret are certainly correct that the myriad interrelated trends pose dangers, perhaps existential, that cannot be overcome without a radical global transformation, which in turn requires a new, overarching narrative. The question is the extent to which top-down policies and bottom-up innovations, whether deliberate or reactive, can generate this narrative and resulting transformation in an increas-ingly complex and fast-paced world.

The Dawn of Everything: A New History of Humanity
David Graeber and David Wengrow. London: Allen Lane, 2021.
£30.00. 692 pp.

Grand narratives about the past are part of what frames our narratives about the present – and future. In *The Dawn of Everything*, archaeologist David Graeber and anthropologist David Wengrow argue that the two main tradi-tional narratives about human cultural origins and development – Thomas Hobbes's dystopia and Jean-Jacques Rousseau's noble savage – are wrong and reductive, and have dire political implications. Instead, they tell a story in which humanity spent the greater part of the last 40 millennia not stuck in social and cultural stasis but moving back and forth between different forms of social organisation, seasonally or sequentially, repeatedly building up and dismantling hierarchies. In the process, they cover themes such as indigenous peoples' critiques of European institutions and world views; whether social inequality had an 'origin'; the source of private property; the differentiation of cultures; and the origins of agriculture, cities, sovereignty, institutions and states. In many cases, they argue that we have been asking the wrong questions. 'If nothing else', they write, 'surely the time has come to stop the swinging pendulum that has fixated generations of philosophers, historians and social scientists, leading their gaze from Hobbes to Rousseau, from Rousseau to Hobbes and back again' (p. 117).

This framework is implicitly (and sometimes explicitly) presented as a new paradigm that would overturn generations of scholarship and analysis. This is a tall order and, in the end, the authors fall short of the mark. Many of their critiques certainly merit discussion and debate, and may incrementally change our understanding of ourselves and our history, but their grandiose claims are over-ambitious, verging on extravagant. They do not, moreover, offer a coherent grand narrative to replace those they reject: 'this book is simply trying to lay down foundations for a new world history [and] … a quest to discover the right questions' (p. 24). It is a big jump from this to overturning 'whole fields of knowledge – not to mention university chairs and departments, scientific journals, prestigious research grants, libraries, databases, school curricula and the like' (p. 525). A degree of humility might be in order.

This is even more the case because Graeber and Wengrow suffer the same failures they perceive in other writers' views of social and cultural origins and evolution when they stray out of their own areas of expertise into other disciplines, for example mediaeval and early modern European history, or human genetics. Their portrayal of dominant theories and scholarship amounts to a series of almost unrecognisable (to the non-specialist with a certain familiarity with the literature) straw men of their own devising, reducing other scholars' nuanced arguments or interpretations to absurd caricatures which they then call things like 'self-evidently quite absurd' (p. 497). And although they claim to be synthesising recent advances in their respective fields, they are by their own admission in the minority even in their own disciplines, in both interpretation and underlying ideological approach.

The Dawn of Everything is absorbing, detailed, interesting and provocative, but in the end unconvincing. At best, the authors make a good case for a careful reassessment of the conventional wisdom. Such efforts are often a useful reality check. But this book is not that reassessment, nor does it persuade that such an undertaking would end in overthrowing the scholarly consensus or popular understanding. Conventional wisdom is correct more often than not. The pendulum swings, but rarely breaks.

The Nature of Conspiracy Theories
Michael Butter. Sharon Howe, trans. Cambridge: Polity, 2020.
£17.99. 202 pp.

**Red Pill, Blue Pill: How to Counteract the Conspiracy
Theories that Are Killing Us**
David Neiwert. Guilford, CT: Prometheus Books, 2020. $28.95.
232 pp.

German literary and cultural historian Michael Butter's *The Nature of Conspiracy Theories* is a superb complement to Thomas Milan Konda's 2019 *Conspiracies of Conspiracies* (reviewed in *Survival*, vol. 62, no. 3, June–July 2020). Butter's book was, in fact, the earlier, published in German in 2018 as *'Nichts ist, wie es scheint': Über Verschwörungstheorien*. This translation was produced by Sharon Howe, who deserves much credit for its fluid and engaging style. Like Konda's book, Butter's is meticulous and precise, but Butter brings a deep knowledge of non-US conspiracy theories lacking in Konda's US-focused study, and offers a broader definition of conspiracy theories that allows for different insights.

One such insight is that, despite appearances, we are not living in a 'golden age of conspiracy theories' (p. 7); in fact, they were widely accepted and normal until around 1950, when they began to be marginalised and stigmatised. Winston Churchill, for example, believed a single, centuries-old Jewish-led conspiracy lay behind the French and Russian revolutions, with the goal of establishing a global communist state. Abraham Lincoln believed there was an organised conspiracy, including leading political figures, whose goal was to introduce slave-holding across the entire US. Conspiracism began to be delegitimised after the Second World War, first in the academy, as social scientists considered the causes of totalitarianism in Europe, and later as this discussion entered the popular consciousness. By the 1960s the reversal was essentially complete, at least in North America and Europe. What we are seeing now is a third phase, in which conspiracism as a mindset is contested, viewed as 'simultaneously legitimate and illegitimate knowledge' (p. 8).

Butter characterises conspiracy theories as internal or external according to whether the purported conspirators are fellow citizens or foreigners; internal conspiracies can be top-down or bottom-up according to whether the conspirators already hold power or are seeking to obtain it. Recent conspiracy theories tend to be internal and top-down, for example the belief that the US government orchestrated the 9/11 attacks. Theories can be event-based or systemic, the former focusing on specific plots behind events such as 9/11 or suspicious deaths, the latter on particular groups that are seen as the hidden hand behind a whole series of events. Super-conspiracy theories combine the two. What distinguishes theorised from real conspiracies are mostly size and complexity, and a grossly simplified, Manichaean world view. There is an odd dynamic in which some theorists fetishise expertise, or at least its outward trappings, while others reject it as elitist. This is to some degree correlated with the de- and relegitimisation of conspiracism, as well as with the rise of the internet and the popularisation of knowledge and dissemination of ideas. Butter also explores in detail how conspiracy theorists argue and why they believe.

Why does this all matter? In his final chapter, Butter discusses how belief in conspiracies can lead to radicalisation, harassment and violence, make people reject life-saving medical knowledge, and undermine trust in institutions. He cites, but does not analyse in detail, the 1995 Oklahoma City bombing led by Timothy McVeigh; the 2011 Utøya murders in Norway by Anders Breivik; the 2016 murder of British MP Jo Cox; and attacks on synagogues in Halle, Germany (2016), and Pittsburgh, Pennsylvania (2018), and on the Al Noor Mosque in Christchurch, New Zealand (2019). The plot to kidnap, try and execute the governor of Michigan in 2020 and the storming of the US Capitol in 2021 both came after the book was written. The author points out, however, that there are plenty of non-violent conspiracists, and plenty of violent groups in which conspiracism plays no part. Butter nevertheless argues that some conspiracy theories are particularly prone to lead to violence, and all conspiracy theories stand in the way of actually understanding the world. Dialogue with believers in conspiracy theories has proven vain, but improving general levels of critical thinking and literacy in history and the social sciences are, he says, fundamental to any strategy to counter their spread.

David Neiwert's *Red Pill, Blue Pill*, in contrast, is more concerned with individual psychology to help understand why people fall into conspiracism and, crucially, how other people can bring them back from the abyss. The title is a reference to the 1999 film *The Matrix*, in which the main character is offered the choice of a red pill that will free him from the virtual world in which he is trapped, so he can free the rest of humanity, or a blue pill that will return him to this virtual prison. The metaphor has been widely adopted by conspiracy theorists of all stripes, who see themselves as the only ones (other than the conspirators) who understand what is going on, unlike the mass of blue-pilled 'sheeple'.

Neiwert covers some of the same contextual ground as Butter, and indeed Konda, but is less concerned with typologies, history and theory, and more focused on the details of particular acts of violence. He spends about half the book covering in much greater detail than Butter individual cases of conspiracy-fuelled violence, including most of those mentioned by the latter, as well as some others. His prescription is not a blue pill to 'honestly awaken people to an embrace of traditional reality and normative versions of factuality and reason' (p. 146) – he agrees with Butter that this is a pipe dream – but slow, empathic one-on-one engagement with believers, in the knowledge that it will often fail, or even make things worse. Neiwert offers a set of 15 approaches anyone can use in engaging friends or family who have fallen down the rabbit hole, which elaborate practical ways to implement Butter's more general suggested approach. He ends with, again, a more detailed elaboration of the general principles applied at the societal or governmental level. Despite numerous points on which Neiwert and Butter would disagree, their differing approaches are complementary and form a greater whole. The contrast between Butter's well-written but scholarly and Neiwert's journalistic but well-informed styles also means that, even where the books cover the same ground, they never feel repetitive. Along with Konda's 2019 book, they form an essential triptych for understanding conspiracism in the twenty-first century.

Power to the Public: The Promise of Public Interest Technology
Tara Dawson McGuinness and Hana Schank. Princeton, NJ: Princeton University Press, 2021. £14.99/$19.95. 187 pp.

Technology – and specifically information technology (IT) – is more than simply hardware, software or even the two acting in tandem. As IT specialist turned public servant Tara Dawson McGuinness and public servant turned 'tech translator' Hana Schank use the term in *Power to the Public*, technology also comprises the organisational structures, processes and culture required to design and use such tools to collect and analyse the right data to deliver the desired results or goals. The emerging practice of public-interest technology is 'the application of design, data and delivery to advance the public and promote the public good in the digital age' (p. ix).

McGuinness and Schank draw on case studies from governments at all levels, such as individual cities' efforts to deal with the homelessness crisis, US states' public-welfare systems and the digitisation of US immigration to illustrate both best and worst practices. In the recent case of economic relief during the COVID-19 pandemic, they contrast national efforts in the US and Germany to the same end. The pattern that emerges mirrors that of successful profit-driven technology companies such as Amazon or Uber: a focus on customer needs through constant feedback and testing; continuous real-time data collection and analysis to inform decisions and tweak both design and delivery; and starting with small pilot projects to get things working and to improve them before scaling up to massive roll-outs.

One message that comes through loud and clear is that technology is all too often a solution in search of a problem, and one that frequently creates more problems than it solves. Organisations are always succumbing to 'the siren song of the flashiest, sexiest new thing' (p. 72), confusing the tool with the product. Paradoxically, managers and bureaucrats tend to emphasise technology, while engineers and technocrats tend to emphasise problem-solving methods and organisational processes and culture. Sometimes the solution turns out not to be a new app, website or database, but something as simple as adding a line to a form or stapling two forms together so they don't get lost. 'Public interest technology', the authors conclude, 'despite the name, is not about fancy technology' (p. 68). Rather, it is a mindset that considers goals before gadgetry.

Actually changing how organisations, bureaucracies and governments work is a huge task. Public-interest technology is slowly advancing through networking and the power of example. The smaller and simpler the organisation or level of government, the easier this is, but to do more than nibble around the edges will require more. McGuinness and Schank understand the difficulty, and suggest a two-pronged approach: spreading the word about the success stories they discuss in the book, and investing in education, training, recruiting and rewarding the right people. In essence, public service should be made both competitive and cool again. To do this – in effect, to reinvent government – is a worthy but daunting goal. McGuinness and Schank have done their part by showing that public-interest technology can in fact help solve some of the world's most intractable problems, if it can be realised.

Middle East
Ray Takeyh

**Worlds Apart: A Documentary History of US–Iranian
Relations, 1978–2018**
Malcolm Byrne and Kian Byrne. Cambridge and New York:
Cambridge University Press, 2021. £22.99/$29.99. 283 pp.

The documentary record assembled in this book is an important addition to our understanding of how US–Iran relations have evolved over the past four decades. Too often, assumptions are made regarding this important relationship without the necessary archival foundation. The US government must bear its share of blame as it has been too slow in releasing documents. Its declassification rules are too cumbersome and its bureaucracy too sluggish. *Worlds Apart* reflects the paucity of available records, as most of the original documents it presents pertain to the early periods. For the most recent presidencies, it relies on public declarations that are already easily accessible. This is not a criticism of the authors but of the United States' archival administration.

One of the persistent claims made by scholars of Iran is that America missed various opportunities to normalise relations with a willing Iran. Even a casual reading of the documentary record reveals that the story is not so much one of near misses but rather of a fundamental divergence of perspectives between two governments with differing views on the Middle East. The fact is that every US president since the Islamic Revolution hoped to lessen the tensions with Iran and even find some pragmatic accommodation with the Islamic Republic. These gestures were routinely rebuffed by the theocratic state. The lingering influence of the revolution and Iran's poisonous factional politics militated against mending ties with the 'Great Satan'. Iran was never the foremost priority of any US administration, but its mishandling did damage to both the Carter and Reagan presidencies.

Paradoxically, historical evidence does not always adjust our impressions of the past. Jimmy Carter is seen by many as the president who 'lost Iran'. Yet, as this volume reveals, Carter may have had the toughest stance against the Islamic Republic. As with all his successors, he tried to mend fences with the new revolutionary regime, but once the hostage crisis took place, he quickly switched tracks. Recent documentary disclosures reveal that Carter even issued a 'presidential finding' in December 1979 calling for regime change in Iran. This important piece of evidence is not included in this volume, but there are enough documents marshalled here to disabuse us of some inaccurate views on Carter.

Survival | vol. 64 no. 2 | April–May 2022 | pp. 186–191   https://doi.org/10.1080/00396338.2022.2055835

One of the persistent misjudgements of successive US administrations is to see in Iran's bewildering array of factions an opportunity to strengthen the forces of moderation. Americans have believed that by adjusting their policy tools they can somehow alter the internal balance of power in Iran. The Islamic Republic has remained impervious to such entreaties, inviting some Americans to try even harder. It was such an impulse that led the Reagan administration into the disastrous Iran–Contra affair.

By injecting primary sources into the Iran debate, *Worlds Apart* allows us to see things as they are, as opposed to how we wish them to be.

A Self-fulfilling Prophecy: The Saudi Struggle for Iraq
Katherine Harvey. London: C. Hurst & Co., 2021. £35.00.
365 pp.

As America geared up to invade Iraq in 2003, there were contending views on what the future of that country would look like. The proponents of the invasion insisted that Iraq had all the necessary ingredients for democratic rule: a middle class, high rates of literacy and an array of reliable political actors, even though most of them were exiles. The opponents painted a very different picture, and feared that a looming sectarian conflict would only benefit the Shia state next door. The author of this compulsory and readable, if uneven, book identifies a new culprit for Iraq's mishaps: Saudi Arabia's King Abdullah.

In Katherine Harvey's telling, post-war Iraq need not have shattered into a sectarian hellscape, an experience from which it has never really recovered. To be sure, America made its share of mistakes. The most significant sin was the original one: the author recites the usual catechism about an arrogant George W. Bush leading a country shell-shocked by the 9/11 tragedies into an unwise war of choice. The US occupation is sensibly censured here for its many mistakes and misjudgements.

But it is King Abdullah who emerges as the principal villain of this tale. Iraqi prime minister Nuri al-Maliki was not the Shia chauvinist he is sometimes portrayed as being, but an Iraqi nationalist desperate to escape the clutches of Iran. He sought inroads into the Sunni world that were blocked by Abdullah. After an initial flirtation between the two, Abdullah insisted that Maliki had lied to him and refused to accept the hapless Iraqi leader's many entreaties. Of course, the Saudis were relentlessly hostile to the new order in Iraq and missed many opportunities to establish a working relationship with Maliki. And it must be said that during his tenure as prime minister, Maliki did at times try to clamp down on Shia forces, usually his peer competitors. But the Sunni world was not unanimously hostile to Shia Iraq. Jordan, Egypt and many of the Gulf sheikhdoms did try to accommodate the new order.

Among the curious omissions of this book is that there is little about Iran or the United States. Even though Maliki was rebuffed by the Saudis, he still enjoyed the backing of a superpower with ample troops on the ground. Should he have sought a more nationalistic path, there were many in America ready to cheer him on. And given that Iran is viewed as the ultimate winner of the self-fulfilling Saudi prophecy, there is little here on its actions and designs. How effective were the Iranians in creating a chaotic situation in Iraq that would ultimately redound to their advantage? Was it inevitable that Iran would emerge as the most significant outside power in Iraq given its own misapprehensions? There are no inevitabilities in history, and the Iranians were often surprised by the twists and turns of Iraqi politics. The author's account would have been more convincing if it were multilayered, encompassing the roles played by both America and Iran. Still, the focus on Saudi miscalculations is enough to recommend this book for students of this most unfortunate of wars.

Presidential Elections in Iran: Islamic Idealism Since the Revolution
Mahmoud Pargoo and Shahram Akbarzadeh. Cambridge and New York: Cambridge University Press, 2021. £22.99/$29.99. 186 pp.

The office of the presidency sits in an uncomfortable place in the maze of institutions that constitutes the Islamic Republic. It is an elected post beholden to the citizenry, and yet its authority is hemmed in on all sides by unelected institutions, most importantly the office of the Supreme Leader. But that is not where the misfortune of the presidency ends. The judiciary exercises its power without deference to the president, and the security organs, particularly the Revolutionary Guard Corps, do not see themselves as accountable to the chief executive. All this is not to suggest that the president is powerless. He commands important sectors of the bureaucracy, and his bully pulpit can still galvanise the populace. Of all the actors on Iran's public stage, the president is the only one who can claim a popular mandate as registered by a nationwide election.

Given the centrality of elections to the influence of the presidency, the authors have chosen a timely and important subject. In the 1980s, when the authority of the founder of the revolution, Ayatollah Ruhollah Khomeini, was beyond reproach, elections were a means of displaying one's loyalty to the system. They were frequently lacklustre events, with the few contenders for the job praising the theocracy and in some cases each other. The task at hand was not to lay out an agenda but to prove one's fealty to the Supreme Leader. Turnout was usually low as there was little to excite the masses.

All this changed in the aftermath of Khomeini's death in 1989. The constitutional revision undertaken at that time eliminated the office of the prime minister and thus elevated the importance of the presidency. Suddenly, elections had to be about something other than proving one's revolutionary ardour. Every Iranian presidency since then has been about something. Hashemi Rafsanjani talked of economic reconstruction in the aftermath of the Iran–Iraq War. Mohammad Khatami exhilarated the public by calling for an Islamic democracy. The firebrand Mahmoud Ahmadinejad injected populism into the nation's bloodstream. Finally, Hassan Rouhani insisted that the path to Iran's economic rehabilitation was an arms-control agreement with the 'Great Satan'. The most recent presidential election of Ebrahim Raisi is not covered in the book, which is a pity given that he harks back to the republic's early days.

The authors' thesis seems to be that in order to appeal to large swathes of the public, the candidates for the presidency had to abandon the old revolutionary rhetoric and talk about issues of the day. This finding is both sensible and true, but it ignores the fact that none of the presidents managed to enact their agenda. The unelected branches of the state stood firmly behind the revolution and its values. All the presidents who tangled with the shadowy government were made irrelevant. The Islamic Republic has perfected the art of turning its presidents into dissidents.

Since Raisi's presidency began the system seems to be coming full circle. He is a laconic, unimaginative leader who seems more than willing to yield to the Supreme Leader. He has little in the way of an agenda or vision for the future. That is why his campaign for the presidency was one of the least competitive since the dark days of the 1980s.

Call to Arms: Iran's Marxist Revolutionaries
Ali Rahnema. London: Oneworld Academic, 2021. £35.00. 505 pp.

Ali Rahnema's *Call to Arms* is a thoughtful and important contribution to our understanding of the reign of Shah Mohammad Reza Pahlavi. Too often, historians of modern Iran draw a clear line between the 1953 coup that toppled the nationalist prime minister Mohammad Mosaddegh and the 1979 Islamic Revolution that led to the overthrow of the Pahlavi dynasty. The intervening quarter-century is casually excised from the historical record. For many, it has seemed sufficient to say that the coup so compromised the shah's legitimacy that the monarchy's collapse was a foregone conclusion. But as Rahnema demonstrates, much did happen between 1953 and 1979, including the rise of a Marxist guerrilla movement that should have called into question many of our assumptions about the shah's rule at the zenith of his power.

The Iran of the 1970s was considered by many as a stable and predictable authoritarian state. The shah had consolidated his power. The old left, led by the communist Tudeh Party, was all but destroyed. The remnants of Mosaddegh's National Front were a shell of their former selves, and the clerics were confined to the seminaries. The parliaments and cabinets that once checked monarchical excess were mere rubber-stamp entities. The economy was growing, and the shah was a master of geopolitics. The rise of a modern middle class was considered a pillar of strength for the monarchy. And yet, it was from that middle class that a youthful movement pressing for violent change emerged.

Marxism was the opiate of university students in 1970s Iran. Although they may have soured on the Soviet Union, they venerated the Cuban revolutionaries, North Vietnamese guerrillas and even Mao Zedong's China. Iran's Marxist forces sought to emulate Mao's tactic of starting in the countryside, attacking remote military bases and police installations. Eventually, they penetrated Iran's urban centres with their targeted killings and symbolic acts of violence. Given the lack of conventional political avenues for the expression of dissent, they insisted on violence as a harbinger of change. The regime unleashed its security organs, which managed with difficulty to gain the upper hand. If the old adage is true that guerrillas succeed if they can survive, then Iran's Marxist warriors were remarkably effective. They bedevilled the shah's secret police and even impressed the monarch with their resilience.

The more searching question is the relationship between the rise of urban guerrilla warfare and the populist revolution that soon followed. The guerrillas' intellectual leaders assumed that their high-profile attacks would convince a large segment of the public that the shah's regime was neither as powerful nor as menacing as it seemed. By sacrificing themselves, they would diminish the fear factor that often helps hollowed-out autocracies linger. They could shatter the veneer of stability and provoke fissures within the system, inviting a larger popular backlash. By this account, the guerrillas were far more effective and forceful agents of change than is often assumed. They may have lost all their battles, but they won the ultimate war.

Mohammed bin Salman: The Icarus of Saudi Arabia?
David B. Ottaway. Boulder, CO: Lynne Rienner Publishers, 2021. $29.95. 230 pp.

Books on Saudi Arabia seem to be proliferating. The rise of Crown Prince Muhammad bin Salman (MbS) has invited close scrutiny, and the narrative of most books about him is the same, beginning with the emergence in the Kingdom of an impetuous moderniser seeking to upend the establishment. He is celebrated in the West for taking on the old order, particularly its austere religious culture and expansive welfare state. Then comes MbS's order to murder the dissident journalist Jamal Khashoggi. Suddenly the entire enterprise of reform is called into question. David Ottaway's book falls largely within this genre. With a journalist's eye for detail and an accessible writing style, Ottaway has produced a useful primer that adds little to what is already known.

The question at hand is whether an autocrat with a penchant for cruelty can reform a society in desperate need of change. Saudi Arabia's national compact, whereby the state provides cradle-to-grave welfare provisions in exchange for political passivity, is exhausted. The old men who ruled the Kingdom for so long did not seem to fully grasp this reality. The growing population and the sheer inefficiency of the administrative state had made such bargains untenable. Change had to come to Saudi Arabia, and MbS was astute enough to grasp that. But his temperament seems to have gotten the better of him. As an absolute ruler, he assumed that liberalising the social sphere and importing Western cultural products would garner him the indispensable support of the youth. He believed that glossy brochures produced by Western consulting firms constituted a real platform for economic reform. As the author convincingly demonstrates, such halfway measures were not sufficient.

MbS's record is hardly an enviable one. His impetuosity led him to involve himself in a war in Yemen that drained Saudi resources without producing results. Saudi diplomats are now mulling around Baghdad hoping that their summits with the Iranians, who have the upper hand in the conflict, will ease their pain. Unfortunately for them, Persian Shi'ites rarely rescue errant Wahhabis. At home, the political atmosphere is suffocating: civil society remains repressed and opportunities for the expression of dissent are non-existent. This is hardly a recipe for long-term stability.

In one area, MbS seems to be having greater success. His pariah status after the murder of Khashoggi seems to be fading. Western businesses and politicians are once more returning to the Kingdom. Oil tends to tranquilise public outrage. Saudi Arabia is still one of the largest producers of a commodity that remains central to the global economy. Any claims that alternative energies or suppliers are about to supplant Saudi oil reserves are exaggerated. So long as MbS remains the master of the petroleum kingdom, his many sins will be forgiven by Western chancelleries and corporate boardrooms.

United States
David C. Unger

Phantoms of a Beleaguered Republic: The Deep State and the Unitary Executive
Stephen Skowronek, John A. Dearborn and Desmond King.
Oxford: Oxford University Press, 2021. £18.99. 288 pp.

This insightful book offers an original and important frame for understanding the internal dynamics of the contemporary American state. By examining the decades-long contest between advocates of state depth (also known as the 'deep state') and advocates of the unitary-executive theory, it makes possible a more coherent and historically grounded view of the defining struggles of the Trump administration. Rather than take sides in the debate, the authors critically examine the theoretical weaknesses and practical excesses of each, and point to the dangers their escalating confrontation poses to American democracy. Their aim isn't to indulge in originalist hair-splitting, but to restore a workable government in the United States.

The unitary-executive theory bases itself on the first sentence of Article II, Section 1 of the US Constitution. Most of Section 1 details the complicated rules of presidential selection. But the first sentence reads: 'The executive Power shall be vested in a President of the United States of America.' It does not say 'all' the executive power, but it does say 'the' executive power. If nothing else, the framers meant to establish the kind of executive power the Articles of Confederation conspicuously lacked, and they meant to lodge that power in a single individual, not disperse it among an executive council or share it with, say, the Senate – all ideas discussed, and ultimately rejected. The framers did not envision a popularly elected president, but one indirectly elected by state-chosen electors, as the rest of Section 1 goes on to detail – a point conveniently forgotten by unitarians who fetishise the president as the only nationally elected official.

Normative notions of state depth, by contrast, are based not on constitutional text, but on constitutional principles and the informal norms established as successive American governments have tried to reconcile the expanding powers of an imperial presidency with the core constitutional concept of checks and balances. Unitary executive power wielded solely by a president is arbitrary power, but attempts to regulate that power by administration officials deliberately thwarting the chosen policies of an elected president are undemocratic.

These two warring conceptions of the executive can be traced back to the presidency of Andrew Jackson (1829–37), but the issue has become especially acute since the explosive expansion of executive agencies under Franklin Roosevelt.

Survival | vol. 64 no. 2 | April–May 2022 | pp. 192–200   https://doi.org/10.1080/00396338.2022.2055836

The growth of executive power during the New Deal, from regulatory agencies to national-security policy, effectively marginalised Congress. As the concentration of government within the executive branch proceeded, struggles for decisive governmental power shifted terrain, from contests *between* the executive and legislative branches to contests *within* the executive branch. These took shape as battles between the concepts of state depth and the unitary executive.

These battles escalated during the 1970s, when the Vietnam War and Watergate spurred successive congresses to try to rein in the imperial-presidential pretensions of the Nixon White House. While the War Powers Act, impeachment hearings and the Church Committee intelligence investigations were all congressional initiatives, deep-state actors such as 'Deep Throat', later identified as FBI official Mark Felt, and former White House counsel John Dean also played prominent roles. Supporters of the imperial presidency in the subsequent Ford White House, including Dick Cheney and Donald Rumsfeld, watched in anger and frustration as presidential powers ebbed, but both men returned to the fray more successfully later on.

Set in this larger context, Donald Trump's peremptory removals of such executive-branch subordinates as FBI director James Comey, secretary of state Rex Tillerson, attorney general Jeff Sessions, national security advisors H.R. McMaster and John Bolton, ambassador to Ukraine Marie Yovanovitch and countless others, along with the president's undisguised contempt for the quasi-independent inspectors-general (the executive-department watchdogs put in place after Watergate), take on a consistency and coherence that otherwise might be hard to see.

Trump is no constitutional scholar – few presidents are. But he surrounded himself with credentialled partisans of the unitary theory, such as attorney general William Barr, who kept assuring him that Article II gave him power to demand that executive-branch officials place the president's demands for personal loyalty above any loyalty to their own ideas of American interests and constitutional duty. Such advice confirmed Trump's instinctive view that many, if not most, executive-branch officials were part of a deep-state conspiracy to thwart the results of the 2016 presidential election.

Stephen Skowronek teaches political science at Yale, where co-author John Dearborn is a postdoctoral associate. Desmond King teaches American government at Oxford. Together they have managed the impressive feat of rendering abstract constitutional arguments into highly readable prose. They also maintain an admirable tone of scholarly objectivity, pointing out excesses on the part of Trump's opponents as well as those of the former president. The result is one of the most illuminating books thus far on the Trump presidency.

After the Apocalypse: America's Role in a World Transformed
Andrew Bacevich. New York: Metropolitan Books, 2021.
$26.99. 224 pp.

If you've never read a book by Andrew Bacevich, *After the Apocalypse* is an excellent place to start. Bacevich, an emeritus professor of international relations at Boston University and a 23-year military veteran, now serves as president of the Quincy Institute for Responsible Statecraft. He has used that platform to argue for a radically less ambitious, and therefore, in his view, radically more solvent US foreign policy, based on what he sees as a more realistic assessment of contemporary America's true national-security interests and capacity to act effectively in the international arena.

Bacevich writes vividly and clearly. Though he has covered some of the same territory in previous books, of which there are more than a dozen, he can be relied on to plough new analytical ground. He does not counsel isolation from the planet's pressing problems, from infectious diseases to rampant climate change. He favours active American encouragement of global trade and investment, educational and scientific exchanges, and environmental cooperation. What he inveighs against is the squandering of America's resources in hubristic and futile foreign military adventures. Those resources, he argues, would be better employed addressing real, non-military threats to American and global security in cooperation with others.

Bacevich is not alone in arguing for a smaller, more focused US military footprint. In their very different ways, Barack Obama, Donald Trump and Joe Biden have at least paid lip service to this goal. But unlike these recent presidents, Bacevich isn't calling for mere tactical adjustments in order to make the post-1945 exceptionalist model of American empire more sustainable. He builds his argument on a radical re-examination of American history and national identity, encompassing issues of racial inequity, climate disaster and the COVID-19 pandemic. As he puts it: 'Changing times render obsolete the past that we know and require the discovery of a "new" history better suited to the needs of the moment' (p. 9). The key word here is 'discovery'. Bacevich's 'new' American history has been there all along, much as the Western hemisphere was there before the arrival of Christopher Columbus.

Informed by this rediscovered history, Bacevich calls for a massive redirection of will and resources away from efforts to reshape other countries using American military power and toward more robust and better-funded efforts to counter domestic economic inequalities, racial injustices, unaffordable healthcare and crumbling infrastructure.

To fund this, Bacevich calls for a wholesale strategic withdrawal from regions he considers peripheral to today's American national-security interests – Europe and the Middle East, for example. Just because these regions were once central to American security, it does not follow that they remain so today. Needless to say, any downgrading of such hallowed strategic priorities would be hotly contested. But while there is room for argument about which regions constitute today's core strategic interests, Bacevich persuasively argues that America cannot continue to sustain a Cold War and post-Cold War model of global force projection that is out of date, has lost its domestic legitimacy and has played out disastrously on a succession of foreign battlefields.

The organising theme of this book portrays the year 2020 as a metaphoric stand-in for the biblical apocalypse, a year when all the bills came due for the misconceived and misbegotten policies of the recent past. COVID-19, economic disruption, protests over the police killing of George Floyd and Trump's disastrous presidency become stand-ins for the four horsemen of war, pestilence, famine and death, who in the biblical narrative signal the ushering in of the end times. Obviously, this cannot be taken literally, nor is it meant to be.

Bacevich's underlying argument deserves to be taken seriously. From the bipartisan sins of commission in invading Iraq to the bipartisan sins of omission in meeting the challenges of COVID-19 and climate change, the author sees signs of a broader failure of America's ruling elites – one that goes far to explain the widespread popularity of Trump. Bacevich sees Trump's policies and presidency as an unmitigated disaster, but he isn't content to blame Trump's political rise solely on James Comey's curiously timed press statements, Vladimir Putin's armies of internet trolls or Hillary Clinton's serial obtuseness as an electoral campaigner. Those factors helped put Trump over the top in 2016, but Bacevich suggests that, without the repeated prior failures of bipartisan elites, Trump would never have been within striking distance. The clear implication of Bacevich's analysis is that, without the kind of deep-rooted policy changes no top Democrat or Republican now proposes, a Trumpian reprise, in one form or another, is a real possibility.

The Plague Year: America in the Time of Covid
Lawrence Wright. New York: Knopf, 2021. $28.00. 336 pp.

The definitive account of America's COVID-19 experience has yet to be written and, with the pandemic now entering its third year, it may never be. Meanwhile, this well-reported, highly readable account of what *New Yorker* writer Lawrence Wright designates the 'plague year' of 2020 serves its purpose well. Wright, the author of ten previous, well-received non-fiction books, does not limit himself to the story of the pandemic, its victims and the medical efforts to contain it: as the subtitle promises, he tries to paint a picture of America. Wright largely delivers on that ambitious promise, although this reviewer would have preferred more emphasis on the medical story and, to the extent possible, less on the political – although the two are closely intertwined.

The medical story, which Wright skilfully recounts, features the scientists whose efforts to identify and model the virus made possible the extraordinarily rapid development of effective vaccines. It also includes the front-line medical workers who battled exhaustion, despair and the threat of becoming infected themselves to keep overwhelmed hospitals functioning. Most poignantly, it encompasses some of the hundreds of thousands of promising lives abruptly cut short by this new and deadly plague.

The political story is necessarily a story of the Trump administration, and its frequently, but not always, bungled responses to the COVID-19 catastrophe, as viewed through the eyes of Wright's journalistic sources. These include people such as Matthew Pottinger, the former *Wall Street Journal* reporter who served as Asia director of Trump's National Security Council; Matthew's wife, Yen Duong Pottinger, who fled Vietnam with her family as an infant and later became a Columbia University medical researcher; and Matthew's brother Paul, an infectious-disease doctor in Seattle. (Matthew and Paul's father, J. Stanley Pottinger, held high positions in the Justice Department under presidents Richard Nixon and Gerald Ford, which tells us something about the continuity of America's governing elites.)

Wright also recounts the perceptions of Dr Robert Redfield, who headed the Centers for Disease Control and Prevention from 2018 through the end of the Trump administration, and Deborah Birx, the White House Coronavirus Response Coordinator for most of 2020. These sources are well chosen and illuminating, usefully shifting the focus away from more familiar marquee characters such as Dr Anthony Fauci. More than once, Redfield and Birx saw their pleas for stronger preventive policies shot down by president Trump or vice president Mike Pence, while Fauci and Birx continued to publicly front for the administration's chosen policies.

Their stories illuminate the many connections between the AIDS fighters of a generation ago and the COVID fighters of today. Before COVID-19, Birx was the US global AIDS coordinator. She had studied at Fauci's clinic and worked with Redfield at Walter Reed Army Medical Center. These and other scientists and administrators understood that navigating the often treacherous political waters sometimes required subordinating their own scientific instincts to the whims and needs of the politicians whose choices would affect the lives of millions.

Wright shines new light on some of COVID's darker medical mysteries. He offers the clearest exposition I have seen about the questions surrounding the Wuhan Institute of Virology and its possible connections to the emergence of COVID-19. He tracks the history of the earliest COVID-19 variants in ways that give perspective to current concerns about the Omicron variant.

Wright's cinematic cut-and-fade writing style has its advantages and disadvantages. It sustains reader attention, though sometimes at the cost of analytic continuity. But overall, for readers seeking to learn more about the pandemic that continues to overturn our lives, *The Plague Year* is well worth a look.

The Second Cold War: Carter, Reagan, and the Politics of Foreign Policy
Aaron Donaghy. Cambridge: Cambridge University Press, 2021. £47.99. 288 pp.

In *The Second Cold War*, Aaron Donaghy, who teaches modern international history and US foreign-policy history at University College, Dublin, takes an interesting approach to an under-analysed subject – the 'second cold war' that erupted under Jimmy Carter and Leonid Brezhnev, and ended under Ronald Reagan and Mikhail Gorbachev.

For a time during the Nixon–Ford era of detente, the Cold War was often talked about in the past tense. Almost no one publicly declared the conflict over, but few expected it to come roaring back. But roar back it did, and it is worth trying to understand why that happened, and whether the resulting 'second cold war' was inevitable.

When Carter entered office in 1977 he was a Cold War dove. When he left it four years later, he had become a Cold War hawk. Reagan moved in exactly the opposite direction. For both US presidents, their fourth year in office (1980 for Carter and 1984 for Reagan) marked the decisive turning point.

In both cases, domestic politics contributed to these policy reversals. So, of course, did changes (or at least American perceptions of change) in Soviet conduct. Perhaps most important during the Reagan–Gorbachev period was Moscow's new-found belief that a radical change in foreign and domestic policies was essential to the survival of the Communist regime. This multiplicity of factors makes it impossible to attribute each period's foreign-policy developments solely to shifts in the respective White House strategies.

Donaghy's book offers two central narratives. In one, we see Carter, under pressure from the neo-conservative Henry Jackson wing of the Democratic Party and coached by his hawkishly anti-Soviet national security advisor, Zbigniew Brzezinski, overreacting to the Iranian hostage crisis and the Soviet invasion of

Afghanistan, and swinging sharply to the anti-Soviet right. Four years later, we see Reagan, faced with pre-election polls showing strong public disapproval of his failure to advance arms control, turning away from hawkish advisers such as Caspar Weinberger, Richard Perle and Kenneth Adelman, and listening instead to pragmatists such as George Shultz, James Baker and Michael Deaver. Following their advice, Reagan began efforts to re-engage with the Kremlin even before Gorbachev came to power in March 1985.

In the first case, a president with relatively little experience in foreign affairs listened to hawkish advice and lost his re-election bid. In the second, a president with limited foreign-policy experience listened to pragmatic moderates and won a landslide re-election.

As a journalist who covered the foreign-policy evolution of both presidents in real time, I was disappointed to learn that the opening of archives and the publication of memoirs over the past 35 years has added so little to the basic story known at the time. That is not Donaghy's fault. His footnotes reveal that his scholarly research was admirably thorough, but it has added little new information or analytical insights to the historical record.

The Storm Is Upon Us: How QAnon Became a Movement, Cult, and Conspiracy Theory of Everything
Mike Rothschild. New York: Melville House, 2021. $28.99. 320 pp.

Mike Rothschild is an investigative journalist who has been studying QAnon, the online conspiracy-theory phenomenon centred on the prognostications of 'Q', for years. He has collected an impressive amount of material, which he presents in *The Storm Is Upon Us*. QAnon is an elusive subject: Q is, as the name suggests, anonymous, and thus cannot be interviewed. Instead, Rothschild has relied on interviews with Q believers, whom he characterises as delusional, and their frequently distraught family members.

Q communicates through vaguely phrased internet posts or 'drops', which offer predictions of future events, such as the arrest and execution of 'deep state' liberal enemies. None of these predicted events is known to have occurred, but the vague or elliptical phrasing of many drops allows followers to keep the faith. Q has also alluded to having personal connections with military intelligence and Donald Trump – claims that, again, cannot be definitively confirmed or refuted. Those who want to believe – a large and growing number of people that Rothschild estimates to number well over one million – will believe.

So what is a reader, or a reviewer, to make of a book like this? Despite Rothschild's diligent reporting and informed speculations, the reader is left wondering how many people are actually involved in the QAnon movement, how deeply, and with what real-world consequences. Whatever the precise answers to these questions, there is no doubt that QAnon has a significant following, and that some of its followers, by their own admission, took part in the pro-Trump violence on Capitol Hill on 6 January 2021.

The Storm Is Upon Us does not purport to be a work of social science, but it draws heavily on the large body of social-science literature that tries to explain extremist politics and conspiracy-theory thinking as psychological pathologies. This is a well-established school of analysis that reaches back at least to the 1950 classic *The Authoritarian Personality* by Theodor Adorno, Else Frenkel-Brunswik, Daniel Levinson and Nevitt Sanford. But pathologising political belief and behaviour, even extreme behaviour, risks missing underlying experiences and beliefs that are not merely psychological. What is it about QAnon that believers find politically appealing? If QAnon beliefs are to be classified as pathologically abnormal, who gets to decide which political beliefs do and do not qualify as normal? Pathological behaviour is not always accompanied solely by pathological beliefs.

In his concluding chapter, Rothschild offers extensive guidance for how to lead people away from QAnon, based on the advice of experienced counsellors. Most of this is built on sensible suggestions such as avoiding wholesale challenges to QAnon thinking and not getting into back-and-forth arguments about specific predictions or drops. Such advice may be helpful to people who have lost friends or relatives to the closed world of QAnon belief.

Rothschild deserves much credit for his efforts to understand and explain QAnon, whether it is best classified as a cult, conspiracy theory, pathology or fringe (for now) political movement.

Copyright © 2022 The International Institute for Strategic Studies

Ukraine: The Shock of Recognition

Dana H. Allin

I

In *The Age of Extremes*, Marxist historian Eric Hobsbawm reflected on the
'exceptional and comparatively short-lived' anti-fascist alliance of roughly
1933 to 1947. Its unity was manifest in an early product of the young
American sample-survey industry. In January 1939, a Gallup poll found
that, in the then still hypothetical event of war between the Soviet Union
and Germany, 83% of Americans favoured a Soviet victory – a result that
'would have amazed all US presidents before Franklin D. Roosevelt, and
will amaze all readers who have grown up since the Second World War'.[1]

America and Soviet Russia were, after all, avatars of capitalism and
communism, respectively. These two ideologies had riven the Western
world of the early twentieth century even without factoring in that
'Stalinist tyranny was at that time, by general recognition, at its worst'.
And the counter-intuitive American embrace of Russia as a natural ally
could not really be explained, Hobsbawm argued, by the 'range of international relations or power politics'.[2] This was, rather, an 'international
ideological civil war', and one in which, 'as it turned out, the crucial lines
… were not drawn between capitalism as such and communist social revolution, but between ideological families: on the one hand, the descendants
of the eighteenth-century Enlightenment and the great revolutions including, obviously, the Russian revolution; on the other, its opponents'.[3]

Dana H. Allin is Editor of *Survival* and IISS Senior Fellow for US Foreign Policy and Transatlantic Affairs.

Survival | vol. 64 no. 2 | April–May 2022 | pp. 201–208   https://doi.org/10.1080/00396338.2022.2055838

The ideological family fighting fascism was broad. It stretched from the British conservative Winston Churchill and French Catholic conservative Charles de Gaulle, through Roosevelt and his social-democratic kin in Europe, to the Italian communist leader Palmiro Togliatti and, most awkwardly but also importantly, to Josef Stalin himself. It encompassed openly racist white GIs from Alabama and underground communist resistance fighters in France.

Ideological consciousness in this global coalition varied, of course, approaching zero for most of the millions of fighting men and women. Hobsbawm's true insight, however, was that the global, international civil war was waged not – or not only – on the basis of realpolitik, but also because governments and nation-states, trade unions and businesses, politicians and political parties, artists and intellectuals, church leaders and generals could unite around a visceral recognition that they were fighting an axis of powers led by a 'Hitler Germany [that] was both more ruthlessly and manifestly committed to the destruction of the values and institutions of the "Western civilisation" of the Age of Revolution, and capable of carrying out its barbaric project'.[4]

Almost a century later, it appears that a similarly visceral recognition has galvanised Western populations who are, broadly speaking, descendants of the Enlightenment. It is a shock of recognition. To wake up on the morning of 24 February 2022 was to feel, moreover, on top of shock, a degree of foolishness. One felt foolish for being shocked. After all, the Biden administration had been saying for weeks that the best US intelligence indicated that Russia would launch a full-scale invasion of Ukraine. There were almost 200,000 Russian troops mobilised on Ukraine's borders. What was anyone expecting?

The answer is that many still imagined that Russian President Vladimir Putin would make decisions on the basis of a rational, if not reasonable, assessment of actual Russian interest. He might have made some gains with continued threats and more limited incursions. NATO leaders were ready to talk and, in fact, travelled to Moscow and Geneva to do so. Turning the NATO clock back to 1997 was not going to happen, but acceptable accommodations to defensible Russian concerns were in the realm of possibility. Instead, Putin plunged his country into a war of incomprehensible nihilism, into dramatic international isolation, and into what looks to be a gut-wrenching economic depression. His delusions about Ukraine have been shattered, if not abandoned. Russia can destroy its neighbour, but it cannot subjugate it.

The West, meanwhile, has surprised itself in unity and purposeful outrage. What neither side can know, of course, is how this might end.

II

When the Cold War began, the alliance against fascism ended, or at least fractured. Yet a kind of shell and even some spirit of the original alliance survived. It was embodied in the United Nations, which did function, after a fashion, even with an often-paralysed Security Council. It was embodied in the early detente promoted by John F. Kennedy and Nikita Khrushchev after near catastrophes over Berlin and Cuba, and expressed in classic Enlightenment language in Kennedy's American University oration of coexistence.[5] The alliance survived in the parallel dimension of Rooseveltian realpolitik: where Roosevelt had imagined shifting combinations of his 'Four Policemen' (Britain, China, Russia and the United States) ganging up on one another to keep the peace, Richard Nixon refined the art of triangular diplomacy with rival communist powers.[6]

The Enlightenment coalition either survived or was reborn in the late 1980s with Mikhail Gorbachev's glasnost and perestroika, accommodations to the West and palpably sincere visions of a 'Common European Home'. In 1987 Gorbachev signed with Ronald Reagan the Intermediate-Range Nuclear Forces (INF) Treaty to eliminate a whole class of ballistic and cruise missiles from their respective arsenals. In 1988, Gorbachev unilaterally withdrew thousands of troops and many tank divisions from Central Europe. In 1989 Moscow made clear to its Warsaw Pact satellites that it would not support the violent suppression of peaceful revolutions, or punitive action to stop the haemorrhage of East Germans to the west. Out of these decisions the breach and destruction of the Berlin Wall ensued, perhaps inevitably, at the end of that year. In 1990 Gorbachev and his foreign minister, Eduard Shevardnadze, agreed to the reunification of Germany.

The 1990 negotiations about reunification entailed questions about the future of NATO. These questions would trouble relations between Russia and the West for the next three decades. At the outset the Soviets received mixed messages about NATO not moving east, though they certainly got no promises in writing and possibly heard in those messages only what they wanted to hear, especially as Moscow was now desperate for financial aid as part of the overall package from West Germany. Thereafter, as the idea of NATO enlargement took hold in the Clinton administration, it produced not only Russian anger but also a spirited debate in the West and especially in the United States.[7] Since there have been vestiges of that debate in the run-up to Putin's 2022 invasion, it is advisable to understand the spirit of the 1990s arguments.

In part the opponents were arguing in the spirit of structural realism which, to their pro-enlargement critics, is detached from considerations of right and wrong. A prominent realist opponent of enlargement was the elder diplomat, strategist and historian George F. Kennan, who warned that it would be 'the most fateful error of American policy in the entire post-Cold War era'. Kennan first became famous as an anti-Soviet hawk who worried about the illusions of higher-level Roosevelt- and then Truman-administration officials regarding the possibilities of post-war cooperation with Moscow. His 1946 'Long Telegram', sent from the embassy in Moscow where he was chargé d'affaires, helped to dispel those illusions. Some seven years later, however, back in Moscow as US ambassador, Kennan sent another long telegram to Washington, this one concerning the Atlantic Alliance. He wrote:

> Surely as one moves one's bases and military facilities towards the Soviet frontiers there comes a point where they tend to create the very thing they were designed to avoid. It is not for us to assume that there are no limits to Soviet patience in the face of encirclement by American bases. Quite aside from political considerations, no great country, peaceful or aggressive, rational or irrational, could sit by and witness with indifference the progressive studding of its own frontiers with the military installations of a great-power competitor. Here again, a

compromise must be struck, and one which will inevitably fall somewhat
short of the military ideal. This compromise must be struck with a view
to the peculiarities of the Russian mentality and tradition.[8]

Realism in these terms suggests some need for the accommodation of
genuine monsters, for Kennan was writing about and insisting on a kind of
strategic empathy, for Stalin's Soviet Union no less, and it would be historically impossible to accuse Kennan of illusions about Stalin or his regime.[9]

Yet it was not monsters that American opponents of NATO enlargement
wanted to accommodate in the 1990s, and their opposition had more than
structural realism at heart. The collapse of the Soviet Union, when it happened, was not the defeat of Stalinists. It was the failure of men of evident
goodwill – such as Gorbachev and Shevardnadze – to effectively reform
communism. Historians such as Kennan and John Lewis Gaddis had a
humanist, Enlightenment appreciation of the historical moment. Gaddis
argued (in one of the first *Survival* articles I edited) that enlargement vio-
lated 'principles of strategy ... so basic that when stated they sound like
platitudes', starting with '*the magnanimous treatment of defeated adversaries*'.[10]

This, to put it mildly, was not the view from Budapest or Prague or
Warsaw or other European capitals that had been recently released from
Soviet domination. The former Warsaw Pact members wanted NATO
membership for a clear and obvious reason: whatever the sincerity and
current intentions of the Gorbachev and then Yeltsin governments, they
feared Russia and wanted to be protected against it. Enlargement was in
large measure demand driven.

Historically, both sides of this debate may claim vindication. It is true,
in somewhat tautological terms, that NATO and the West failed to create a
post-Cold War security architecture that accommodated Russia. It remains
arguable that the principle of an open alliance to include, in theory, every
country on Russia's border – a principle regrettably reiterated in NATO's
Bucharest Declaration of 2008 that Georgia and Ukraine 'will be' members
of NATO[11] – was maximally provocative to Russia and minimally reassur-
ing to Ukraine, and thereby more destabilising than stabilising. Pointing to
Putin's depravities as refutation of the realist critics is no more dispositive

than pointing to Adolf Hitler's evil as invalidating John Maynard Keynes's critique of the punitive consequences of the Treaty of Versailles.

That does not mean, by any measure, that the ongoing war is NATO's or the West's fault. They may have failed to accommodate Russia simply because the task was impossible. And certainly those former Warsaw Pact and Baltic states that achieved NATO membership must now feel vindicated in their determination to push for it. They can point, moreover, to considerable evidence accumulated since more or less the beginning of this century that Putin's main concern about Ukraine wasn't Kyiv's NATO aspirations so much as its increasing Western orientation and even democratic development.

Both narratives can be true at the same time. This is the tragedy of the security dilemma. The overriding *moral* fact is that war has come to Europe because the Russian state, led by and largely embodied in Vladimir Putin, decided that an independent Ukraine was intolerable.

III

The axis around which these narratives now revolve is the courage and determination of Ukraine. It is by fighting and, to the world's astonishment, winning – to the extent of inflicting massive Russian casualties and stopping Russian advances – that Ukrainians have both forged their nation and defined the world's stake in its success.

Ukraine has made itself a kind of analogue to the Spain of 1936–39, but with two key differences. The Spanish Civil War was a precursor battle against fascism, but while the Soviet Union supported the Spanish Republic, the Western powers did not. Ukraine has not been so abandoned; on the contrary, Western military aid has been steady and decisive, while the economic punishment of Russia is devastating.

The second difference is countervailing. While the Spanish Republic was defeated, and Czechoslovakia dismembered, the Western powers of France, Britain and America did eventually enter and win a cataclysmic war with Germany and its allies. This will not happen – at least will not happen intentionally – unless Russia attacks a NATO ally. President Joe Biden made this clear before the war. My colleague John Raine has rightly called this an 'escalation trap' that gives Russia huge room for horrifying destruction and argued that NATO should find a way to escape it.[12] Yet escaping it at acceptable risk may be impossible. The US and its treaty allies probably cannot directly fight Russians for Ukraine because Russia has nuclear weapons.

Ukraine's President Volodymyr Zelensky, the Jewish former comic actor whom Putin grotesquely accuses of heading a 'Nazi' government, has eloquently challenged those limits. But he has also understood them – and signalled a willingness to negotiate with Russia on the question of NATO membership. As this issue of *Survival* went to press, talks were ongoing, with reports of an Austrian or Finnish model of armed neutrality being on the table. It was impossible at this juncture to say whether Putin would relent at anything short of annihilation. After his enraged assault on Russia's neighbour, however, one thing is clear: a stable and secure neutrality might be viable only because Ukraine has shown its determination and capability to defend itself.

The NATO states, with the support of much though by no means all of the rest of the world, have also demonstrated unity and determination. Given the abysmal performance of the Russian army against Ukraine, a Russian attack against a NATO country would appear manifestly foolish and therefore highly unlikely. We must concede, however, that stable expectations of what is likely or rational have come unmoored. This issue contains articles by John L. Harper and Lawrence Freedman that recall the Nixon diplomacy of half a century ago that produced, respectively, the opening to China and the SALT agreement with the Soviet Union. It occurred during the height of the war in Vietnam, as American soldiers were dying at the hands of a Soviet-armed enemy. Yet diplomacy could be conducted on the assumption of bounded rationality. Now, Putin appears to have escaped those bounds.

Also in this issue, my colleague Nigel Gould-Davies assesses Putin's war as a strategic failure that will damage him immensely. This seems right. Less clear is how this defeat will be translated into a Western success. 'But if one does not make war, one must sooner or later make peace', wrote de Gaulle in the last volume of his memoirs on the necessity of detente with the Soviets.[13] This must also be true, sooner or later, of twenty-first-century Russia. But we do not know how, for there is no *Stunde Null* and no clear path back to the world we have lost.

Notes

1 Eric Hobsbawm, *The Age of Extremes: The Short Twentieth Century, 1914–1991* (London: Abacus, 1994), p. 143.

2 *Ibid.*

3 *Ibid.*, p. 144.

4 *Ibid.*, p. 145.

5 'For, in the final analysis, our most basic common link is that we all inhabit this small planet. We all breathe the same air. We all cherish our children's future. And we are all mortal.' John F. Kennedy, commencement address at American University, Washington DC, 10 June 1963, https://www.jfklibrary.org/archives/other-resources/john-f-kennedy-speeches/american-university-19630610.

6 See John Lewis Gaddis, *Strategies of Containment: A Critical Appraisal of Postwar American National Security Policy* (New York: Oxford University Press, 1987), p. 10. On Nixon's diplomacy, see John L. Harper, 'Nixon in China, February 1972: Revisiting the "Week that Changed the World"', *Survival*, vol. 64, no. 2, April–May 2022, pp. 45–51.

7 The best history of these events is M.E. Sarotte, *Not One Inch: America, Russia, and the Making of the Post-Cold War Stalemate* (New Haven, CT: Yale University Press, 2021).

8 George F. Kennan, 'The Soviet Union and the Atlantic Pact', Foreign Service Dispatch 116, from American Embassy, Moscow, to Department of State, Washington, 8 September 1952, reprinted in George F. Kennan, *Memoirs: 1950–1963* (New York: Pantheon Books, 1972), pp. 141–2.

9 Less than two weeks later, Kennan spoke to a press gaggle at Tempelhof Airport in Berlin and emitted an outburst about conditions in Moscow that got him declared *persona non grata* and barred from returning even to collect his family and belongings. *Ibid.*, pp. 145–67.

10 John Lewis Gaddis, 'History, Grand Strategy and NATO Enlargement', *Survival*, vol. 40, no. 1, Spring 1998, pp. 145–51 (emphasis in original).

11 NATO, 'Bucharest Summit Declaration', 3 April 2008, https://www.nato.int/cps/en/natolive/official_texts_8443.htm.

12 John Raine, 'Time for NATO to Find a Way Out of the Escalation Trap in Ukraine', IISS Analysis, 11 March 2022, https://www.iiss.org/blogs/analysis/2022/03/time-for-nato-to-find-a-way-out-of-the-escalation-trap-in-ukraine.

13 Charles de Gaulle, *Memoirs of Hope* (London: Weidenfeld & Nicolson, 1971), p. 201.

Copyright © 2022 The International Institute for Strategic Studies